THE
Hound & Horn
LETTERS

THE
Hound & Horn
LETTERS

Edited by
MITZI BERGER HAMOVITCH

Foreword by Lincoln Kirstein

THE UNIVERSITY OF GEORGIA PRESS
Athens

Copyright © 1982 by the University of Georgia Press
Athens, Georgia 30602
Set in Linotron 202 Monticello
Designed by Dwight Agner

The paper in this book meets the guidelines for permanence
and durability of the Committee on Production Guidelines
for Book Longevity of the Council on Library Resources.

Printed in the United States of America

Grateful acknowledgment is made to those who hold copyright on the
individual letters in this collection and have given permission for their
use: Nancy T. Andrews; Bernard Bandler; the Beinecke Rare Book and
Manuscript Library, Yale University; Brown University Library; the Es-
tate of Harry Crosby; Mrs. Dudley Fitts; the Estate of Michael Gold; the
late Caroline Gordon; Alexander R. James; Maria Jolas; Lincoln Kir-
stein; James Laughlin; the Estate of T. E. Lawrence; Dwight MacDon-
ald; the late Archibald MacLeish; the late A. Hyatt Mayor; the Estate of
Marianne Moore; Seán O'Faoláin; Frank Oppenheimer; Mrs. Kenneth
Patchen; the late Katherine Anne Porter; Stephen Spender; the Estate of
Gertrude Stein; Alan Stroock; Mrs. Edmund Wilson; the Estate of Wil-
liam Carlos Williams; the Estate of Ezra Pound; and the late Allen Tate.

Library of Congress Cataloging in Publication Data

Main entry under title:

The Hound and horn letters.

Includes index.
1. Hound & horn.   2. Authors, American—20th
century—Correspondence.   I. Hamovitch, Mitzi
Berger.   II. Hound & horn.
PN4900.H6H6   816'.52'08   81-16172
ISBN 0-8203-0607-X   AACR2

Contents

Acknowledgments

I would like to thank the following people for their assistance: Professor John Thompson, English Department of the State University of New York at Stony Brook, whose idea it was that I edit the letters in the *Hound and Horn* Archive and whose guidance was invaluable; the readers of my doctoral dissertation, Professors Peter Shaw, Rose Zimbardo, and Charles Hoffmann; Lincoln Kirstein, for granting me permission to edit the letters and for answering faithfully my numerous requests for information; Dr. Bernard Bandler, Professor Francis Fergusson, the late A. Hyatt Mayor, Alan Stroock, and Doris Levine Fish, for their time in talking to me about the *Hound and Horn*; Donald Gallup, former curator of the Collection of American Literature at the Beinecke Library, Yale University, for his cooperation; Malcolm Cowley and Dr. Leon Edel; Dr. Virginia Hlavsa, who read an early draft and made many helpful suggestions; Dr. Lynn Buck, for her encouragement; Ann Fitzgerald, who was of invaluable help with research and typing; the reference department of the Great Neck Library, particularly Elsa Reznick Prigozy; the secretarial and reprographic services at Queens College, City University of New York, particularly Rose Marie Callahan and Celia Rutsky; and most especially my husband, for his great encouragement and support throughout this project.

Two books that helped immeasurably in my work were *The Hound and Horn: The History of a Literary Quarterly* by Leonard Greenbaum

(The Hague: Mouton, 1966) and *The American Literary Review, A Critical History 1920–1950*, by G. A. M. Janssens (The Hague: Mouton, 1968).

M.B.H.

A Note on the Editing

Permission was withheld for the use of letters from T. S. Eliot and Yvor Winters, and some restrictions were placed on me regarding the choice of material for *The Hound and Horn Letters*. The trustees of the Ezra Pound Estate requested that I limit my choice of letters to a third of his correspondence with any one editor of the *Hound and Horn*. Allen Tate asked that I limit the number of his letters selected for this collection to fifteen out of the over one hundred letters in the archive.

In one instance, I was asked by the writer to remove a passage that he did not wish published, a request with which I complied. Otherwise, I have made deletions—signified by ellipses—in my selection of letters from the *Hound and Horn* Archive only to avoid repetition or to eliminate material that was not of general interest. Ezra Pound's noted idiosyncrasies of spelling, punctuation (including his use of virgules— the diagonal slash—underlining, and capitalization), and expression have been preserved to convey to the reader a sense of the force, vigor, and urgency of his correspondence.

Hound & Horn
Forty-eight years after

I graduated from Harvard College in 1930. I'd lived in Boston, Massachusetts, since 1912. It is perhaps hard to understand the feeling that I still have about Boston—and Cambridge. When I went to school, the nineteenth century was only terminating its cultural and intellectual hegemony. I felt and feel I am a man of the nineteenth century. Although Harvard was in few ways comparable to Oxford or Cambridge of the same epoch, I consider I had a "classical" education—of a kind—and so did the young men with whom I came to be associated in several thoughtful pursuits. Most of us took our formation from Harvard as it existed before the "House System" was instituted in 1931, when I was leaving Cambridge. But when I was a freshman, and for some four years after, the minds I most admired were still under the influence of Charles William Eliot, Charles Eliot Norton, George Santayana, John Livingston Lowes, Alfred North Whitehead, Charles Grandgent, and Irving Babbitt. Reading Ms. Hamovitch's kindly words documenting some of our efforts, I find myself brought face to face with a character I have trouble in recognizing: myself. The casual reader may be brought to believe that one of the founders of the magazine under survey was one of a corps of intellectuals. In a very real sense, I personally never had intellectual pretensions. I started the magazine as a "Harvard Miscellany," intending it to be a kind of historical or archeological survey of a site, its buildings, traditions, and the men who made them. That it developed more broadly was not, at first, foreseen by me. I abandoned the magazine after seven years, not entirely because my interests had altered and I was otherwise magnetized (by the ballet). The real reason I did not fight to continue *Hound & Horn* and made only feeble efforts to have several interested groups pick it up was that I didn't give a damn for politico-philosophical tendencies which I felt were devouring the magazine's space, and I was neither equipped to deal nor interested in dealing with them. I felt inadequate, and still do, with those delighted by ratiocination, with energies that mentate as sport.

I was an adventurer; *Hound & Horn* was my passport. If the truth were known, and, at a time when burgeoning "modernism" was a mandatory stance, my idiosyncratic models were Balzac's Lucien de Rubempré, Bulwer Lytton's Pelham, and Benjamin Disraeli's Coningsby. I wrote an (unpublished) romance entitled "Choice of Weapons," which portrayed the luxurious perplexities of a contemporary young dandy, a provincial who would conquer the great city. This character couldn't decide who or what he wanted to be or do; the fun was in the choice. Should he become a diplomat (like Harold Nicolson, whom I knew and admired), or a painter (like John Singer Sargent, with whom my father had contact), or a poet and/or critic (like Conrad Aiken and John Brooks Wheelwright, who were advisors). Wheelwright was my strongest mentor; an architectural critic, a Brahmin of Boston's best, an Anglican Trotskyite, and a most interesting theological poet, he knocked a lot of ambitious nonsense out of my head and told me life was not a career but a service.

In 1926, my freshman class was addressed by Harvard's president emeritus and editor of the famous five-foot bookcase of the World's Best Books. He was very old, very eminent, very tottering. His advice to the rich and clean young gentlemen already tenderized by St. Paul's, St. Mark's, St. George's, Phillips Exeter, and Phillips Andover (with a few from the Boston Latin School) was "*Flee introspection.*" I wasn't listening with great attention. At first I thought he said "Free introspection." No—he reiterated: "Flee introspection." Over the years I mused on that accumulation of sagacity which prompted such drastic advice and tried, on and off, to arrive at what he intended. Advising a crop of rich youths to avoid self-examination, if that's what he meant, was barely necessary. The boys I knew didn't take drugs, at that time, but they certainly drank, like fish. I would, in the next four years, meet few undergraduates who could be tormented by self-examination. Most were on impalpable launching-pads, which Harvard has never been slow to provide, that would propel them with minimal deviation into their destined and ultimate operations. They would be occupied by business, the law, medicine; a few might teach. The very notion of introspection was almost as alien to the majority as political, visual, or musical curiosity. They were (the ones I knew and liked) physically brilliant, self-assured, charming, mannerly, gentle, good-natured, and kind. They had absolutely no idea of, or interest in *Hound & Horn*. My occupation with the magazine, which took about half my time (at the expense of decent academic grades), was in a world apart. It was diverting to pass from one world to another. I imagined the other world resembled the Harvard class of 1859, whose members included the friends of Henry Adams and Roonie Lee, in those halcyon days when a Bostonian and a Virginian were still friends just before war. Not that war, or even the Wall Street crash or the Great Depression, ever impinged on our conscience or consciousness. But the boys, who in my time knew one another as "The Lads," belonged to a Hamiltonian dynasty of the rich, wellborn, and able. As for their ability, I never knew what happened to them; when I played with them, their charm seemed a kind of genius which spelt unlimited possibility. As for what they thought of me—they didn't think of me, or anything else. But I should say that they, as a class or representative group, were neither stupid nor snobbish; they were, according to those who would make *Hound & Horn* whatever it became, mindless. Not only had they fled introspection; their innocence, animal spirits, instincts, and endowment lacked any mechanism with which to manipulate abstract notions, for they saw no reason to occupy themselves with anything unnecessary to their satisfactory and circumscribed physicality.

My co-founder and co-editor, Varian Fry, held "The Lads" in high contempt. To him, they were the enemy. He was an excellent Greek and Latin scholar, a formidable pianist with a good background in elementary philosophy. This was before the age of Wittgenstein and Popper. When I told him I was auditing Professor Whitehead's course in metaphysics, Varian said that contemporary philosophy was nothing but epistemology, and I shouldn't try to put my abstractions in order since I was as incapable of rational analysis as the dumbest of "The

Lads." He was quite right; when *Hound & Horn* began to fill itself up with quasi-political or proto-Marxist exegesis, I became increasingly uncomfortable. It would, of course, be an inverse sort of vanity to insist on one's being feeble-minded. But I could only feel myself attracted to what I personally could use. Later, when through Jack Wheelwright, Eliot, and others I became interested in Christian theology, it was poetry rather than the dogmatics which inspired faith. Reviewing Kierkegaard's "Either/Or," Wystan Auden wrote, "In contrast to those philosophers who begin by considering the *objects* of human knowledge, essences and relations, the existential philosopher begins with man's immediate experience as a *subject*, i.e., as a being in *need*, an *interested* being whose existence is at stake."

As for visual taste and the interest *Hound & Horn* manifested in painting, sculpture, and architecture, as far as I was concerned, it came from an intimacy with the magnificent palace of the Boston Public Library, of which my father was, for many years, president. The splendor of design and craftsmanship in one of the greatest of many great buildings by Charles Follen McKim and Stanford White still share, fifty years ago, in the brilliance of its original conception. My father was responsible for the cleaning of Puvis de Chavannes's murals, and he spoke with John Singer Sargent over the completion of his wonderful vault depicting comparative religion, now shamefully ill-used and defaced. While the library had been planned in the old century, it represented to me the apex of concrete perfection in a rational material plan, on the highest level of imaginative competence, from Edwin Austin Abbey's series of Arthurian murals in the Delivery Room to Augustus Saint-Gaudens's golden marble memorial lions on the grand staircase, the inlaid brass zodiac in the entrance hall, and the richness of the mahogany paneling in the Directors' Room. While McKim and White looked back to Leon Battista Alberti and Giacomo da Vignola, so Professor Grandgent made Dante a contemporary voice, and while Sargent was the antithesis of painting that our Harvard Society of Contemporary Art fostered in an effort parallel and comparable to the magazine, it was neither Pablo Picasso nor Henri Matisse who were my models, but rather Hans Holbein, Corneille de Lyon, and Jean Auguste Ingres.

As an adventurer, on a small scale, I embraced the advance-guard taste of Alfred Stieglitz and progressive Manhattan galleries. Essentially this was opportunism. The fun was in the energy expended in a crusade, and the opportunities this afforded to have contact with movers and shakers. I curried favor with Ezra Pound, although apart from his oft-quoted passages, I could never make head nor tale of the *Cantos*. As for the Southern Agrarians, their economics seemed childish, their regionalism stubborn and perverse, but I was daft about the ambiance of the Civil War and was deeply in love with both General J. E. B. Stuart and his tragic young aide, Major John Pelham. I had toured the principal Virginia battlefields and extravagantly admired Allen Tate's "Ode to the Confederate Dead." In fact, my natural bent toward historicity, my consciousness of a living past, was reinforced by a very active and beautiful familial society which extended from Beacon Hill in Boston to Shady Hill (C. E. Norton's old home), Cameron Forbes's estate in Milton, and the lovely houses of Shaws, Lowells, and Ameses in Concord. In our late twenties, my nineteenth century was indeed alive. Identification with a society of living and thinking New England dynastic actors gave a security and assurance prompting freedom of action, a sense of inevitability of possibility achieved which I do not think any other locus in America then offered.

Wheelwright was also a poet, although a very eccentric metrist. His architectural training, his residency in Florence, his assumption of authority as a man of the world as well as being heir of Adams Brooks and Chardons,* kin to half of old Boston, and his attachment to the odd orthodoxy of the Cowley Fathers, brought me closer, at least in thought, to T. S. Eliot who, more than any one person, was responsible in my mind, for the pattern of what a magazine might be—when I came to be conscious of what that was. His magazine, the *Criterion*, was indeed, for me and many of my generation, "A standard of judging; a rule or test by which anything is tried in forming a correct judgement respecting it." I was fifteen years old, in boarding school, when an older friend, a senior on his way to Yale, gave me a copy, volume 1, number 1, of a new magazine. It had no pictures. Its contents included an essay on "Dullness" by George Saintsbury, a sketch of a

---

* "Wheelwright's mother was a Brooks whose father was a Chardon; he was also connected with the Sturges, Cabots and Adams as most of those proper Bostonians were." (Letter to me from Lincoln Kirstein, 30 August 1981.)

novel by F. M. Dostoevsky, an essay on Tristram and Isolt by T. Sturge Moore, and a longish poem entitled "The Waste Land" by the magazine's editor, T. S. Eliot. It is impossible to recapture the effect this work had on me, and my friend. We had no education in *The Golden Bough* or *From Ritual to Romance*; the poem then bore neither notes nor the dedication to Ezra Pound; it was quite unexplained and inexplicable. But it was magic; it seemed to fuse past and present, to make certain assertions about renewal or repetition of seasons and epochs. It became a text from which we quoted at increasingly frequent and appropriate moments.

In school I had written a certain amount, but I had had no real desire to be an "editor." The *Criterion*, later the *Dial*, were models of what magazines might be; both seemed so elevated and comprehensive in their spectra that, at the start, *Hound & Horn* aimed to have been modestly enough, a mere "Harvard Miscellany." But we printed a trial issue and secretly hoped that somehow it would please Eliot. Five years after I first read "The Waste Land" I was taken to a *Criterion* luncheon in London by the scholar and critic Bonamy Dobrée. Mr. Eliot was charming; he did not need to frighten me; I was already scared—but he promised help. I imagine that Dobrée eased my way. In any case, Eliot seemed to me, at the time, the most important authority in the world for anything and everything that could occupy me, and strangely enough this included theater. Those who read his essay on Marie Lloyd and the English music hall will recognize the scope of his theatrical appreciation, while this was years before his own plays. Varian Fry and I manfully campaigned to get Eliot appointed to give the Charles Eliot Norton lectures; we were tolerantly laughed off; not until years later did he come to Harvard for exactly this purpose.

It must appear that I had little contact with "life," or rather that *Hound & Horn* at its start was a rich boy's dilettante toy more than a genuine literary assemblage or an aspirant to academic experiment. My father felt I should not enter college without some knowledge of "life" as he had lived it in his youth. He was a poor boy who lived by his wits; his father had been a lens-grinder from Jena who had emigrated to Rochester, New York, after the troubles of 1848. Father and son had a large sense of craft; lens-grinding is something of a jeweler's trade. I wanted to be a painter, preferably a portrait painter (like Sargent or Holbein), but I found myself in a stained-glass factory which turned out windows for the National Cathedral in Washington and Saint John the Divine in New York. I designed some roundels with figures of jazz-band players. They were conceived after the renderings of Viollet leDuc, but I had been given *Mont St. Michel and Chartres* by my sister, who as a graduate student at Radcliffe had finished a dissertation on Henry Adams; I felt comfortable combining the thirteenth and twentieth centuries. More importantly, I became involved with the craftsmen and manual laborers responsible for making stained-glass windows. Situations arose which led toward the unpleasant eventuality of a strike. Although I was an unpaid apprentice, nevertheless I could not help taking sides, identifying myself with a man who had befriended me and who was the leader of the labor action. I had assumed that beauty was imagined, invented, or created in "beautiful" surroundings, or under "beautiful" conditions. We know the Hans Christian Andersen story of the flower-pot and the flower, the furnace that fires the clay, as well as the dunghill that breeds the blossom. I had some sleepless nights trying to decide how, or what, to risk in the dispute over wages and conditions. I found, of course, I had nothing to gain or lose and it made absolutely no difference how I acted about what I felt. Anything I suffered or agonized over was sheer luxury. And yet the atmosphere in the shop was ugly, my presence embarrassing (to me), the issues obscure. However, I did get inklings of human extremity, degrees of despair. These, then, I found as well as words well arranged also contributed to "literature." So, in a way, my education started before I was a freshman, and a certain confidence in being able to talk with and feel for more than one class of person was useful.

I mention this in order to explain my degree of interest in the nature of Marxism, articles about which began to get themselves printed in the later years of *Hound & Horn*. As for the philosophical or economic basis of Marxist theory, or the position of its various factions or political strategems, I never gave a damn. But I did become involved with some individuals actually in the field, who interested me personally. There was a southern boy, an organizer of sharecroppers, of whom I saw a great deal. He seemed to me an up-dated representative of confederacy of the same ilk as Stuart or Pelham. I was more interested in people than notions, and hence it was almost a relief when the maga-

zine was terminated. However, if serving no other purpose, it was edu-
cational. It did provide a passport of a kind which was to be used on
less flabby material. It also left me highly critical of similar ventures,
for I note in them the tendency to which we also were susceptible, mu-
tual self-service and support of coterie predilections.

I recall very little of individual editorial conferences. I remember, in
the first years, driving up to Portland, Maine, to read proof at the
Southworth Press, under the direction of Fred Anthoensen, a printer
of taste and sympathy for our not very lucrative contract. I spent a con-
siderable amount of care on format and decorations. The Widener Li-
brary's rare-book room, which encased the fine collection of young
Harry Widener, and the course in book design led by George Parker
Winship made us conscious of the importance of the looks of a page of
print. Eliot's *Criterion* was designed (and published) by an eminent
English printer, R. Cobden-Sanderson, although his presentation was
far more chaste than ours. Rockwell Kent, whom I then admired as a
latter-day William Blake, made decorations for us at what he called
"children's prices"; later, W. A. Dwiggins drew some printers' "flow-
ers," which I thought very pretty and other editors felt very silly. My
own silliness increased in mathematical proportion to the emphasis on
Humanism, Agrarianism, and Marxism. Varian Fry was tacitly ex-
cluded early on as being "impossible," and he left. I really had little to
do with the magazine in its last years, except to fulfill ordinary obliga-
tions and to pursue the inertia of habit. There is a good short essay
(about as long as its subject is justifiable) in the Yale University *Ga-
zette* for January 1965 which anatomizes the intellectual skeleton that
projected our tables-of-contents. It was by Leonard Greenbaum, then
an assistant professor of English at the College of Engineering at the
University of Michigan at Ann Arbor. This was the first historico-
critical piece about the magazine that had an impersonal stamp; he
called *Hound & Horn* "an adventure in ideas." I have called myself an
adventurer, but with myself the adventuring was more with people
than notions, although the people may have been characterized by con-
geries of ideas entangling them.

I remember several hideous scenes involving refusals of contribu-
tions, misplaced and unacknowledged manuscripts, unpaid bills, and
disagreements about payments to needy or politically important con-

tributors. The concluding article in a series by Adrian Stokes, a writer on the Italian Renaissance promoted by Ezra Pound and subsequently an art historian of note, was killed by me, for no other reason than that I felt it unreadable. After the magazine accumulated a fragile reputation of its own and began to be taken seriously (up to a point), I withdrew, both out of a sense of inadequacy facing the dominant interests, however divergent, of Bernard Bandler, Richard Blackmur, and the contributors they preferred, and because they bored me. I was not very responsible; I felt that the pieces, reviews or verse that I wrote myself which essentially interested neither of them, must seem frivolous. I have described elsewhere how Bandler aspired to be (after college) a new Aristotle. Actually, he turned out to be a distinguished psychiatrist, but his intellectual ambition was daunting. Dick Blackmur worked in Maurice Firuski's excellent Dunster House Bookshop and conducted informal seminars with undergraduates who came to find the latest books recommended by the *Criterion*, the *Little Review*, or *transition*. Firuski loved fine printing and published limited editions, beautifully presented, of texts he admired, older ones by George Santayana and new ones by the promising Archibald MacLeish. Blackmur had the day-to-day burden of keeping shop. The Dunster House Bookshop was of the same rare quality of Heywood Hill's on Curzon Street, Basil Blackwell's in Oxford, and Terence Holliday's on Forty-Ninth Street in New York. Such shops which were also gathering places of men interested in ideas seem hardly to exist today, even on the university level. These were less "advance-guard" than a place where the best of the academic energy was available as lively amenities.

Dick Blackmur wrote lucubrations on smallish white paper pads, in a hand that was not crabbed, but miniaturized, square and clear. There was no crossing out or emendations; his notes always stood ready for the printer. One day, he protested when I said he was the best educated man I'd ever met, and the reason for this was that he'd never been able to go to Harvard. Nevertheless, this was a deprivation that troubled him through his life, and my flattery, and that of others later, was small consolation. He rejected the compliment bitterly, saying he could not teach himself Sanskrit. At the time, I had no notion of why Sanskrit was important; to me the whole subject of semantics or linguistics was about as germane to my idea of fun as Thomist philosophy. I loved the persona of Eliot but rarely knew what he was talking about. Blackmur ended up at Princeton; I prized his poetry more than his prose and am happy his poems are now published. They are poignant and precise, concentrated and elegant. He was a great influence in our minuscule world, and his handwriting—cramped, delicate, and precise—perfectly reflected this influence.

In writing this note, I have found it necessary to make a distinction between what I personally felt about *Hound & Horn* and whatever intrinsic or objective value the collective activity of seven years at a certain juncture in a particular place may have had. Ms. Hamovitch's selection of documents is probably as representative a reliquary as can be managed. For myself, it seems mostly juvenalia; what I prize most in recollection is the encouragement, advice, and friendship of half a dozen collaborators. The magazine helped me clear my mind and decide on several things I finally found that I did not want to do. It provided a series of heady flirtations with current fashions in thinking; more importantly, it gave one a sense of the vitality of a few working intelligences who were interested enough in general principles to apply these to particulars. The magazine, which at its start called itself "a Harvard Miscellany" and dropped this title later as jejeune, was indeed exactly that. Without Cambridge it could not have happened. At least nothing like it was to appear in New Haven, Princeton, Chicago, or Ann Arbor. The magazine could never compare in quality to the *Criterion* under Eliot, the *Dial* under Marianne Moore, the *Little Review* under Jane Heap, or *transition* under Eugene Jolas. It borrowed elements from all of these, whose editors were senior to ourselves. Looking back, I most regret our rejection of Hart Crane's "Tunnel" section from "The Bridge." Perhaps I learned most, at least whatever good I may have done in writing verse, from Yvor Winters. My most constant stimulation and awareness of discovery came from A. Hyatt Mayor. The single piece prompted by myself which I feel does me most credit was a translation of some of the great *sura* of the Koran, done by an anonymous scholar whose heavy effect on me determined the structure of my subsequent development.

Lincoln Kirstein

THE
Hound & Horn
LETTERS

Introduction

A number of the leading writers and critics of our time—Ezra Pound, Archibald MacLeish, Katherine Anne Porter, E. E. Cummings, Marianne Moore, William Carlos Williams, Allen Tate, Stephen Spender, and others—wrote these letters, for the most part, during the life span of the *Hound and Horn*, 1927–1934. Therefore, besides being personal, they reflect some of the literary, cultural, and ideological concerns of a tumultuous period in American history, the high prosperity of the late twenties and the deepening depression of the early thirties.

A brilliant literary quarterly, the *Hound and Horn* was founded by Harvard undergraduates Lincoln Kirstein and Varian Fry and was named after two lines from a poem by Ezra Pound, "The White Stag."

> 'Tis the white stag, Fame, we're a-hunting
> Bid the world's hounds come to horn!

Irritated by its policies several years later, Pound nicknamed the magazine the Bitch and Bugle; Kirstein wrote about the name, "Even up to seven years later confused people would send us advertisements of prize beagles and airedales thinking we were a hunting magazine."[1]

Readers of a certain age can still remember today the pleasure with which they read in its pages the modernist fiction of Erskine Caldwell, Kay Boyle, Stephen Spender, and Seán O'Faoláin, and the experi-

---

[1] The material quoted from Kirstein and Fry, unless otherwise noted, is taken from Lincoln Kirstein, "The *Hound and Horn*, 1927–1934" (with a letter from Varian Fry as a note), *Harvard Advocate* 121, no. 2 (Christmas 1934).

I

mental poetry of E. E. Cummings, William Carlos Williams, Wallace Stevens, Marianne Moore, and others. It is no less absorbing today to browse through issues of the *Hound and Horn* and encounter as if freshly written Foster Damon's essay on *Ulysses*, Lincoln Kirstein on the Diaghilev period, Lewis Galantière's review of Hemingway's *A Farewell to Arms*, Katherine Anne Porter's unforgettable short story "Flowering Judas," and Edmund Wilson's "The Ambiguity of Henry James," the now-classic Freudian interpretation of *The Turn of the Screw.*

Drawings by Picasso and Gaston Lachaise were reproduced in the magazine as well as photographs by Harry Crosby and Walker Evans, then an unknown photographer whose camera artistry was discovered by Kirstein. Some of the finest critical writing of the period could be found in the *Hound and Horn*—Allen Tate's important reviews of Eliot's "Ash Wednesday" and of Edmund Wilson's *Axel's Castle*, of Hart Crane's "The Bridge" as well as an evaluation of Crane's work after his suicide. Richard Blackmur's critical essays included his "Critical Prefaces," reprinted later as the introduction to Henry James's *Art of the Novel*, and studies of T. S. Eliot, E. E. Cummings, Wallace Stevens, and Ezra Pound. Yvor Winters's reviews of the poetry of T. Sturge Moore, Robert Bridges, and the *Oxford Book of Sixteenth-Century Verse* provided material later for his critical work *Primitivism and Decadence*. In the *Hound and Horn* letters, we read about works that are classics today being commissioned by the editors of the magazine or suggested as possibilities by their authors. We see, too, another aspect readers never see—the hectic, confusing, humorous, often slapdash life behind the impressive and somewhat august facade of one of the leading American literary magazines of its time.

The letters have a revealing personal aspect as well: Katherine Anne Porter announcing her (now famous) story "Flowering Judas," hoping it will prove suitable for publication; Lincoln Kirstein commissioning E. E. Cummings (whom he saw as the American Cocteau) to create a choreodrama for a ballet based on *Uncle Tom's Cabin* to be choreographed by George Balanchine (Balanchine, it is discovered later in the letters, is lukewarm to the idea, and besides, the translator of Cummings's libretto into Russian for Balanchine does not think too highly of Cummings's English!); Archibald MacLeish highly amused by Ernest Hemingway's letter to the *Hound and Horn* in answer to an essay critical of his work; T. E. Lawrence, seeking to deflect Kirstein's adulation by protesting that he is "just an ordinary man"; and, in a little paragraph tucked away in a letter to Cocteau in December 1929, Kirstein describing to Cocteau his inadvertent witnessing of Diaghilev's funeral, while he was visiting the Church of San Giorgio dei Greci in Venice.

In the 1920s, America was breaking away from its colonial status in the Western world of letters and establishing itself as an artistic force, with the writing of Eliot, Pound, Hemingway, Faulkner, and Fitzgerald. To that end, Kirstein's letters encourage the publication of hitherto unpublished American writers. In fact, for a time, he refused the writing of non-Americans, with the exception of Stephen Spender, who had become a friend and whose work he greatly admired. This policy provoked an exchange between editor A. Hyatt Mayor and Alan Stroock, business manager of the magazine. A query from Mayor about the reason for Kirstein's refusal to publish photographs by the French photographer Eugène Atget elicited the reply that Atget was not American. "Ask Kirstein if Diaghilev was an American," wrote co-editor Bernard Bandler to Stroock, urging the publication of Atget. Stroock wrote plaintively to Mayor, "The Pope and Henry VIII are at it again." Atget was not published.

Although expatriation was still in evidence in the early thirties (with Ezra Pound as foreign advisor to the *Hound and Horn* writing from his home in Rapallo, Italy, T. S. Eliot in London, and Katherine Anne Porter living in Paris), Archibald MacLeish had returned to the United States from Paris and was working for *Fortune* magazine, Malcolm Cowley, contributor of poetry to the *Hound and Horn* and chronicler of the expatriates of the twenties with his book *Exile's Return*, was an editor of the *New Republic*, and Lincoln Kirstein wrote that he had just returned from Europe and didn't "want to go abroad again for years and years and years." After three concentrated months in the midst of the so-called culture capitals, he said, "I am convinced more than ever, that this country is the one place to do something" (to Yvor Winters, 31 August 1933).

Because of Kirstein's catholicity of interest, the letters record major events in the worlds of art, architecture, dance, film, and photography in the late twenties and the early thirties. Reference in Marianne Moore's letters to H. A. Potamkin's brilliant *Hound and Horn* essays on the film genius of directors René Clair, Georg Wilhelm Pabst, Vsevolod Pudovkin, and Sergei Eisenstein remind us of the excitement of the movies for an earlier time. Editor A. Hyatt Mayor's letters mention his essays on Picasso's method, before Guernica, and on the role of the newly created Museum of Modern Art, built in 1929. The Matisse frescoes in the Barnes Museum in Merion, Pennsylvania, were being installed (1933), and Russian choreographer Leonid Massine was creating dances for the audiences at Radio City Music Hall, much to Lincoln Kirstein's disgust. However, underlying the brilliance and glitter of the arts is the ominous presence of the rising war machine in Hitler's Germany. Hitler's *Mein Kampf* was translated into English and reviewed as *The Battle* in the *Hound and Horn*, winter issue, 1933, by M. R. Werner, who wrote, "Such a man will probably push Germany and Europe to destruction, for Hitler, along with many of his adopted countrymen, lacks creative imagination and can only wish to destroy."

The *Hound and Horn* owed its existence to a burgeoning of little magazines that began in the second decade of the century. When Harriet Monroe founded *Poetry* in Chicago in 1912, she led the way to a renaissance of little magazines that had a profound effect on American letters. Floyd Dell and Max Eastman initiated *The Masses* (1912–1917), a left-wing literary magazine and precursor to the leftist magazines of the thirties. Alfred Kreymborg's *Glebe* (1913–1914) and *Others* (1917–1919) and Margaret Anderson's *Little Review* (1914–1929) were all founded to encourage the writing of talented unknowns who would not have been brought to public attention otherwise. In fact, 95% of our post-1912 poets were introduced by these magazines.[2] Added to writers whose names were famous—such as Edwin Arlington Robinson, Edgar Lee Masters, and Sara Teasdale—were new discoveries, Carl Sandburg, Vachel Lindsay, T. S. Eliot, Wallace Stevens, Marianne Moore, John Reed, John Gould Fletcher, Maxwell Bodenheim, and Robert Frost.

Along with the wish to encourage new talent was a strong desire to

[2] Frederick J. Hoffman, Charles Allen, Carolyn F. Ulrich, *The Little Magazine* (Princeton, N.J.: Princeton University Press, 1947), p. 8.

rebel against the old, traditional forms of expression as well as against the social and cultural standards of the time. At Ezra Pound's instigation, *Poetry* published the revolutionary poetry of the Imagists in 1912 and Eliot's "Love Song of J. Alfred Prufrock" in 1915. The *Little Review* prided itself on its serialization of parts of James Joyce's *Ulysses*, 1918–1920, long before the novel was allowed publication in the United States in 1933. In 1922, the *Dial*'s publication of Eliot's "Waste Land" assured Eliot's place in the world of letters. In short, the most exciting avant-garde writing of the second and third decades of the century was made available to the public through the little magazines. They published what the commercial magazines, *Scribner's*, *Atlantic Monthly*, and *Harper's*, were not ready for.

Most of the little magazines (so called because of their relatively minuscule readership) were short-lived; they lasted for a year or two, if that. Sometimes just one issue sufficed to express its editor's message, the demise occurring because of lack of funds, because of the dearth of usable material, or simply because of the accomplishment of the editor's mission. Because the *Hound and Horn* could rely on regular funding, it had continuity that enabled it to undertake long-term projects. It could also afford to remain detached from the demands of the marketplace and thereby remain aloof from current movements and fads, if it chose. A distinguished representative of those magazines that sought to retain a degree of political detachment in the thirties, the *Hound and Horn* was one of the very few that remained uncommitted to a left-wing or Marxist position. This, no doubt, in large part accounts for the timeless quality of its articles and reviews and its enduring readability.

Background of the *Hound & Horn*

The *Hound and Horn* began because Harvard undergraduates Lincoln Kirstein and Varian Fry were led to believe that they would not be accepted on the editorial board of the *Harvard Advocate* and so decided to publish their own literary magazine, funded in large part by Kirstein's father, the president of Filene's department store in Boston. Despite the editors' youth and inexperience, they founded a magazine that was to become one of the most highly regarded literary and critical journals in the country; later, the funds that supported it were diverted into the establishment of the School of American Ballet, seedbed for the world-renowned New York City Ballet, of which Kirstein is director, and choreographer George Balanchine is artistic director.

For their fledgling magazine, subtitled "A Harvard Miscellany," Kirstein and Fry initially planned a series of critical articles about outstanding Harvard alumni: T. S. Eliot, Henry James, George Santayana, Henry Adams, and others, each to be accompanied by a bibliography. A two-part critical essay on Eliot by Richard Blackmur, with bibliography by Varian Fry, was published in volume 1, but after that the project was dropped until vol. 7, number 3, an issue on Henry James. Although I was not given permission to reprint T. S. Eliot's letters, the letters from the editors to Eliot will give the reader a clear idea of the working relationship between the young *Hound and Horn* editors, in their very early twenties, and the encouraging, world-renowned alumnus, editor of *Criterion*.

Besides being scholarly, the magazine aimed to be modernist, to bring "to the consciousness of Harvard the recent developments in art and literature it seemed to us to be ignoring, to its own cost," as Varian Fry wrote.[3] "I was an admirer of Joyce, Kirstein of Eliot. We had both read Gertrude Stein, looked at Picasso, listened to Strawinski [*sic*]. They seemed to be important, and we felt that Harvard undergraduates ought to know more about them than they did. It was to hail the new and glittering world they and their influences were creating, and to bid farewell to the stodgy in the nineteenth century and its heavy hand on the twentieth, that I . . . wrote that first editorial."

From its parochial beginnings as a Harvard journal, the *Hound and Horn* became overly ambitious and highbrow, Fry thought, when Bernard Bandler, a recent Harvard graduate and assistant in the philosophy department, "bringing Humanism with him," and Richard Blackmur, then a bookstore clerk, became editors in 1929. Fry wrote, "In our effort to be mature, we came to scorn . . . college boyishness, and

---

[3] In a further attempt to introduce modernism to Harvard, Lincoln Kirstein, John Walker III, and Edward Warburg, of the banking family, founded the Harvard Society for Contemporary Art in 1928. It is generally credited with being the forerunner of New York's Museum of Modern Art.

much of what we published was certainly above the heads of our intended audience, as it was sometimes above our own." Varian Fry left the magazine after a "family quarrel." He was to achieve recognition later when, as representative of the Emergency Relief Committee, he helped over 1,500 persons escape from German-occupied France in 1940–1941.

In the winter of 1930, the magazine moved to New York, to a small office on East 43rd Street, and became national in scope. The *Hound and Horn* sold for 50 cents a copy and cost 40 cents to print. "We lost about eight thousand dollars a year. If we had ever twenty-five thousand dollars a year to spend we could have made it pay for itself in two and a half or three years, I'm pretty sure. . . . We never sold many more than 4000 copies of an issue, but had nearly seven hundred libraries all over the world on our list." Initially, the magazine paid $7.50 a page for poetry and $3.50 a page for prose, while the *Dial* (1917–1929) paid $20 a page for poetry and $10 a page for prose, the reason it could command the best writing of the period. "We always tried in giving our poems to the *Dial* to make them just over a page," said Malcolm Cowley to me in an interview in 1978. Most of the little magazines did not pay anything at all in the 1920s—*transition* paid 50 cents a page, the *Little Review* paid nothing.

The *Hound and Horn* was considered by many to be the successor to the *Dial*, with its emphasis on criticism and modernism, and it modeled itself for a time after T. S. Eliot's London-based *Criterion*. Ezra Pound hoped that the *Hound and Horn* would be less cautious than its paradigms, and Richard Blackmur answered, "You ask, Is the *Hound and Horn* ready to do what the *Dial*, and *Criterion* won't? Answer: I don't know. But certainly, seriously, we are trying not to do certain things those magazines do do . . ." (20 May 1929, Chap. I, Letter 2). And later in the same letter, Blackmur wrote, "I quote your paragraph—'I take it the Hound and Horn exists for licherchoor only,' and say I think so. That is why we publish almost nothing but criticism, there not being much of the other available." What the *Hound and Horn* wanted for "licherchoor" was previously unpublished American writing of a certain caliber, and Blackmur's complaint was familiar to publishers looking for good new talent. By 1933, modernist fiction was finding a market in the higher-paying magazines like *Scribner's,* and Yvor Winters was advising Kirstein to concentrate on the areas of poetry and criticism, where the magazine could still afford to compete for superior material.

The mainstay of the magazine was Lincoln Kirstein, who, independently wealthy, could afford to make a career of the unprofitable *Hound and Horn*, but a number of brilliant young men came and went as editors, on their way to establishing their names in the world of letters, the arts, academe, or, as in the case of Bernard Bandler, psychiatry. Richard Blackmur, first managing editor of the *Hound and Horn*, was able to leave his position as bookstore clerk to pursue his writing of critical essays and poetry as a result of his work for the magazine, but in 1930, there was no longer money enough to pay him, and he resigned. He continued, however, to write for the magazine. A. Hyatt Mayor and Francis Fergusson, characterized by Lincoln Kirstein as "two of the magazine's chief props" and both involved with the American Laboratory Theatre, became editors in 1930. Mayor left the *Hound and Horn* to work in the Print Department of the Metropolitan Museum; he later became curator of prints. Francis Fergusson has had a distinguished career as a professor and literary critic. Ezra Pound, who was active in over one hundred little magazines, became foreign advisor from his base in Rapallo, from 1930 to 1931; from 1932 to 1934, Allen Tate, as southern editor, brought Agrarian philosophy and the New Criticism to the magazine, and Yvor Winters, western editor, introduced his own brand of rigorous criticism and an intense approach to poetry.

The Impact of Humanism

The influence of Bernard Bandler on the *Hound and Horn* was great. That he had a profound effect on Lincoln Kirstein was evident. "He had a mind that was so fluent, so much the master of intellectual and philosophical abstractions, so deeply involved with the real business of the spirit, that when he first talked to me at any length I was exhausted for two days. He wrote an essay on W. C. Brownell and others on Charles du Bos and Irving Babbitt. He might have been a rabbi or a priest, and is now doctor of medicine. His influence on the *Hound and*

Horn, at least from a critical point of view, was its formulating one," wrote Kirstein in the *Harvard Advocate*.

Bandler's strong enthusiasms led the *Hound and Horn* down an erratic path, committing the magazine at first to Humanism and then to Agrarianism. His keen interest in Henry James resulted in the publication of the most memorable issue of the magazine, a homage to James. In 1932 Bandler withdrew as editor to study medicine and is now an eminent Boston psychiatrist.

For Bernard Bandler, Irving Babbitt, professor of French literature at Harvard, was the true Humanist—a man of erudition, humanity, and scholarship. Babbitt and Paul Elmer More, the founders of American Humanism, conceived of Humanism as an attempt to define the nature of man through an evaluation of life and literature. They saw the literary movements Romanticism and Naturalism as the *bêtes noires* that had encouraged an overindulgence of emotion and a weakening of the intellect and the will. Modern-day chaos was the result. Unless man could be prevailed on, through individual control, to curb the evil side of his lust for power, for knowledge, for sensation, civilization was doomed. To achieve happiness, man should become "ethically efficient" and restrain his temperament and impulse. Babbitt advocated an inner check or vital control (*frein vital*) to subdue the natural man, while an outer control was to be brought about by a kind of aristocracy in taste, manners, education, and decorum. Humanism aspired to cultivate "one's humanity" through "moderate and decorous living" and inner "poise." There was to be nothing in excess, and the avoidance of "uniqueness, spontaneity, and above all, intensity."[4]

The weakness of Babbitt's philosophy was that he nowhere made clear just how man was to control his lower nature, nor did he present a program whereby man could achieve an aristocracy of behavior. However, the movement held great attraction for many people because of its advocacy of order and decorum in a time of increasing loss of restraints and questioning of traditional values, the period characterized by F. Scott Fitzgerald as "the greatest, gaudiest spree in history." Like all such movements, however, it provoked a great deal of controversy. Several literary journals—particularly the *Bookman* and the *Forum*—

[4] Irving Babbitt, "Humanism, an Essay at Definition," *Humanism and America*, ed. Norman Foerster (New York: Farrar, 1930), pp. 28–29.

published articles that explained and defended Humanism. The *Hound and Horn* entered the fray, propelled into it both by Bandler's enthusiasm and by T. S. Eliot's counterproposal, when he was invited to write on Henry James for the magazine, that he write on Humanism instead. Six articles on Humanism by Eliot, Allen Tate, Bernard Bandler, and others were published in the *Hound and Horn*, but finally Bandler became disillusioned about the subject; he found its goals undefined and its program vague. In a conversation with me in 1975, Bandler reminisced, "Babbitt was wonderful in the classroom, a man who had an exciting mind, *enormous* learning, *great* erudition." But as for Humanism, "it was very hard to define; that was the great weakness. It was surprisingly thin in terms of anything constructive. But it wasn't until I began to write my essay that I saw how thin it was." And Bandler guffawed as he remembered an incident when, as Babbitt and he were walking down a street in Paris, they were approached by a beggar. Without hesitating, Babbitt reached into his pocket and gave the man some money, "quite a humanitarian thing to do," recalled Bandler, "at a time when the word 'humanitarian' [with its implication of undisciplined emotion] was anathema to Humanists." The impact of the movement that critic Gorham Munson labeled as "the only movement in contemporary American thought of international importance" was short-lived.[5] Humanism as a program for the *Hound and Horn* was dropped, and Eliot wrote Tate in 1930 that he was "so sickened by the kind of publicity which these philosophical discussions have obtained in America, and by the reciprocal violence of vituperation, that I never want to hear the word humanism again."[6] The decision to end the Humanist discussion was applauded by most of the correspondents. Ezra Pound had written on 10 January 1930, "One ought to devote *one* obit. to each of these winds . . . and then move out into criticism." Archibald MacLeish wrote, "[I] hope that you will go on with the *Hound and Horn* as a magazine devoted to the arts of writing and painting. All the rest of them are running after the philosophs—the Babbitts and the rest whose only effect on writing . . . is to kill it" (undated;

[5] "The Artist's Stone," *Pagany* 1, no. 1 (Winter 1930), p. 3.
[6] Tate papers, quoted from G. A. M. Janssens, *The American Literary Review* (The Hague: Mouton, 1968), p. 115.

Chap. IV, Letter 13). But one who dissented was Seán O'Faoláin, who commented, "Good Christ, why do you drop a good thing like that? I had hoped for more solid things from the *Hound and Horn* than this news-sheet impatience for something new, fresh, etc. No number should be published which does not contain, as the *Criterion* aspires to, at least one article of *permanent* value as a contribution to knowledge. But you Americans don't know what permanent means. Didn't you invent the phrase semi-permanent?" (3 July 1930; Chap. IV, Letter 25).

Ezra Pound

From his home in Rapallo, as foreign advisor from 1930 to 1931, Ezra Pound bombarded the editors of *Hound and Horn* with letters, urging the publication of poetry and fiction by his newest protégés, Louis Zukofsky, Basil Bunting, and Robert McAlmon, and increasing his attack on American society. "God eternally damblast a country that spends billions interfering with people's diets and that cannot support a single printing press which will print stuff that people like me want to read; i.e. regardless of immediate fiscal profit . . ." (3 August 1930; Chap. I, Letter 19). "Bloody bureaucracy etc. low grade mutts allowed to govern. Billions for prevention of normal diets and nothing for education." Pound's aesthetic prescription at this time included propagandistic devices. "The american short story can just as well develop in portraying the kinds of sonvabitch that get elected or appointed to posts in which they can retard or ruin the nation." "Make the bloody freshman do a portrait of his congressman, not of his aunt Jemima" (8 February 1930; Chap. I, Letter 8).

A kind of Poundian cultural center had been created at Rapallo, with visits from Yeats, pilgrimages from Pound's disciples, would-be poets, editors of little magazines, and "old Ez's scholars," who followed him in his enthusiasms for the Renaissance to his obsession with modern banking. New sections of the *Cantos* appeared from time to time, as well as other works of literary criticism and political writing. Pound also began his one-man campaign of reform, writing to magazines all over the world in his effort to spread the gospel of Social Credit economics.[7]

After the death of the *Dial* in 1929, Pound allied himself with the *Hound and Horn*, hoping to find a fresh outlet for his ideas. In his letters, we see Pound trying to relive the heady days of early experimentalism, when he had done so much to break ground for the new work of the Imagists H. D., Richard Aldington, and F. S. Flint, of D. H. Lawrence, Robert Frost, James Joyce, T. S. Eliot, William Carlos Williams, and others. Although Pound did what he could to foster the publication of Zukofsky and Bunting and the commissioning of new material from Wyndham Lewis, he was not too successful. Kirstein, responsible for the editorial policy of the magazine, thought Bunting derivative of Pound and, of Zukofsky's work, published a three-part essay on Henry Adams and some poetry.

Pound's *Cantos* XXVIII–XXX and some of his vituperative letters, under the heading of "Correspondence," were printed in the magazine. His targets were familiar—the shortsightedness and philistinism of the American government and the American or "Murkn" people, the stodginess of academe, the "cretinity" of the publishers, and the Old Guard conservatism of the American Academy of Arts and Letters that was reluctant to make room for such exciting moderns as Ernest Hemingway, Theodore Dreiser, and Eugene O'Neill. What exacerbated his feelings still further was that two essays he sent to the *Hound and Horn*, his own "Terra Italica" and a translation of Cocteau's "Mystère Laic," were not accepted by the editors. The editors thought the "Terra Italica" confused and disjointed in style and, in the main, repetitive of those letters of Pound's that were printed in the magazine; they found the translation of Cocteau's "Mystère Laic" awkward. Irritated by what he considered a tremendous error in judgment and further angered by a delay in the return in the "Terra Italica" and the possible loss of the "Mystère Laic," Pound withdrew from the *Hound and Horn* in disgust. "You will probably discover that the ms/ has been mislaid in transferring your offices from one palatial office to another. I

[7] Pound's economic belief stemmed from Major C. H. Douglas's theory of Social Credit, which stated that the interest charges established by the banking system (Pound's "usura") led to an imbalance between production and purchasing power, thereby generating underconsumption and unemployment.

wish I had never heard of yr/ magazine and I think you a god damn fool not to have printed the M.L. both for its integral quality and for its value proportionally to what you do print," wrote Pound to Kirstein on 8 July 1931 (Chap. I, Letter 32).

"We found the Mystère Laic. As I read it over I was overwhelmed with a sense of guilt that we had not published it. . . . So few of the things we publish have anywhere nearly its distinction and lucidity," Kirstein wrote to A. Hyatt Mayor in August 1931. Kirstein did not entirely discard the possibility of a reconciliation, but Pound was too "fed up at working for two years for a pair of rich fahrts and not getting paid" to prolong the association.[8]

"Artists are the antennae of their race," Pound wrote. His ideal society was that in which artists were honored prophets, and his urgent tone and frantic style of communication were a measure of his obsessive need to convert the reader to his world view. As Eliot wrote, "Pound often presents the appearance of a man trying to convey to a very deaf person the fact that the house is on fire. . . . He has a passionate desire not merely to write well himself, but to live in a period in which he could be surrounded by equally intelligent and creative minds. Hence his impatience."[9]

During the thirties, life was rigorous for many artists; Pound, who had contributed so greatly to the arts, sadly lacked recognition of a practical sort. James Laughlin, today the head of New Directions Press and publisher of Pound's work, then a Harvard undergraduate on the editorial board of the *Harvard Advocate*, wrote Kirstein in 1933 asking him how much "Pound charges for a Canto." Kirstein's facetious yet poignant reply was, "I dare say you could get it for nothing except postage . . . as I remember, I paid Pound for three cantos, one hundred dollars. He would take the same now, or probably less" (5 October 1933; Chap. V, Letter 28).

In the end, the association between Ezra Pound and the *Hound and Horn* proved too heady, and "finally, in spite of his lovely poems and his marvelous letters, we couldn't face the attendant coterie of lame duck discoveries he was always capriciously harboring, and we were relieved

---

[8] Zukofsky papers. Cited in Janssens, p. 124.
[9] *The Literary Essays of Ezra Pound*, ed. T. S. Eliot (Norfolk, Conn.: New Directions, 1954), p. xii.

to let him be obscene about us in other 'little magazines,'" wrote Lincoln Kirstein in the *Harvard Advocate*, 1934.

Allen Tate, Agrarianism, and the New Criticism

Allen Tate's advocacy of Agrarianism was primarily a desire to emphasize the gentility, traditionalism, and graces of the antebellum South to mitigate the encroachment of the industrial mechanization of the North. Tate felt, as well, that the South "provided a usable myth, a frame of reference for his own poetry—some of the best of which, he was to admit later, was written during the Agrarian phase." [10]

As southern regional editor for the *Hound and Horn* from 1932 to 1934 and as an Agrarian, Allen Tate sought to add to the roster of contributors to the magazine the friends who had worked with him on the *Fugitive*, an outstanding little magazine published in the years 1922–1925 in Nashville, Tennessee. Among the group were John Crowe Ransom, Robert Penn Warren, Donald Davidson, Andrew Lytle, and others. An essay by Davidson, "Sectionalism in the United States," stressed the importance of maintaining the autonomy of various sections of America. Book reviews by Andrew Lytle and Frank Owsley on the fathers of secession, Edmund Ruffin and Robert Barnwell Rhett, and on Agrarian philosophers Thomas Jefferson and du Pont de Nemours, and by Paul Buck of Allen Tate's two biographies, *Jefferson Davis* and *Stonewall Jackson*, were published as well, but essays by Ransom and Warren were received too late in the life of the *Hound and Horn* for publication.

Personally interested in the Agrarian cause, Bernard Bandler wrote Tate 10 November 1931 (Chap. VI, Letter 6), "Fergusson, Mayor, and I sat down with *I'll Take My Stand*[11] to do our type of *New Republic* editorial, but I laid down my Davidson's chapter and thought it

[10] *Fugitives' Reunion*, ed. Rob Roy Purdy (Nashville, Tenn.: Vanderbilt University Press, 1959), p. 180. Quoted by Janssens, p. 133.

[11] *I'll Take My Stand* was a collection of essays published in 1930 by twelve Southerners, members of the "Nashville group," who advocated an Agrarian way of life, as suggested by the small farms of the old Middle South, in an effort to forestall the increasing encroachments of the modern industrial age.

was pretty good, and Mayor weakly confessed he liked Ransom, and Fergusson was impressed with whatever he read, so instead of doing you in an editorial, we all but bought tickets for Nashville. I . . . would like to see the movement in action." Writing to me in 1975, Dr. Bandler stated,

> As to the attraction of Agrarianism, I had great admiration for the writings of the *Fugitive* group. . . . I felt strongly that art and literature emerged from the basis of a community and its culture. Even exiles like Joyce drew sustenance from their native soil such as Dublin, and the South had been an American culture just as had been the New England of Hawthorne and Melville and Emerson. So the Fugitives had an American past although romanticized. The idea of indigenous communities and cultures was one of the reasons that led me to propose regional editors for the *Hound and Horn*.

Lincoln Kirstein himself was bitten by the southern bug. "I never gave a damn about Agrarianism. I was mad for the Civil War and never got anywhere with my book on [John] Pelham [Civil War hero]. I went all over the Virginia battlefields; some of this comes into my book about Robert Gould Shaw[12] [the New Englander who led the first black platoon to fight for the Union in the Civil War]" (letter to me, December 1975).

It is as a critic, however, that Allen Tate left his mark on the *Hound and Horn*. His letters give insight into the writing of some of his reviews, particularly of Eliot's "Ash Wednesday." Tate stresses the importance, in a critical review, of adhering to a close technical analysis of the poem, rather than presenting a moralistic, historical, impressionistic, or other kind of reading. He objected particularly to the kind of criticism then used frequently by some critics in reviewing "Ash Wednesday," of analyzing the poem in terms of Eliot's psychological needs and religious conversion, rather than dealing with the poem as an entity in itself. A case in point is the fascinating exchange between Alan Stroock and Tate. When Stroock wrote to Tate (September 1930), "We should have liked to have had more attention paid to a critique of the poem as poetry, than to a defense of T. S. Eliot," Tate replied, "It is

[12] *Lay this Laurel*, with photographs by Richard Benson (New York: Eakins Press, 1973).

not so much a defense of Eliot as the plea for a sound critical proce-
dure. Edmund Wilson's review of 'Ash Wednesday' [in the *New Re-
public*] seems to me to be very unsound; it ends up with some very
disconcerting speculation on Eliot's private life which has no signifi-
cance at all. When a man of Wilson's great gifts succumbs to the zeit-
geist, it is surely powerful enough to justify comment at length. I will
rewrite the review. . . . I see your point of view perfectly." Stroock was
bringing Tate back to the business at hand, which was a reaffirmation
of the kind of technical criticism Tate had begun to advocate in the late
twenties, a forerunner of what Ransom was to label the "New Crit-
icism" in his book of that name, published in 1941.

In a letter dated June 1931, Lincoln Kirstein said to the composer
Roger Sessions, "I feel the *Hound and Horn* has a definite function to
fill which, generally speaking, is to provide as good technical criticism
for intelligent laymen as possible, the minimum of rhetoric and rhap-
sody." That he achieved his goal is borne out by John Bradbury, who
wrote that after the *Hound and Horn* had ceased publication, there was
no other organ in America with critical standards approximating those
it had advocated.[13] And in *The Little Magazine*, Frederick Hoffman
wrote that "the *Hound and Horn*'s Art, Book, and Music Chronicles
were equaled only by those in T. S. Eliot's *Criterion*."[14]

Yvor Winters

The scope of the magazine was enlarged still further when Yvor Win-
ters became a regular contributor to the *Hound and Horn* in 1930 and
western regional editor from 1932 until the magazine's demise. The
Hound and Horn provided a forum for Winters's aesthetic theory. In its
pages he set in final form, in his reviews of T. Sturge Moore, Robert
Bridges, and the *Oxford Book of Sixteenth-Century Verse*, his idea that
"moralism"—that is, the ability to distinguish between truth and false-
hood by which the poet evaluates experience—is essential to a work.[15]

[13] *The Fugitives* (Chapel Hill: University of North Carolina Press, 1958), p. 103.
[14] Hoffman, Allen, and Ulrich, p. 208.
[15] Preface to *Primitivism and Decadence* (1937; rpt., New York: Haskell, 1969).

His idea of a great poet is one who is able to weld both style and mood to content. Winters considered that the critic's main aim should be evaluation and that he should develop the ability to decide on the merits of compared poems, stanzas, lines, metaphors, and even words. To that end, he made lists and was constantly ranking poets and various aspects of their poems in a huge assessment that ranged through the centuries.

Because of a clause in his will forbidding publication of his letters for twenty-five years after his death, which occurred in 1968, I am unable to include any of the over two hundred letters in the Archive at Yale. One day, some fortunate editor will have access to Winters's letters, highly judgmental, at times vitriolic, always vigorous, and filled with his dogmatic and precise evaluations.

His letters to Kirstein show him in the process of judging and commenting on writers and their works. He found T. Sturge Moore superior to Yeats, Robert Bridges one of the eight or ten greatest poets in the language, and Howard Baker one of the four finest poets under forty writing in America. He was as adamant as Pound in stressing the importance of standards and values in the literature and life of a society, and he was witty, too. In discussing William Carlos Williams's *A Voyage to Pagany* (1928), he characterized the current fuss about being an American, about whether or not to live in Europe or America, as tiresome. One should take one's nationality casually, "as the Greeks took their liquor and sex, without too much worry." Like the Humanists, Winters saw Romanticism as the villain in modern literature, but he denied emphatically any connection with them. Ironically, although he emphasized the need for rationality, clarity, and logic, Winters argued only his personal enthusiasm when he urged the publication in the *Hound and Horn* of the writing of his students at Stanford (Albert Guérard, Jr., and J. V. Cunningham, winners of the short story and poetry contests, respectively, sponsored by the magazine) or of those who wrote for his magazine, *Gyroscope* (Howard Baker, Janet Lewis, and Grant Code, all of whom were published in the *Hound and Horn*).

Writing about Robert Fitzgerald's review of his book of poems *The Proof* in *Hound and Horn*, volume 4, number 2 (January–March 1931), Winters took issue with Fitzgerald's judgment that he belonged to the Symbolist school of poets. Those writers who most influenced him as a poet, he stated, could be divided into two groups. The first group, consisting of Thomas Hardy, Emily Dickinson, and Baudelaire, affected his attitude toward experience, and the second group, William Carlos Williams, Wallace Stevens, T. Sturge Moore, and Robert Bridges, formed his style. He wrote in 1930 that of all the fiction published in the *Hound and Horn*, Katherine Anne Porter's "Flowering Judas" was the only one that interested him, but he claimed he did not read fiction much and therefore might be a poor judge. He himself wrote only one short story, a superb tale of metaphysical horror, "The Brink of Darkness," published in volume 5, number 4 (July–September 1932). Later, as editor, in 1932, he wrote Allen Tate that Tate's first short story, "The Immortal Woman," came close to being a very fine story but needed a great deal of rewriting. He pointed out obscurities and lack of clarity in the narration of the story. Tate took these criticisms seriously, for, although he replied that the relationships in the story were deliberately obscure—that obscurity was the subject of the story—Tate wrote Kirstein that he had revised the story considerably. "I know it is vastly improved, and I fear after my counter-attack on Winters I have really taken a good deal of his advice."

Kirstein wrote in the *Harvard Advocate*, "Particularly to me personally, Winters was a great aid in all matters relative to verse . . . poetry, he used to rail at me—he felt as a 'life and death matter.' My editorial taste was constantly in a state of burning shame from his explicit and explosive letters."[16]

The *Hound and Horn* never measured up to Winters's exacting standards. In 1933 he wrote Kirstein that higher-paying magazines like *Scribner's* were ready to "risk it" and were taking away from the *Hound and Horn* the better short stories, leaving them "a rotten lot." *Hound and Horn* could compete with other magazines, however, in criticism and poetry. Winters advised that they certainly not abandon fiction but need not publish "messy stuff" in desperation.

When Kirstein announced in July 1934 that he was ceasing publication of the *Hound and Horn*, Winters commiserated with him on the magazine's demise. He noted that his supporters, notably his fa-

---

[16] *Harvard Advocate* 121, no. 2 (Christmas 1934).

ther, should receive due reward in Paradise, despite the fact (he added typically) that as an editor, Kirstein made many more mistakes than he should have.

The Depression and Marxism

In the early 1930s, the realities of the deepening depression were making themselves felt on the determinedly aesthetic *Hound and Horn*. Katherine Anne Porter wrote to Bernard Bandler on 12 December 1929 (Chap. IV, Letter 35), "It occurs to me that you probably pay on publication [instead of on receipt of manuscript] and if you do, this would be so sad for me. I shall ask you to suspend your rule this once in my favor. [The editors did not.] Existence, in a purely material sense, is for me, I assure you, precarious." Kenneth Patchen wrote to Kirstein (Chap. V, Letter 31), "I am working in the Cambridge Rubber Co. My job is to unload drums and crude rubber from a conveyor two men to a drum; drums weigh 500 pounds. Thirty-five cents an hour 7:30 until 5. . . . I am utterly done in at the close of each working day but in spite of this I shall write." In a more humorous vein, Lincoln Kirstein responded to Mrs. Lucy Porter, Glenveagh Castle, Garton, County Donegal, Ireland, 21 December 1931 (Chap. V, Letter 13), "You say that you feel that 'if a magazine has money to sustain an office on the most expensive street in the world, it can easily continue without feeling the loss of my withdrawal.' . . . Since your letter suggests that you are interested in what we are trying to do and are only ceasing your subscription because you wish to curtail your expenses, will you allow us to continue our extravagance in offering you a complimentary subscription?"

During the years of economic ills and political commitment in the 1930s, the *New Republic* provided a forum for writers of liberal persuasion, while the *New Masses* and *Partisan Review* were perhaps the best known of the magazines further to the left.

Bernard Bandler left the *Hound and Horn* in 1932, but he reappeared in the office in the fall of 1933 to urge Kirstein to keep the magazine clear of politics. Kirstein wrote later, "Had the magazine continued it would have been definitely left. My two painter friends,

Philip Reisman and Ben Shahn, and Harry Potamkin [the *Hound and Horn*'s film critic], encyclopedically informed about the movies and the first practising communist I had ever met who literally burned with his ideas of social abuse and exploitation, had shown me the great richness in revolutionary subject matter. The *Hound and Horn* was, even up to its end, pretty consciously isolatedly artistic, and I don't think it was a bad thing at all." [17]

The aesthetic stance of the *Hound and Horn* could not long remain unassailed, however, during the politically turbulent 1930s. Granville Hicks, left-wing contributor to the *New Republic*, incorporated into his review of Lincoln Kirstein's first novel *Flesh is Heir* a criticism of the magazine as being a "leisure-class" publication put out by those who prefer "not to face the grave social problems of the present day." [18] He accused the editors of nurturing an intellectual preciosity both to fill their time and to bolster their feelings of elitism. He labeled the magazine's fiction as "direct and almost childishly behavioristic accounts of naive and bewildered persons" "quite unrelated to the subtle and dignified philosophy, the impressive erudition, the pretentious self-discipline of the articles." [19]

Hound and Horn editors Bandler, Mayor, and Kirstein refuted Hicks's attack with facts, not ideology, in a brief letter, supplying Hicks with a list of the names of editors and contributors who were *not* members of the leisure class (Richard Blackmur, Francis Fergusson, A. Hyatt Mayor, E. E. Cummings, John Cheever, and so on). They said merely, in response to the criticism of their fiction, that "the editors can choose books for a review, select the reviewers (Mr. Hicks has written for the *Hound and Horn*), and assign articles to be written, but with the short stories, they can only publish what to their taste are the best of those submitted" (June 1932; Chap. V, Letter 20).[20] After

---

[17] *Harvard Advocate* 121, no. 2 (Christmas 1934).

[18] Published in 1932 and reissued in 1975 by the University of Southern Illinois Press, Carbondale, Ill., *Flesh is Heir* is a fictionalized autobiography recounting episodes in the life of a sensitive young man in the 1920s. It includes an account of Diaghilev's funeral, which Kirstein inadvertently witnessed. Kirstein's second novel is *For My Brother: A True Story by Jose Martinez Berlanga as Told to Lincoln Kirstein*, published by the Hogarth Press (London, 1934).

[19] "Inheritance Tax," *New Republic*, 20 April 1932, pp. 278–79.

[20] "Correspondence," *New Republic*, 25 May 1932, pp. 48–49.

their response, Dudley Fitts wrote to Kirstein, "I thought you came off rather badly with the incredible playboy from Troy, New York" (30 May 1932; Chap. III, Letter 11). Kirstein replied, agreeing with him but adding, "We were merely pointing out errors in fact of what Hicks said. All this is good publicity and it proves in a way that people do consider the magazine as something worth quarreling with" (4 June 1932; Chap. III, Letter 12).

Hicks replied with more of his leisure-class attack, and the exchange ended with a letter from the editors of the *Hound and Horn* stating that they were doing a greater service to man by providing him with timeless art, in the company of others like Homer, Racine, Shakespeare, than by entering the class struggle.

Michael Gold, editor of *New Masses* and the writer whose name is synonymous with the proletarian writing of the thirties, sent a "roughhouse piece" to the *Hound and Horn*, "part of a novel on unemployment," a "mass novel," which he found "damn hard to do. Some of your esthetes ought to examine this problem of technique. . . . Dos Passos has made about the only start in this country, and it's not quite successful" (Chap. V, Letters 21 and 22). Kirstein was interested in publishing it but, after advice from A. Hyatt Mayor, dropped it; "the point is this: do you want to give the H&H a party political bias? . . . I think our detachment is our real virtue and value to this time when detachment has almost perished from the world" (Mayor, undated; Chap. V, Letter 23). But Kirstein himself wrote for Communist publications and befriended Communist activists. "I flirted with a lot of young Communists in the early Thirties. . . . I wrote a lot for *New Theatre*, a CP publication. I was much involved with a young CP activist called Wirt Baker; he was a boy who had been in jail in Alabama whom I liked personally" (letter to me, November 1975).

Henry James Issue and the End

When the *Hound and Horn* was a "Harvard Miscellany," the editors had planned a Henry James issue, but it was not until Bernard Bandler bought the Henry James "scenario" (so called in the magazine) for

The Ambassadors at an auction in 1931 as a wedding present for
A. Hyatt Mayor—"the only act of generosity I've ever regretted," he
told me—that the idea was given impetus.

The penultimate issue of the *Hound and Horn*, the "Homage to
Henry James, 1843–1916," was volume 7, number 3 (April–June
1934). It took almost three years to gather the articles for the issue and
the final list of contributors is quite different from the originally pro-
jected group. Many writers were approached for articles for a proposed
Spring 1932 Henry James issue, among them Eliot, Pound[21] (who
had written five essays for the *Little Review* Henry James issue in 1918),
Tate, Winters, Edith Wharton, Bernard Berenson, Ford Madox Ford,
Conrad Aiken, and Gertrude Stein. Some writers, like Eliot, refused
because they felt they had nothing to say at the time; others, like
Gertrude Stein, did not finish their articles on time.

With outstanding articles such as "The Critical Prefaces" by Rich-
ard Blackmur, "The Ambiguity of Henry James" by Edmund Wilson,
"Drama in the *Golden Bowl*" by Francis Fergusson, "The School of
Experience in the Early Novels" by Stephen Spender, "James and the
Almighty Dollar" by Newton Arvin, "Henry James in the World" by
Edna Kenton, "James as a Characteristic American" by Marianne
Moore, and the publication of James's scenario to *The Ambassadors*
with bibliographical notes by Edna Kenton, the issue is a collector's
item. The noted Henry James scholar Leon Edel wrote me in June
1975: "it resulted in the publication of some very fine essays that
would not have been written until long after if at all. . . . It is my great
regret that I was not qualified then to participate in that fine sym-
posium." It was this issue that renewed American interest in Henry
James.

Kirstein's love for the ballet began to dominate his life from 1933
on, and money used for the *Hound and Horn* was diverted to estab-
lishing ballet in America. Excited by European ballet, Kirstein had
dreamed of being a dancer, but when his good friend and "dominant

[21] Ezra Pound wrote Hyatt Mayor in October 1931 suggesting that when the edi-
tors of *Hound and Horn* had "finished commemorating the illustrious dead, they
might make a memorial for [him]." And in October 1933, when Kirstein wired
Pound again asking him to contribute to the James issue, he received a postcard
from Melbourne, Australia, Monday, January 15: "Rudyard Kipling has agreed to
write an ode for the dedication of the city's Shrine to Remembrance."

companion," Muriel Draper, mother of Paul Draper the famed tap-dancer, told him he would never be one because he was "too old, too tall, too rich," he turned his energies toward "tasty management" instead; he would found an American ballet company. On the advice of Pavel Tchelitchev, artist and set designer for Diaghilev's then defunct Ballets Russes, he offered the directorship of what was to become the School of American Ballet to George Balanchine, who had been dancer and choreographer for Diaghilev. With additional funding for two years promised by Kirstein's college friend Edward Warburg of the banking family, a theater proffered by A. Everett "Chick" Austin, director of the Wadsworth Atheneum in Hartford, Connecticut (this part of the offer was turned down by Balanchine, who preferred to remain in New York), and artistic freedom guaranteed by Lincoln Kirstein, Balanchine agreed to come to the United States, and a historic union was formed.[22] The life of the *Hound and Horn* was over. However, because of the interest inherent in Kirstein's correspondence with Stephen Spender, the last chapter in this collection contains a selection of letters that extends beyond the metamorphosis of magazine into ballet to recount the growth and change in the lives of two men at a time when they were creating important places for themselves in the world of arts and letters. The epilogue brings *The Hound and Horn Letters* to a close with several letters describing the demise of the magazine, but it is a mythological death only, because offstage awaits the birth of one of the cultural glories of New York—the New York City Ballet.

[22] Lincoln Kirstein, *The New York City Ballet* (New York: Alfred A. Knopf, 1973), pp. 13–20.

CHAPTER I

Ezra Pound

I
RICHARD BLACKMUR
TO EZRA POUND
16 March 1929

Dear Mr. Pound:

This is a very late thanks for your note of January twenty-second. I turned over the information about your first Cantos, to my friend and I imagine he is in the process of getting a copy, trusting to a very Puritan God indeed to let it slide, from ignorance, through the Boston Customs. I saw yesterday, which is what reminded me of your letter, a copy of the first sixteen bound up in red velvet like the Second cantos. I suppose this is *not* a reprint.[1]

I don't think that your great grandmother's family is sufficiently removed to keep you out of a *Harvard Miscellany*.[2] In the first place, both "Harvard" and "Miscellany" were unwise words to have chosen and really, I think, mean nothing except to advertisers. As soon as we can manage it, we will drop the "Harvard Miscellany" part of the title altogether. We are not restricted in any way to Harvard men, or college men, or American men, or men at all; and we should very, very much like to have something of yours. Particularly myself, I should like to have a new Canto, one with a Greek or Latin reference if possible. I am as bald as this about it only because I altogether realise how impertinent it is of us to ask you for anything at all. But believe us, if you can see your way clear to let us have something, we shall be a long time in your debt.

24

Ezra Pound (1885–1972) was born in Hailey, Idaho, but lived for most of his life as an expatriate in London, Paris, and Rapallo, Italy. "Make it new" was his dictum, and he saw the little magazine as a vehicle flexible enough to accomplish that goal. He strove ceaselessly to gain acceptance for the experimental in literature, persuading Harriet Monroe, editor of *Poetry*, for which he was foreign correspondent from 1912 to 1918, to publish T. S. Eliot's "Love Song of J. Alfred Prufrock" and Margaret Anderson to print Joyce's *Ulysses* in installments from 1918 to 1921 in the *Little Review*. As foreign advisor to the *Hound and Horn* from 1930 to 1931, Pound pressed for the publication of the work of his newest protégés, Louis Zukofsky, Basil Bunting, and Robert McAlmon, and plied the editors with his idiosyncratic letters, urging an editorial policy aimed to open readers' eyes to the weaknesses eroding American life and art. Pound's *Cantos* XXVIII–XXX and some of his vituperative letters, under the heading of "Correspondence," were printed in the magazine, but the relationship between Pound and the *Hound and Horn* ended when several essays—*Terra Italica* and a translation of Jean Cocteau's *Mystère Laic*—were rejected by the editors.

Unless specified otherwise, all of Pound's letters were written from Rapallo, Italy.

Richard P. Blackmur (1904–1965), managing editor of the *Hound and Horn* in 1929–30, wrote for the magazine poetry, book reviews, important essays on T. S. Eliot, E. E. Cummings, Ezra Pound, Wallace Stevens, and the "Prefaces to Henry James," published as an introduction to Henry James's *Art of the Novel*. He was working in Maurice Firuski's Dunster House Bookshop in Cambridge, Mass., when Lincoln Kirstein and Bernard Bandler asked him to be editor of the magazine. "He was very clever, taught me about 'modern literature,' he was good to work with, a superintellectual," wrote Kirstein to me (2 July 1975).

[1] *A Draft of XVI Cantos*, published in Paris by William Bird, Three Mountains Press, 1925.

[2] Blackmur may have had in mind Pound's grandmother, Sarah Angevine Loomis, who was said to come from a family of "charming people, an old lady from upper New York State once told Pound, in fact the nicest people in the county, but horse thieves." Noel Stock, *The Life of Ezra Pound* (New York: Pantheon, 1970), p. 2.

2   RICHARD BLACKMUR
              TO EZRA POUND
              20 May 1929

Dear Mr. Pound:

I am very sorry that there are no Cantos available at the present time, but I hope before the next batch appears in book form that you may be able to let us have one or more. It is not, of course, the sort of thing that we can persuade you about.

Rates for the *Hound & Horn* at present are three dollars and fifty cents a page, for prose; and seven fifty, for verse. We can't stretch these rates any further until we stretch our subscription list enormously; and

I am afraid we can't stretch the subscription list until we can dig up enough first-rate but poverty-stricken contributors to appeal to, or fool seven or eight thousand people. Payment is made definitely on publication. This last we hope to improve shortly, making payment on acceptance.

I have had you put down for a free perennial subscription. You probably won't like us very much. On the other hand, you may like certain parts of us a good deal. I don't know.

You ask—Is the *Hound & Horn* ready to do what *The Dial* and *Criterion* won't?? Answer: I don't know. But certainly, "seriously," we are trying not to do certain things those magazines do do, but I can't tell for sure whether we are trying to do what they won't, in your sense. . . .

About the republication of your prose, in revised and rearranged form, I don't think of anything that any of us can do which would be of any practical help. I suppose the first thing would be money, and that is what we are most short of. I remember talking with Pat Covici[1] last fall about some such project. We found that it would cost quite a good deal to take care of, although not nearly the eighteen thousand that your god damned fool mentioned. I also mentioned the matter to Dunster House Bookshop where I used to work, where again it was a question of money. However, if anything does turn up which looks like a good stimulant, I will hop on to it.

I quote your paragraph—"I take it the *Hound & Horn* exists for licherchoor only," and say I think so. That is why we publish almost nothing but criticism, there not being much of the other available.

---

[1] Pascal Covici (1888–1964), Pound's Chicago publisher.

3   UNSIGNED, BUT IN ALL
       PROBABILITY RICHARD
       BLACKMUR TO EZRA POUND
       2 October 1929

Dear Mr. Pound:

It is very hard for me to answer your very gracious letter without an appearance of ingratitude and ungraciousness. When you suggest an overt alliance between us, we can only, on the face of it, eagerly accept; but when we begin to consider the probable terms of such an alliance, it is difficult not to be immediately aware of much that might happen to irritate, even exacerbate, in a truly political fashion, that alliance. In many cases our tastes would strongly differ; and we simply haven't got either the money or the space to publish anything we don't all agree upon. I can imagine nothing more disagreeable to either of us than the circumstances of our refusing to publish material you had engaged in all good faith. And I can imagine nothing more insolent on our part than an attempt to correct or control your taste. —Of course I don't mean that anyone must think a thing supremely good, or consonant with private prejudice, to make it publishable. The question is often, what ought to be published, despite, or even because of, its flaws; and there we might disagree.

On the other hand. It is useless of me to repeat to you that you, in the *Little Review*, *The Egoist*, and elsewhere, have unearthed more good people than all the rest of the editors put together; so that there is nothing we can be more grateful for than your offer to take up again that habit for our sake. If we had the money for a "supplement" or a special number, to be edited by yourself, decision would be simple: you would receive complete authority and plenty of space. But we can't do that. What we can do is this: take everything you send us (especially poems and stories), do our best to agree with you, and publish so much as we can of it. It ought not to be hard to assent to your choice most of the time; and as we're going to stretch the number of pages, we ought to have room for a good deal. This would amount to your gracing us as Contributing Editor. I do hope you will proceed with us on this basis. The advantages, I know, are all ours. . . .

The death of the *Dial*[1] did do us considerable good (plus all the harm that comes of having to read the bunk that would have been submitted to it). I mean we have Burke, Cowley, Williams, and possibly a few others.[2] Perhaps without the *Dial*, you might be able to let us have a Canto: I hope one of the swell greek ones if such there be; or some short poems. Or anything. You spoke previously of some criticism; a part of a rewritten *Spirit of Romance*.

My regards to your father, whom I have never met, but have had several charming letters from.

[1] Publication of the *Dial* ceased in July 1929.
[2] Kenneth Burke (*b.* 1897) was music critic of the *Dial* from 1927 to 1929, and of the *Nation* from 1934 to 1936. Parts of *Towards a Better Life, a series of Declamations or Epistles* (1932) appeared in *Hound and Horn* prior to publication.

Malcolm Cowley (*b.* 1898) was associate editor of the *New Republic* from 1929 to 1944 and is literary advisor at the Viking Press.

William Carlos Williams (1883–1963), poet, contributed widely to avant-garde magazines. His poems "Rain" and "In a Sconset Bus" were published in the *Hound and Horn*, vol. 3, no. 1 (Oct.–Dec. 1929) and vol. 5, no. 4 (July–Sept. 1932).

4   EZRA POUND TO
RICHARD BLACKMUR
20 November 1929

Dear Blackmur:

I shd. be pleased if you cd. put through this group. Think it better to print a group than a single poem. Man worth printing; worth printing so that one can make out where he exists etc.

At any rate you can give this precedence in time over other mss. I have sent on (as question of space don't arise).

Bunting was asst. edtr. on *Transatlantic.*[1] Present address:—
Villa Aschiere; Rapallo.

The longest poem prob. better than the other two, but still I think stuff stands better in group. Certain amt. of texture or fibre (rather than thin snap of the accelerated).

[P.S.] I mean distinct personality comes out of the group of poems ergo more interesting as group than single poem which might merely be accident.

[1] Basil Bunting (*b.* 1900), British poet, was assistant editor of Ford Madox Ford's *Transatlantic Review*, published monthly in Paris from 1924 to 1925, which contained the writing of Hemingway, Robert McAlmon, E. E. Cummings, Pound, Gertrude Stein, and James Joyce.

5   EZRA POUND TO
THE EDITORS OF *HOUND & HORN*
7 January 1930

Messieurs:

   . . . I shall be sending on (as per his[1] request) not one Canto but three. It becomes increasingly difficult as the poem proceeds to make *brief* detachable fragments which are complete or intelligible in themselves. XXVIII and XXIX are transitional, or at least don't seem to me to have any shape without the very short XXX, which, in turn is (most of it) too lyric to stand alone.[2]

/   /   /

You might let me know whether you want my private criticism of present number (i.e., private and confidential let us hope impersonal and for office use only).

On 10 Jan. 1930, Pound wrote the editors approving the idea of *Hound and Horn* reprints of important articles and put forth some practical suggestions concerning their printing and distribution. He suggested two tentative titles for reprints: "Fenollosa on the Chinese Written Character," published at the end of his *Instigations* and out of print, and his *How To Read*, and he stressed the importance of making the price as low as possible. Ernest Fenollosa (1853–1908), an American who had gone to Japan in the 1870s as an instructor in rhetoric at the Imperial University, had fought against the increasing Westernization of the Japanese arts and, as a result, had been appointed the Imperial Commissioner of Art in Tokyo. After his death, Mrs. Fenollosa, impressed by Pound's "Contemporania" and other poems, offered Pound the opportunity to edit her husband's literary papers. Among the notebooks and translations was Fenollosa's essay "The Chinese Written Character as a Medium for Poetry." Pound spent much time trying to find a publisher for it, finally placing it in Margaret Anderson's *Little Review* (Sept.–Dec. 1919). Pound's *How to Read*, published 13, 20, and 27 Jan. 1929 in the *Herald Tribune* and as a book in 1931, offered a list of works, the reading of which, Pound thought, would help to develop clarity of thought. Pound maintained that if people who have influence use language improperly, "the whole machinery of social and individual thought and order goes to pot."

    About the current Jan.–March 1930 issue, Pound stated that he approved Tate's "killing off" the Humanist debate (in his article "The Fallacy of Humanism," printed in the *Criterion* originally as "Humanism and Naturalism"); Pound criticized the Humanist movement, headed by Irving Babbitt and Paul Elmer More— "One ought to devote one obituary to each of these winds . . . and then move out into criticism." He suggested sending *Hound and Horn* magazines to a list of possible subscribers.

[1] Blackmur's.
[2] Cantos XXVIII–XXX were first published in *Hound and Horn*, vol. 3, no. 2 (April–June 1930).

6   EZRA POUND TO
         LINCOLN KIRSTEIN
         3 February 1930

Dear Kirstein,

. . . I shan't find another Gaudier[1] if you are reproducing art? or having art notes, you might keep a look out (selective) for Hiler[2] show in N.Y., I believe, Miro; Arp, Max Ernst;[3] and for Man Ray's painting (people know about his photography/ or the things he does on photograph paper without a camera, but his painting is insufficiently known).[4] Judging from what I now take to be your general line and direction I think Aldington[5] might have something for you. He has shaken off the fetters of the Times and is doing excellent critical journalism. . . .

In the case of GOULD[6] there is certainly a tremendous lot of weeding to be done. Perhaps I regard all america as a mad house and am grateful for any clear manifestation of symptoms. (Which same wd. be merely an added bore if they occurred geographically nearer oneself.) . . .

[1] Henri Gaudier-Brzeska (1891–1915), the sculptor who had linked his name with that of Sophie Brzeska, with whom he lived. Of his death in World War I at the age of twenty-three, Pound wrote, "Gaudier-Brzeska has been killed at Neuville St. Vaast, and we have lost the best of the young sculptors and the most promising. The arts will incur no worse loss from the war than this is. One is rather obsessed with it." *The Letters of Ezra Pound*, ed. D. D. Paige (New York: Harcourt, Brace, 1950), p. 61. Pound later published *Gaudier-Brzeska: A Memoir* (1916).
[2] Hilaire Hiler (1898–1966), American painter, arts editor of Samuel Putnam's *New Review* in the 1930s.
[3] Joán Miró (1893–1974), Spanish painter, among the most prominent of the Surrealists.

Hans Arp (1887–1966), Alsatian sculptor and painter who with Tristan Tzara founded the Dada movement in Zurich in 1916. In the 1920s, he joined the Surrealists, participating in their first exhibition in Paris in 1925.

Max Ernst (1891–1976), German-born painter who in 1921 moved to Paris to become a founder of the Surrealist group.
[4] Man Ray (1890–1977), American-born painter and photographer. This no doubt refers to Man Ray's Rayograms (photographs without a camera). "By placing ob-

jects on a piece of photographic paper and lighting them from a particular angle, he created new poetic vistas." Hans Richter, *Dada* (New York: McGraw-Hill, 1965), p. 98.

[5] Richard Aldington (1892–1962), British writer, one of the original group of Imagists, editor for a time of the avant-garde *Egoist* (1914–1919), married to the poet H. D. (Hilda Doolittle).

[6] Joe Gould (1889–1957), a classmate of E. E. Cummings at Harvard, called himself "the last of the Bohemians." A widely recognized "character" in Greenwich Village, he claimed to have compiled an "Oral History of Our Time," consisting of millions of words recounting things people had told him. Cummings wrote the poem "Little Joe Gould has lost his teeth and doesn't know where."

7
EZRA POUND TO LINCOLN KIRSTEIN
4 February 1930

Dear Kirstein

I have just recd. Taupin's[1] *Influence du Symbolisme Francais sur la Poésie Américaine* (1910–20).

Certainly the most serious job that has been done on Am. lit. hist. of that period.

I take it you'll review it.[2] Before dealing with the decade 10–20, it might be well (I dunno) even to translate the chapters on the preceding hell.

H & H. might review it in sections, or Zuk[3] might translate the 300 pages if there were a poss/ publisher.[4]

(There are certain errors; scholastic haste, etc.) BUT I think it wd. be a valuable service to KILL off and annihilate and finally besmirch Harper Bros. If there are any putrid survivors of the regime that you are prob. too young to remember they might at least be made to die with Taupin's estimate of them in their ears. . . .

I haven't yet decided on modus of correcting minor errors re/ 10–20. He has made me more or less the protagonist of the whole show. (with thanks in opening note for "conseils personnels".) He was here two afternoons and I wrote him one letter[5] or possibly two (in which case I think one was merely a formal note saying I wd. see him or answer questions. At least thass all I can remember.) . . .

[1] René Taupin.
[2] Reviewed by Yvor Winters, in vol. 4, no. 4 (July–Sept. 1931). Although giving Taupin high marks for compiling a valuable history of the period, Winters concluded that "Mr. Taupin's critical faculties are inadequate to his task; his knowledge of English poetry appears superficial. Were it not for these deficiencies he might have written a final and authoritative work; as it is, he has merely provided a great deal of invaluable material for one."
[3] Louis Zukofsky (1904–1978), poet and author.
[4] In Letters 20 and 22 of this chapter, Pound and Kirstein mention a translation by Dudley Fitts that was not published.
[5] See *Letters of Ezra Pound*, ed. Paige, p. 216.

8　　EZRA POUND TO LINCOLN KIRSTEIN
8 February 1930

Dear Kirstein

I.　　　　　　　　　/ / /

... I strongly suggest that you read Fenollosa on the "Chinese Written Character" (the last item in my *Instigations*)[1] and try, harder than the publik yet has, to understand the importance of the thought in it.

II.

I suggest you get hold of my "How to Read" (N.Y. Herald "Books" Jan. 13, 20, 27 of last year 1929) and try to see that it is not merely a set of articles or even the summary of what I have learned in the past 27 years; but the solid basis of a new critical method which will absolootly bust up, acid test; put an end to a certain kind of merdacious faking; make forever impossible for Clive Bell's[2] and their like to shit on every honest man's doorstep with impunity.

... returning to my How to Read. Consider it (I think in third part). Make the g;d; critic present his credentials; his ideograph.

There is here a new crit. system. It has not been used in france and one cd make it definitely a start, a date, and give H & H just as clear a chronological position as Taupin says the L. R.[3] had. ...

A couple of positive ideas of this sort; prob. more valuable than detailed application of them in sniping what's already printed and can't not be helped. (Lord; yes; I know how an edtr. gets landed with stuff he don't want and can't dodge (hence the uses of Margaret Andersons[4] who decline to be bound by social decency or non-lit morals and who by reason of appearing insane can with impunity annoy by appearing irresponsible. . . . Have never made a secret of wanting to civilize the damn country. Poetry is now as good as that of any contemporary nation and a bloody sight better'n England's. Prose novel (eg. in parts of Hem's Farewell[5]) as good as european.

You people can get the crit. at least up to french level.

After that one might spread still further into the peripheries. I don't think it is your function to deal with the further-out. Take limited objective. Leave the "cleansing of govt." to some other periodical (or periodicals).

What I have said in *Exile* 4.[6] damn well needed saying. Bloody bureaucracy etc. low grade mutts allowed to govern. Billions for prevention of normal diet and nothing for education etc.

/   /   /

If you want to tell me (it won't go any further) what yr. circulation is, and how solid yr. finances are I might be able to calculate what I consider reasonable risk. I don't believe the Dial gained a damn thing by its excess of caution. It cost 'em oodles of money; enormous deficits to do what I believe cd. have been done at something between a tenth and a half the expense. I may be wrong; but . . . .

Also point made in *Exile*. The american short story can just as well develop in portraying the kinds of sonvabitch that get elected or appointed to posts in which they can retard or ruin the nation. That is the gangrene the literature of diagnosis must study; alle samee Kings in greek tragedy. Important because their life or disease affects larger group. (have elaborated this elsewhere).

Make the bloody freshman do a portrait of his congressman not of his aunt Jemima. This is not a timeless hunk of crit. it is an indication of a or the job to be done next in the Am. short story.

Instead of Harding as done in *Revelry*[7] we want Cal.[8] done as Hem. or McAlmon[9] might if they wd. (or rather as someone else must). They don't happen to know. . . .

[1] *Instigations*, 1919, includes Pound's notes on modern French poetry, his essays on Henry James and Remy de Gourmont, the *Egoist* series on translators from the

Greek, reviews of Eliot, Joyce, and Wyndham Lewis, his essay on Arnaut Daniel, together with his translation of Daniel, and other pieces. It also marked the first book publication of Fenollosa's "Chinese Character as a Medium for Writing Poetry," edited, with notes by Pound.

[2] Clive Bell (1881–1964), writer, married to Vanessa Stephen, sister of Virginia Woolf. Perhaps Pound's antipathy toward the "Bloomsbuggars" can be explained in part by Forrest Read's theory: "Pound jibed [in *New Review*, Jan.–Feb. 1931] as subeditor, at the Homeric explicators and psychological analysts of *Ulysses*; he probably had in mind Stuart Gilbert's *James Joyce's Ulysses*, 1930, as well as the *Nouvelle Revue Française* for which Larbaud had written his article on *Ulysses*, and the Bloomsbury group . . . Virginia Woolf, John Middleton Murry, Aldous Huxley, Herbert Read, etc., who were interested in psychology, in the stream-of-consciousness, and in the unconscious as it was being exploited in surrealism." From *Pound/Joyce: The Letters of Ezra Pound to James Joyce*, ed. Forrest Read (New York: New Directions, 1967), pp. 237–38.

[3] The *Little Review*.

[4] Margaret Anderson (1891–1973), founder of the experimental magazine *Little Review* (1914–1929).

[5] Ernest Hemingway's *A Farewell to Arms* (1929).

[6] *Exile*, Pound's little magazine published four times, semi-annually (1927–1928).

[7] Samuel Hopkins Adams's *Revelry* (1926), a novel based largely on facts of the Harding administration.

[8] Calvin Coolidge.

[9] Robert McAlmon (1896–1956), novelist and short-story writer, editor of the magazine *Contact* with William Carlos Williams, from 1920 to 1923.

9   EZRA POUND TO BERNARD BANDLER
13 February 1930

Cher B

. . . Don't know whether you have revd. Hemingway's *Farewell to Arms*.[1] I thought *Sun Also Rises* a let-down; at least a damn bad slump from what I hoped Hem. wd. do. But parts of *Farewell* seem to me as good as Mérimée[2] or anyone else. I don't think this is bias, as I had not expected to approve, and had neglected to get the book until chance pushed it under my nose. . . .

[1] Reviewed in vol. 3, no. 2 (Jan.–March 1930) by Lewis Galantière, who saw Hemingway as hampered both by his fear of showing emotion and his need to depict "ideal" behavior. But he found the war story successful and the writing "the best Hemingway has done."

[2] Prosper Mérimée (1803–1870), French writer.

10   EZRA POUND TO
                HOUND & HORN
                26 February 1930

HOUND AND HORN. Secret archives. Doc. I.

Private and confidential report on "Winter 1930," as much of it as I have had time to consider.

. . . Huxley[1] is largely blah, and is not out of place in Vanity Fair. Dobrée[2] don't at all believe in. London Bloomsbury.

. . . Hicks[3] possible, even a possibility.

Josephson.[4] No further than 1918. (cf. my H. J.[5] number of Lit. Rev.). I don't believe Josephson has any further to go. Waste of space printing finished (ended) reviewers when you have untried talent of such promise as found elsewhere in the number. (Hicks has already ticked off Munson,[6] Josephson and Munson both seem to me rather dated already).

Merrill Moore,[7] apart from Fitts eulogy;[8] they say he has a vein of sorts. Fitts deserves a chance I think; I believe he has found it uphill going, he means to be constructive. I shd. vote to give him his aptmnt. in the edifice. . . .

——H. Read[9] I have already written about. Don't think you need feed him. Dull Englishman, shaped by his milieu. Ils n'existent pas, leur ambience leur donne une existence; Hyatt Mayor,[10] by virtue of comparison of Picasso to P. Francesca; Quercia seems to me to have the seein' eye. Pic. having just the nervous delicacy of outline plus vigour of that Period. etc. I believe Mayor cd. do useful series (continuing) to Wyndham Lewis (if he can see enough of his drawings) Gaudier and Brancusi.

May say, historicly that a few years ago when Vanity F. was trying to purrsuade me to prostichoot myself in their whorehouse I said I wd. ON condition that they do a full page of illustrations of the above four artists. (they to have the right to delete but not alter meaning of my text) they refused. That for Crownies bold jump to the future and leading Noo Yok.[11] Oh yes they wanted me to write etc. But an honest distinction between real art and le chic. no; no; that wd. be too much. . . .

On 27 February 1930, Kirstein wrote Pound, explaining why the *Hound and Horn* chose not to publish McAlmon's stories, stating that he found "too much characterization of unimportant figures and the main line obscured. . . . I have yet to see anything of his in the last three years that I would like to print." He added that he had liked Hemingway's last work, *A Farewell to Arms* (1929): "Some of the descriptions of the retreat, the game of billiards with the old Italian and the last 15 pages seemed to me first rate writing. . . . I don't see how he can help doing something really splendid sometime." He had asked Hemingway to send a story "but I think he's probably forgotten all about us."

[1] Aldous Huxley (1894–1963), British writer, appeared in almost every issue of *Vanity Fair* beginning in January 1921, analyzing morals, religion, the elementary schools, etc.

[2] Bonamy Dobrée (1891–1974), born in London, editor and writer, professor of English at the University of Leeds from 1936 to 1955.

[3] Granville Hicks (*b.* 1901), writer, editor of *New Masses*, and author of, among other works, *The Great Tradition* (1935), a Marxist study of American literature since the Civil War.

[4] Matthew Josephson (1899–1978), writer, one of the original group of Surrealist authors and painters, was associate editor of *Broom* from 1922 to 1924, contributing editor of *transition* from 1928 to 1929, and assistant editor of the *New Republic* from 1931 to 1932.

[5] Henry James.

[6] Gorham Munson (1896–1969), writer, edited (sometimes in collaboration with Matthew Josephson and Kenneth Burke) the avant-garde magazine *Secession* from 1922 to 1924.

[7] Merrill Moore (1903–1957) helped to found the southern literary magazine the *Fugitive* in 1922. After becoming a professor of psychiatry at Harvard Medical School, Moore, a prolific poet, continued to write from two to five sonnets a day.

[8] Dudley Fitts (1903–1968), poet, critic, translator, and contributor to the *Hound and Horn*.

[9] Sir Herbert Read (1893–1968), writer and critic.

[10] A. Hyatt Mayor (1901–1980), an editor of the *Hound and Horn*, later curator of the Print Department at the Metropolitan Museum. Pound is alluding to Mayor's article "Picasso's Method" (with illustrations) in vol. 3, no. 2 (Jan.–March 1930).

[11] Frank Crowninshield (1872–1947), editor and publisher of *Vanity Fair*.

11   EZRA POUND TO
LINCOLN KIRSTEIN AND
BERNARD BANDLER
27 February 1930

Dear Kirstein and Bandler:

Note from Cocteau this a.m. says we can have his "Mystère Laic." I haven't seen it, and don't know how long it is. He says it is his best book of critique poetique; and "autour de G. de Chirico." I have naturally told him YES. Unless I hear to the contrary; as soon as I hear from you that the scheme is O.K. and general conditions, re Milan printing etc. feasible; I will put a translator to work on the Cocteau. . . .

12   EZRA POUND TO
          HOUND & HORN
      1 March 1930 and 8 March 1930

H & H public documents

Van Hecke has asked me to help him make up an American number of Variétés. Have you any UNUSUAL photos. of America and American life that you can't use in H. and H.?

I suspect Crosby's bandagiste's window was an exotic.[1] I want by the way a GOOD cigar store Indian; any "social" documents you think of interest; any rare farming snap, early tintype of Al Capone baling Cal[2] out of local swab-up for being dr. and dis. or other revelatory view likely to interest Europeans. Factory machinery and architecture fairly well covered.

Also noted men (in dishabile; if any). Custom House scenes at a premium.

Know Macleish's stuff.[3] He has talent. He also has the disease of facility; and the almost incurable disease of being unwilling to bite on the NAIL. Wants his stuff to be liked WHETHER it is A.1 or not. Saw same symptom in Huxley 13 years ago.

Most dangerous type for health of letters. contagion, good merging into bad. MacL's best is quite as good as the best writer's good.

Also in reckoning potentiality, one has to remember that MacL' starts rather late in life. . . .

Re/Politics. There is NOTHING for you to do directly. Only way to do anything is cultivation of mot juste. AND the encouragement of fiction writers to portray the type of sonofabitch that gets elected by the gorillas. I suggest that every time you accept or reject a short story you ask for stories about the KIND of baboon that gets made president or senator or memb; congress.

Only by heightening the visibility and definition can you do any good. You can't swing an election. What you print now the dailies must use as editorials in 20 years time. System don't matter, all equally good or bad; it is the quality (human) of individuals running the system that is effective.

The highbrow can't poss. have any immediate effect on the mass.

/ / /

By correcting Taupin's errors I merely meant that I can hardly make a direct reply; it wd. be giving too much importance to trifles. . . . (you cd. quote me in footnote to yr. rev. of T as saying that pore ole Amy did NOT pay to get into Des Imagistes and did NOT finance the *Catholic Anthology.*[4]

The other gen. crit. of T. wd. be that one does occasionally think of something before or without reading it in a french opus. (He HAD to take that line as he was a continental writing on a theme; and his sense of order and unity compels him to treat the whole subject from ot. view of said theme.

/ / /

Kreymborg[5] prob wants his book to be bought by ALL those mentioned (poss. subconscious; possibly just Alfred's friendly nature.) NO man will advocate a standard too high to pass at least part of his own work. At least men who will do so are either anonymous and unfindable or else my experience is circumscribed. . . .

Frobenius[6] is expected back from Africa in a week's time. The *Paideuma* is a more serious item because of its length. I think Frob. very important; but am not writing a second letter to him till I hear from you. He is the root and Spengler the top froth.

/ / /

re Macleish. Go ahead and PRINT him, only watch WHAT.

You might ask Hemingway for a poem. He has written three or four good ones. You can't pay his prose price now. . . .

I don't see any use in H. and H. printing Ed. Wilson.[7] Cheapens the periodical. Anyone can buy him for ten cents in Nation or wherever it is he "edits" and he has there plenty of room for his suds. I think he is a bit of a Seldes,[8] floating with current. If he has any ideas or

MEANS anything or means to DO anything he has plenty of place in his own sheet. (? correct me if this is erroneous)

[1] Harry Crosby (1898–1929), writer and editor, and founder with his wife Caresse of the Black Sun Press in Paris. Crosby committed suicide in 1929. He had been assistant editor of the magazine *transition* in 1929. A reproduction of his photograph of the contents of a Parisian drug-store window, showing enema bags, vaginal douches, corn plasters, and trusses appeared in *Hound and Horn*, vol. 3, no. 2 (Jan.–March 1930).
[2] Calvin Coolidge.
[3] Archibald MacLeish (1892–1982), distinguished poet and writer.
[4] Amy Lowell (1874–1925), writer and poet, became principal sponsor of the Imagists with the publication of her three-volume anthology *Some Imagist Poets* (1915/1916/1917). *The Catholic Anthology*, so named by Pound, was published in 1915 and contained the first appearance in book form of Eliot's verse, as well as poetry by Yeats, Pound, and Williams, among others. The title created resentment, and the publisher Elkin Matthews asked Pound: "Why, why will you needlessly irritate people?" Of the book, Pound wrote, "The Jesuits here have, I think, succeeded in preventing its being reviewed. . . . Having forged a donation of Constantine (some years since) they now think the august and tolerant name belongs to them, a sort of apostolic succession." Charles Norman, *Ezra Pound* (New York: Macmillan, 1960), p. 182.
[5] Alfred Kreymborg (1883–1966), poet and editor of the experimental magazine of poetry *Glebe* (1913–1914), and *Others* (1915–1919), a magazine designed to point out that there were "others" writing poetry who were not being published in Harriet Monroe's *Poetry*.
[6] Leo Frobenius (1873–1938), German anthropologist who called the cross-fertilization of culture in space and time "paideuma."
[7] Edmund Wilson (1895–1972), writer and essayist, associate editor of and principal book reviewer for the *New Republic* from 1926 to 1931, and book reviewer for the *New Yorker* from 1944 to 1948. Among his works are *Axel's Castle* (1931), an analysis of the works of Yeats, Eliot, Pound, and Joyce in terms of the French Symbolist movement; *To the Finland Station* (1940), an account of the revolutionary tradition in Europe; and *The Wound and the Bow* (1941), about the dualism of Dickens, Kipling, Edith Wharton, Hemingway, and Joyce.
[8] Gilbert Seldes (1893–1970), writer, drama critic of the *Dial* from 1920 to 1923.

13   EZRA POUND TO ALAN STROOCK
24 March 1930

Dear Mr. Stroock[1]

I hope to 'ell yr. ref. to N.R.F. is an accident. There is nothing I shd. less care to take as a model. The *Mercure de France* is or was a dif. kettle of fish.[2]

I.E. n;r;f; melange of bhoogery and french protestantism with a neo-catholic topwash. HELL. The nearest the frogs can get to blooms-bury. *The Mercure* had for 40 years an intellectual life.

/ / / / / /

I don't honestly think the "slight" dif. in quality of printing matters a damn. Neither Alcan nor Champion[3] cd. exist on fine printing. One is not out for Covici's audience of Chicago butter an eggs men.

No european country can sport intellectual publication save on basis of MINIMUM possible expense. . . .

I (naturally) want you to go hell for leather at much more the *Little Rev.* pace than the *Dial* or *Criterion* pace, but think craft and wiliness demand a gradual acceleration not an explosion. . . .

[1] Stroock was the business manager of *Hound and Horn*.
[2] *La Nouvelle Revue Française* was founded in Paris in 1909 and edited by a group of writers including André Gide and Jacques Copeau: It presented foreign letters, theater and music chronicles, and reviews, but after World War I, during which it had been suspended, it reappeared, with a manifesto written by Jacques Rivière, stressing the importance of keeping the world of art separate from the affairs of the world. The *Mercure de France*, founded in 1890, was characterized by Richard Aldington as "one of the best, if not the best, of the independent literary periodicals in France. Nothing like it has existed in England and America." *Life for Life's Sake* (New York: Viking, 1941), p. 174. On 9 June 1920, Ezra Pound wrote to Carlo Linati, "I *want* (some some immoderation) the *Dial* to do what the *Mercure de France* used to do. But God knows if there is the least chance of success in this enterprise." *Letters of James Joyce*, 3 vols. (New York: Viking, 1957–1966; vol. 1 ed. Stuart Gilbert, vols. 2 and 3 ed. Richard Ellman), 2: 470. The *Mercure* published three issues a month, with almost 300 pages in each issue. Consequently, it was able to cover a number of areas, like politics, which smaller magazines could not.
[3] Small European publishers.

14   EZRA POUND TO LINCOLN KIRSTEIN
[Undated]

Cher K.

I spose it wd. be quite impossible to git a fotograft of that gaspipe speakeasy; or of the coffin one? Secrecy guaranteed as to their locality. But I think Variétés wd. be pleased with a few regimes secs.

/ / /

And IF I did come who wd. pay my rent? who wd. insure the lining of my delicate abdomen? who wd. get my traveling companions across the various state lines?

/ / /

Advertising firm using the licherchoor to help sale of pills?? (Quite right of course; good writing infinitely serviceable)

Have you seen the rubber pipes.[1] I used to hear about that place 30 years ago but have never seen the actual hose.

I don't doubt its existence. If it don't it ought to for the glory of the race. But . . . wd. like the historic evidence.

[1] In writing to Pound about some touring he had done in the low-life of Manhattan, Lincoln Kirstein referred to a Bowery-bum site where the drunks were supposedly served by pipes from barrel to gullet. (Letter to me, 16 September 1975.)

15 EZRA POUND TO THE EDITORS OF *HOUND & HORN* *17 April 1930*

Ed. H. & H.

First impressions re/Spring number.

I. and chiefly: too much space allotted to discussion of trype. Slop 2nd rate.

However clever Mr. Belgion et al. you can NOT go on about Gide, Lippmann, More, Babbitt[1] etc. without some taint of the original merdre or corpse pervading the pages.

/ / / /

Admit you want a critical attitude; etc. for X's sake get hold FIRST of what live matter there is. Let the dead burry itself. Biological analysis must take count of the fact that life is the main thing.

II. McAlmon (all that can be alledged against notwithstanding) is the most important portrayer of moeurs contemporaines that American has. Rot about there being no Telemachus (if they must have a metaphor)[2] he will outlast and outstrip all the Burkes, Fitts, logic-choppers, Munsons etc. all the Bloomsburies and n;r;fs. I admit the difficulties of the EDITOR in dealing wi⁺h McA. I have here a big mss. selected. every damn story has one "impossible" passage or zummat, notwithstanding which you will be getting the Howells and not the H. J. the Aiken[3] not the Eliot if you don't get him in somehow. No use getting one better story by someone who has no future and no general significance. A la longue the greater author shows by being able to stand being presented in bulk. Fitts. crit. of Hemingway wd. not stand a moment against McA.[4]

/ / /

Whether you cd. get a large lot of his stuff and select. Hell, correct his spelling and grammar. ANY British typist wd. do that automatically in typing the mss. . . .

. . . BUT in ten years time the files of *H and H* will be very dead IF they devote too much space to necrology. More, Babbitt, Lippmann are equally dead. To hell with em.

Maritain. Son of a bitch. Digging up Luther, Calvin and Rousseau.[5] Eliot ought to be smacked for drawing attention to him. Valéry (French Bloomsbury).

As editing all right, but don't sink into Criterionism. *Criterion* has printed in seven years about enough live stuff for one, if that. Remark above not intended to disparage Fitts. one of your best critics. but the formula must *include* McA. . . .

The only plus suggestion is that you add McA. SOMEHOW or OTHER and that you keep on reducing the necrology, and kick out the diddlers; people Gide-ized playing with ideas; fooling about with ideas of timid perversion.

If we must have buggars buggars ought to be jovial and exuberant. . . . all this very hasty.

---

[1] Refers to an article by Montgomery Belgion (*b.* 1892), French-born journalist and editor, "God is Mammon," in vol. 3, no. 3 (April–June 1930). Belgion uses two books, *Dieu et Mammon* by François Mauriac (who was responding to a charge by André Gide that he could not be a Christian and a novelist at the same time) and *A Preface to Morals* by Walter Lippmann, as a basis for his article comparing "some expression of current French views with a similar expression of American views" (both countries worshipping Mammon). The More-Babbitt reference concerns a continuation of the debate on Humanism. Irving Babbitt (1865–1933) was professor of French literature at Harvard University and a founder, with Paul Elmer More (1864–1937), lecturer in Greek philosophy at Princeton University, of the

New Humanist movement in America. While the discussion of these matters did not please Pound, the spring issue achieved a high point with the publication of Pound's *Cantos* XXVIII–XXX, Katherine Anne Porter's "Flowering Judas," two poems by Yvor Winters, and book reviews by Francis Fergusson, Dudley Fitts, Richard P. Blackmur, and Yvor Winters.

[2] The Telemachus reference comes from a review by Dudley Fitts of William Faulkner's *The Sound and the Fury* and Thomas Wolfe's *Look Homeward, Angel*. "The shadow of Joyce is heavy upon Mr. Faulkner and Mr. Wolfe, as . . . it is heavy upon us all. . . . We know that in order to say anything, we must first of all learn to write. The instrument is too precious to abuse. And, whether we care to admit it or not, Joyce has been teaching us all over again, its uses, old and new. Ulysses is still looking for a Telemachus."

[3] Conrad Aiken (1889–1973), poet and writer.

[4] Dudley Fitts labels Hemingway's simplicity "intensely rhetorical. When it fails, as in *Farewell to Arms*, it does so for the same reason that *The Sound and the Fury* does, the artifice stifles the emotion."

[5] Refers to Jacques Maritain's *Three Reformers: Luther, Descartes, Rousseau* (1929).

16 ALAN STROOCK
TO EZRA POUND
30 April 1930

Dear Mr. Pound:

Enclosed herewith is our check in the amount of $82.50, in payment for your Cantos[1] which appeared in the Spring issue of the *Hound and Horn*.

In an undated letter, Pound wrote the editors that he was at last sending the Cocteau (*Mystère Laic*). He had been all through the translation and had discussed a dozen obscure points with the "distinguished" author. He suggested they run the whole article in the magazine in one or two issues.

[1] *Cantos* XXVIII–XXX.

17 EZRA POUND TO
LINCOLN KIRSTEIN
25 July 1930

Dear L. K.

. . . Re McA. we don't quarrel, we DIFFER.

The "Myst. Laic" money goes to Cocteau NOT to his goddam booblisher, with a little out for the translation. . . .

The n,r,f, is french bloomsbury, fake, fake catholic, fake protestant; snobbism, family; dishonest business, cheese. Bad as Keynes economics.[1]

No intellectual honesty, no even judgement for all. una bodega oscura. largely personal feelings etc.

In contrast the defunctive *Mercure* once HAD intellectual honesty. and still has vestiges of the tradition. n.r.f. as Larbaud; pompous ignorance unaware of its ignorance, plus affectation.

Thank god I never touched 'em, as thank god I kept out of Eddie Marsh's Georgian amfoologies. . . .[2] as the yellow infants pewk Fry[3] and Clv. Bell are in London; so is the n,r,f, in Paris. i.e., relative to surroundings

[1] John Maynard Keynes (1883–1946) British economist, pioneer of the theory of full employment.

[2] *Georgian Poetry*, an anthology of poetry "heralding a poetry Renaissance" in the words of its editor Edward Marsh, was published in England in five volumes from 1911 to 1922; it contained the poetry of Walter de la Mare, James Stephens, Rupert Brooke, and others.

[3] Roger Fry.

18   EZRA POUND TO
          LINCOLN KIRSTEIN
          29 July 1930

Dear Kirstein

Am back at above as per letter of few days ago. I leave Rapallo when I am foolish and return when I recover my wits.

As to "memoirs"!! Rightly or wrongly, I don't yet regard myself as finished. I trust or hope to go on providing the material for 'em for some time to come, at least in so far as not hindered by forces beyond my control.

If however Mr. Linscott wants to see Rich of Curtis Brown and bid against Harcourt for my *How to Read*, I see nothing to prevent him. They want me to use the 15,000 words of it already printed (summary of my critical conclusions) and expand it into 50 thousand word book. Have had one contract which I sent back, prob. more Rich's fault than theirs. Also the Aquila was contracted to do my collected prose but the

AQUILA has gone bust. Liveright when in Paris said he wd. do it BUT when Rodker[1] counted up the mass. he found there were 500 (five hundred) thousand words. I wanted a folio like Thomas Aquinas or Albertus Magnus.

That work is in a sense my memoirs. I.E. it is the history of the intellectual movement of the past 20 years AS I have seen it.

I think that a reasonable number of univ. libraries wd. have to buy it. The *English Journal* seems very pleased with a 3000 word history of Small Magazines that I have just sent them. I shd. think they wd. support the longer work.

The collected prose contains *Instigations* now out of print and whatever parts of other books I still want to retain. Naturally a lot of stuff that has never been reprinted.

On putting it together for the Aquila I found that it made ONE book. I mean that I have hammered coherently at one major subject and that the material suffers if given in fragments. Just as my poems are much better in one vol. than in small batches.

I am writing this note so that you can forward it to Mr. Linscott. I don't honestly think that an old established house like H. Mifflin cd. lose money on the volume. I don't say they wd. get quick profits. I think they wd. clear initial expenses at once and that there wd. be a slow sale thereafter. I am bound to be accepted as a "standard author" sooner or later.

In The Collected prose, books like *Spirit of Romance*,[2] *Pavannes*[3] etc. have been recast, and are accompanied by biographical notes saying why and when. I included *Indiscretions*[4] which is personal memoir up to age of 4. with reflections.

This letter is in response to Kirstein's suggestion that Pound write his autobiography or memoirs for Richard Linscott, an editor at Houghton Mifflin.

[1] John Rodker, British editor and writer, founder-publisher of Ovid Press, which printed Pound's "Hugh Selwyn Mauberly," in 1920 and limited editions of his *Fourth Canto* (1919) and *Cantos XVII–XXVII* (1927).

[2] *The Spirit of Romance*, published (London: J. M. Dent & Sons) in 1910, contained a collection of Pound's lectures on medieval literature delivered at the London Polytechnic College.

[3] *Pavannes and Divisions*, published (New York: Alfred A. Knopf) in 1918, contained a selection of prose.

[4] *Indiscretions*, an autobiographical "revery," was published in A. R. Orage's magazine *The New Age* in twelve installments, beginning 27 May 1920, and as a book by the Three Mountains Press in 1923 in an edition of 300 copies.

19   EZRA POUND TO
                        LINCOLN KIRSTEIN
                        3 August 1930

                    Costa Più Della Divina Commedia[1]

Dear L. K.

No, I did not dislike the last number. I thought the "Diaghilev"
well done.[2] I mean that you got all there was to be got out of the sub-
ject—perhaps more, but that is a flaw in the right direction.

I think however, that it wd. be a mistake to devote too much of the
magazine to retrospect.

Discussion of W. D. Howells, Eugene O'Neill, Stuart Sherman[3]
or the 1927 humanists is retrospect. Discussion of Henry Adams or
Henry James is not.

The stage is a dangerous subject for either a writer or a review. I
mean that ideas only reach the stage after they have been alive some-
where else. Seven years ago I quoted a remark of Cocteau's "On ne
peut rien plus faire avec Diaghilev. Il a du gout."

A year before that Picabia[4] had made a still more stringent remark
apropos Cocteau's Tour Eiffel. "Il abime tout ct homme. C'est la Tour
Eiffel de Delaunay."[5] This is unjust, because there is a definite act of
energy required to transpose from painting or from literature to the
theatre. But the act originates almost nothing. It is an application. i.e.,
the application of a known thing to something else.

                        / / / /

In reply to your earlier letter. Your statement about live types etc.
amounts to saying that there is good low life in America. There is good
low life anywhere. The lower it is the less it is national and the less it
reflects any credit or interest on the *particular* place in which it exists.

I can only repeat my malediction: God eternally damblast a country
that spends billions interfering with peoples' diet and that can not sup-
port a single printing press which will print stuff that people like me
want to read; i.e., regardless of immediate fiscal profit.

The endowments are sabotaged. Even when some vague and good
natured millionaire "founds" something with allegedly cultural or cre-
ative intent, the endowment is handed over to academic eminences

who are as incapable of picking a first class painter or writer as I shd. be of making a sound report on a copper mine. The one thing they are sure to hate is the germ of original capacity. They will go on backing the Howells, the Tarkingtons and W. Churchills to the end of their ignominious history. . . .[6]

My heading was found in the local pharmacy. I asked for a certain brand of excellent American toilet paper and the pharmacien replied with this epitaph on Anglo saxon civilization.: "E essagerato. Costa più della Divina Commedia." Yes he wd. sell it to me, but really it cost too much. It costs more than the Divina Commedia.

Our race still maintains this proportion in estimate. It is the reversal of the old epigram about hyacinths.

[1] A portion of this letter was published in vol. 4, no. 4 (July–Sept. 1931).
[2] An essay on the Diaghilev period by Kirstein appeared in vol. 3, no. 4 (July–Sept. 1930).
[3] William Dean Howells (1837–1920), author, editor, and critic, an important influence on the school of American realism; Stuart Sherman (1881–1926), writer, editor, and critic, professor of English at the University of Illinois, aligned for a time with Irving Babbitt and Paul Elmer More in the Humanist movement; Eugene O'Neill (1888–1953), playwright, whose powerful dramaturgy was initially responsible for giving American drama a place in world literature.
[4] Francis Picabia (1879–1953), French artist and writer, leading figure in the Dada movement.
[5] Robert Delaunay (1885–1941), French artist whose Cubist painting *The Eiffel Tower* (1910) alluded to the construction of the Eiffel Tower from 1887–1889. It was the highest man-made monument in the world for half a century and was the first monument of modernism.
[6] Booth Tarkington (1869–1946), author of novels about young people; Winston Churchill (1871–1947), American writer of historical romances.

20   EZRA POUND TO
LINCOLN KIRSTEIN
22 August 1930

Dear L. K.

I don't think you can change "Mystère Laic" to mystery of common place. The antithesis IN the work itself is not against mystery of the exceptional but against religious mystery.

Also the glorification of common place has such LOUSY relationships in Henglish and Hengland. Began with or at any rate was going strong with L. Binyon[1] 22 years ago.

It is not what Cocteau means in this vol.

He said something in a note on Satie[2] years ago which might have been brought into line with praise of common place, but even that won't really fit.

In the essay on Chirico[3] it is definitely secular, non-religion mystery.

I doubt very much if I can review the Symons.[4] Have known "poor Arthur" too long. May meet him again; etc.

Thanks for sending the book. will write again re/the matter after I have read it.

Of course IF it carries on from his Spiritual Adventures I cd. say a kind word for it.

You said you had a translator for Taupin (Fitts, I think) but yrs. of 9th inst. is first indication that pub/r had been found.

I believe the *Criterion* is using Zukofsky's essay on me (based on 27 Cantos).

Zuk. has done a good essay on American Poesy since 1920 referring to Cantos 28–30.

His essay on me is I think the most thorough yet done. But i shd. think the Criterion wd. give it enough air.

I dunno if it is Etty/KEtt fer the author to pick his reviewer.

Mssrs. Ford; Williams, Weskott;[5] Eliot and Zuk. have expressed themselves as more or less in favour ditto Mr. Blackmore.[6]

There is allus somethin to be said for a new and if possible un-prejudiced eye.

Mssrs. Kirstein, Hyatt Mayor and who else have inserted criticism in *H. & H.*

I really do not. oh well; Mr. Bunting cd. do the job. He had a very good curse [*sic*] on Brit. Lit. in *Indicé* recently.

As editing it might be better to have it reviewed by someone whom I do not KNOW and who don't know me.

some snotty old academic might be forced to read the work.

Why not let some "prominent American critic" flounder and hang himself. Just strikes me there are three crosses on the cover; not in accepted Xtn. pattern; but still. The Rt. Rev. P. T. Querrrumus of Holyjoke Kawledge can discover several errors in the Greek. I *have* and they were put there AFTER that blighted F. Bernouard[7] sent me the proofs. two rough breafins, an a N dropped and some psyze fer phyze. but they won't affect most of the buyers. The only objection to a prominent American critic is that it wd. take 20 bucks away from some honest man who might have use for the money. No you had never said where you got the title but I had once or twice wondered. or suspected.[8]

There is an allusion to New England huntin' in one of Mister Elyot's pomes also.

Felicitations on prospects of Continuity (title by the late Wm. Wordsworth) Good editing wd. prompt you to get Irving Babbitt, or More or Moore or however he spells it to review Cantos.

I shan't Keatsianly die of the result. I don't suggest Coolidge (Calvin) or Dr. Candam [*sic*][9] because you can't trust them bitches not to start the vice soc. apropos XV and XVI.

It wd. do Babbit and More good to read a serious book in which philosophical questions are seriously considered. Sherman I think is dead? What other trained seals are there.

I have lent my set of *H. & H.* fer ejucatnl porpoises. Failing some big DUDD like Babbitt or More; you might use one of the honest academics whom I noticed in my crit. of earlier numbers of *H & H*. I have forgotten names and you prob. have mislaid the epistle.

But *as editor* some big nasty old noise wd. be the best thing to let loose on XXX. . . .

[1] Lawrence Binyon (1869–1943), English poet, dramatist, and art critic.
[2] Erik Satie (1866–1925), French composer.
[3] Giorgio de Chirico (1888–1978), Italian painter, one of the founders of a school of painting called "metaphysical," which invests the ordinary with an element of mystery.
[4] Arthur Symons, *From Toulouse-Lautrec to Rodin: With some Personal Impressions* (1930).
[5] Glenway Wescott (*b.* 1901), writer and critic.
[6] Blackmur.
[7] François Bernouard, master printer for *A Draft of XXX Cantos* (Paris: Hours Press, 1930).
[8] The title *The Hound and Horn* was taken from a poem by Pound, "The White Stag."
[9] Dr. S. Parkes Cadman (1864–1936), author and religious leader.

21   EZRA POUND TO
                LINCOLN KIRSTEIN
                30 August [1930]

Dear Kirstein

I rushed off proofs of Criterionism espresso before post closed to-day.[1] Hope to get 'em back to you in time to remedy bitched sentence re/*to*, establishing at the start.

also an *if* imbecile for *of*

The edtrs. *H & H* shd. know by now that I am hardly likely to call anyone a damn fool in the conditional. . . . God damn it a FOLIO is a different thing from a series. any harf arsed bastard like Wells or Bennett or the late Hambrose Bierce etc., etc., can write a series of four vols. none of them can do a folio. . . .

My books of poems were crippled, incomplete from the 1909 *Personae* to the Liveright *Collected Poems*, *Personae*. Same thing with the prose. It is NOT a series it is a single chunk, and the components need the other components in one piece with them. There is a dif. between *Ulysses* and a series of Hen. Jas. novels. . . .

You will find mention of *H & H* in note of mine they tell me is due to come out in *English Journal* (of Shy Ka go) in Sept. . . .[2]

/ / / /

You are right about Anabase.[3] It is pewk. I dunno what me frien' Tummus[4] is up to. He sent me proofs of the damn thing some time ago and they went into waste basket. As they had neither his name nor the author's on 'em I was not even tempted to display tact.

Above all else I have abominated "prose poesy", i.e., stuff with no tension and no rhythmic guts. I confess that the "style" or modus of Anabase so putt me off that I did not bother to dig down or speculate as to what T. S. E. might have thought he had seen in the damn thing.

I have ever held the belief that one can tell a bad egg without eating the whole of it.

---

[1] In "Criterionism" Pound argues for timeliness of discussion rather than for "indulging continually in a diet of dead crow," a policy he accuses the *Criterion* of pursuing. "I am against stopping to argue about free will and the immortality of the soul in the midst of an explosion or a shipwreck. . . . It takes as much critical acumen to

pick out the sound and living topics for discussion, to select the vital writers of the present, i.e., May, June, July, 1930, as it does to write elaborate estimates of the failures of 1890 and 1904."

² "Small Magazines," *English Journal*, Nov. 1930, p. 792. Pound wrote, "At the present moment there are a number of free reviews in activity. Of these the *Hound and Horn* appears to me the most solid. It has taken over the heritage of whatever was active in the *Dial*. It has got rid of nearly all of the *Dial*'s dead wood and rubbish. This purgation may endanger its safety. . . . The advance in critical writing which I have mentioned seems to me apparent in Zukofsky's essay on Henry Adams, serialized in *Hound and Horn*, and in Hyatt Mayor's criticism of painting."

³ A long poem by French writer St.-John Perse, published in French in 1924 and translated into English, with an introduction by T. S. Eliot in 1930.

⁴ T. S. Eliot.

22   LINCOLN KIRSTEIN
TO EZRA POUND
10 September 1930

Dear Mr. Pound:

I had a letter from Linscott, saying the following:

"I understand that Ezra Pound has recently completed a definitive edition of his Cavalcanti translation and wants to bring it out with both the Italian and English versions. Do you know anything about it? As I recall the translation is quite swell and I think we would be interested if we could do it in a limited edition jointly with some English publisher."

Our review copy of the "Cantos" has come, and it is very nice looking indeed, except for the rather poor initials. I have been racking my head ever since I got your last letter, trying to find somebody who could give it an adequate review, and I have decided that I do not know anybody, so it will have to be inadequately reviewed. As for the idea of getting some old fogy to do it, the following—we have insulted everybody there is to insult, as far as the academics go. On the basis of Humanism, just yesterday one of our late advertisers decided not to continue, since we do not care to bother with Humanism any longer. P. E. More is more hurt than angry, and, I am afraid, Babbitt is more angry than hurt at our remarks. I don't much want to get somebody like Wilson or Cowley, who would do it anyway for *The Nation*, and most of the people whom I have spoken to about it are rather frightened by the compendious erudition, and so forth. I have been trying to convince them to ignore that completely, and to treat it as a narrative, and almost as a narrative poem. Perhaps Dick Blackmur would be best. He surely would be the most intelligent.

Boni[1] will not do the Taupin, because their business is bad, which is true of every other publisher in New York. I am going to take it, however, to Harcourt, and perhaps he will. Fitts has done a very good specimen of the translation and it could be finished easily.

[1] Charles Boni, of the publishing firm Boni and Liveright.

23   EZRA POUND TO LINCOLN KIRSTEIN
23 September 1930

Dear L. K.

. . . Yes, I guess Blackmur will be as good as anyone. re/ the furrin langwidges, damn it; if the reader will skip the foreign langs. he will generally find that the text is complete without them, they are mostly underlining; precisions of reference; the only way; or the best way to tip the reader that you are thinking of Aeschylus is to quote Aeschylus, etc. . . .

> On Oct. 17, Pound wrote Kirstein, telling him that he was sending him the most important piece of prose ("Terra Italica")[1] since *How to Read*. He felt that it took the place of fifty reviews of various books, such as Spengler, Frobenius, etc., and that it gave an idea of civilization, the "sort of thing the wop of 1930 apparently reads, and buys from his bookstall." He admitted that the essay was elliptical, but "the reader who thinks will see what I want him to find." "Terra Italica" was not published in *Hound and Horn* but in the *New Review* (Winter 1931–1932).

24   EZRA POUND TO LINCOLN KIRSTEIN
22 October 1930

Dear L.K.

. . . I regret to see Galantière and Mortimer on the list of contents. God DAMN Bloomsbury.[1]

Galantière is a snob and a second ratist Anabase as you yourself noted is not worth the attention implied in a 5 page review.

Nicolson again (grant the review is capable); Nicolson himself is suspect, social connections; Mortimer always reviewing ON basis of social connections of the reviewed. There is no *literary* or *intellectual* reason for picking Nicolson's life of his papa from 70 other current biogs. . . .

I may kuss out Fitts for a New England hickory, but Fitts, Tate, even old whats his name the sterile Munson, are in a totally different category far above the Galantières and Mortimers.

Have not yet read the Lozowick, but am willing to take him on faith and glad (until proof to contrary) to see him included.[2]

The Wheelright [*sic*] begins well and sounds as if it wd. be honest.[3] . . .

What about an exchange ad. with Pagany:[4] certainly more respectable than Lunnon Murk/ury and the unspeakable Murry.[5] Evans photos. good; especially Wash Day.[6]

/ / /

What about a little editorial definition / by which I mean 'bout taking Pagany as "the Opponent." . . . DO for godzake, go dig out ole Bill Williams, DONT believe anything he tells you, but indulge in the stimulus of disagreeing with him viva voce. he has the vital sap which our dear friend T.S.E. hasn't.

Pagany appears to think I am the devil of dessication, that is as it should be. Let 'em; and don't waste time arguing the matter.

I take it from Bill's last epistle that he thinks you're nearly as bad as the Dial.

The next important problem is WHO is going to do your article on Apes of God.[7] It wd. be a fine stroke to make ole Bill Water Closet Williams do THAT. His reactions re/Lewis have always been amusing. First strong objection, then conversion, the queery

"How the hell did" I "have sense enough to dig him out of the dung heap with nothing but his hair showing."

Whatever one may think about W. L.'s wasting his time the "Apes" is Hogarth and Rowlandson redivivi, British caricature at its best and without the smirk and stain of the snotten victorian era. . . .

Wheelright is good; have just struck a live sentence. You can do

with more of him. He is not talking about McKim for social reasons.
(or if he is, I am deceived)

[1] Lewis Galantière (1895–1977), writer, critic, and author on modern French literature.

Raymond Mortimer (*b.* 1895), who contributed a monthly London letter to the *Dial*, reviewed Harold Nicolson's *Portrait of a Diplomatist* in vol. 4, no. 1 (Oct.–Dec. 1930): "Not so much a biography of his father, Lord Carnock, as a history of pre-World War I diplomacy."

[2] Louis Lozowick (1892–1973), primarily a painter and lithographer, whose work appeared frequently in the *New Masses*. His article on V. E. Meyerhold and the theater appeared in vol. 4, no. 1 (Oct.–Dec. 1930).

[3] *The Life and Times of Charles Follen McKim* by Charles Moore, reviewed by John Brooks Wheelwright.

[4] *Pagany*, a quarterly published from 1930 to 1933, was edited by Richard Johns; it published among other works William Carlos Williams's *White Mule*, Erskine Caldwell's short stories, a section of John Dos Passos's *USA*, and poetry by Kenneth Rexroth, Conrad Aiken, and Gertrude Stein.

[5] John Middleton Murry (1889–1957), editor of the London *Mercury*, husband of Katherine Mansfield.

[6] Walker Evans (1903–1975), photographer, was introduced to Lincoln Kirstein in 1927 by writer Muriel Draper, and in the decade following Kirstein exerted a considerable influence on Evans's thought and career. Reproductions of four photographs of New York City were published in vol. 4, no. 1 (Oct.–Dec. 1930). Walker Evans was described then as "a Brooklyn photographer who recently had illustrated Hart Crane's poem, *The Bridge*, published by the Black Sun Press."

[7] This book by Wyndham Lewis was not reviewed in *Hound and Horn*.

25   EZRA POUND TO
          LINCOLN KIRSTEIN
          26 October 1930

Dear K

. . . Wish Schwartz wd. have a look at my "Antheil and Harmony." [1] Nobody capable of understanding it has ever been drawn into a discussion of it. Some "like it" and some dud "musical people, composers etc." regard me as a lunatic on acc/ of it. . . .

Richards must be wrong 'un also, or Belgion wdnt. be so interested in him

Vague recollect that I saw a debunk (?) of Richards (I. A.) in *H & H* or do I err? [2]

Only trouble is Rosie Field will neverneverever have the faintest

earthly of WHAT Mr. Schwartz is talkin' about at ATT a Tall. HAVE you
ever met Rosie?

The *Dial's* critiK of MooZeek. . .³

/ / / /

FIRST think is to git honest man who will tell the truth and debunk
the devil. Clarity next requisite (which is after all best guide to intel-
ligence; a few rare spirits have *some* intelligence without being able to
attain clear expression; but they are BLOODY few.)

the ketch iz that the knave HAS to be lucid; so you've got to est. the
honesty first.

(see the Brits. have got a rebel pubctn. called "Experiment" but
have as yet no proof that anyone on it can DO anything.)

Ole Wyndham is by common consent their ablest pamphleteer.⁴
The Apes proves he is NOT YET dead. Pourquoi PAS? I knowIknowI-
know, all these damn books undigested baboo with undigested learnin'
in his insides; but still Lewis wrong is more entertainin' than all the
Criterion right. (not that it ever is RIGHT except during those 5 minutes
every 9 months when Eliot wakes up and is lucid.) Of course you can't
control Wyndham, and nobody cd. depend on him to send in a mss. at
a given time. I suggest the form in which my name shd. NOT appear.

Dear Mr. Lewis

Admiring as we do yr. Apes (or whatever you do admire; admiror,
admiratio etc.) we are damn well tired of seein' the U.S.A. bunked by
Bloomsbury. They have shoved off on us all the shoddy we can stand.

As you are not apparently appearin' in any other American mag. we
shd. be glad to present your work when you find it convenient to send
it to America.

or something of that sort.

We have been labeled "successors to the Dial" but we certainly do
not mean to carry on any sort of Dialish conservatism.

You cd. certainly get some Lewis designs for reprod. that wd. be
useful. You can say; I shd. think with truth; that you wd. have been
glad to use a chunk of Apes if it had been offered you.

You are supplied with critical stuff, or can be; whereas Lewis is
much better in "stories" than in essays. Say quite clearly that if he has
any stories or anything in the vein of the APES you wd. prefer that

FIRST as you have got a bit loaded with crit. After all Cantleman got the *Little Rev.* suppressed before *Ulysses* got into it. Lewis' prose stories at that time were BHLOODY GOOD. Don't mean that *you* are to get suppressed. Lewis is *not* being suppressed now (Privik and confidenshul. IF you can get a decent chunk of W. L. I will TRY to get a chunk of Monsieur Joyce written in plain and decent english or american and not choctaw. This is possibly Icarian, and nothing can be done till I see him in the spring but I hold out the offer . . . about which I request that you *speak to no one* whomsoever (save Bandler if he is supposed as coedtr. to see all this correspondence.)

[1] Herbert S. Schwartz published an article on "Some Problems of Musical Criticism" vol. 4, no. 1 (Oct.–Dec. 1930).
[2] I. A. Richards (*b.* 1893), British psychologist, critic, and educator. He was extremely influential in the development of modern criticism. No essay on I. A. Richards appeared in *Hound and Horn*.
[3] Paul Rosenfeld, music critic of the *Dial*.
[4] Wyndham Lewis (1881–1957), British novelist and editor. Associated with Pound in editing the magazine *Blast* (1914–1918), and in other ventures. He also edited the magazines *Tyro* and *The Enemy*.

26   EZRA POUND TO LINCOLN KIRSTEIN
16 November 1930

Dear L. K.

Nothing is easier than to shrug one's shoulders and say it don't matter. People go on until there is a 1914 or something of that sort. The Am. Acad. don't matter. ALL right, it don't matter. BUT the existence of these otiose old sons of bitches does act as a drag. It is their sins of omission, and as long as they are left in peace the omissions will continue.

They ought to be given a pillar of infamy by someone young enough to be free from the charge of wanting to be one of them.

A list of their infamous names ought to be published. PLUS what they stand FOR. which includes art. 2II. and every other infamy of American literary taste. . . . Perhaps a list of the things these 40 farts have NOT done for American art and letters wd. be as eloquent as anything.

27   EZRA POUND TO
LINCOLN KIRSTEIN
November 1930

Dear K.

    . . . About academicism. I am prob. scary because of my past life. I went to England in 1908, I was told I was a poet and that I cdnt. write English (by which the sonzvof bitches meant Oxfordese of 1892) and I steadily descended to the level of Henry Newbolt as you can verify by an obsolete vol. called "Canzoni" (still Admired by Mr. Aldington)

    This may be the mystic death and dark night of the soul, and may be the purrfect writer has to pass through it;

        but fer gardzake git thru it as quickly as possible.

without some desire for perfection I suppose one wd. remain with Vachel Lindsay and the *New Masses* poets

/   /   /

    Zno use. An ecervelé like Mike Gold[1] has got something we haven't. A rotten Russian film I saw last night "The burning of Kazan" has got something we haven't.

---

[1] Michael Gold (1893–1967), editor of *New Masses* from 1928 to 1932, a writer best known for his novel *Jews without Money* (1930), a classic of tenement life on New York's Lower East Side before World War I.

28   EZRA POUND TO
LINCOLN KIRSTEIN
22 January 1931

No, my dear Linc.

    I am NOT startin' a magazine. Three mags. requested me to officiate at baptism, churching, epiphany, etc., and short of actual refusal I declined; that is to say I advised against swelling list of edt. boards. Putnam seemed to think my name wd. help him pay his rent (so thass' thaat. I await his first number.)[1]

    as fer invektin' go ahead. If there is a bigger corpse lyin' in the road, go bury it, or kill it if it ain't a corpse. After all it's your magazine. No need to eliminate yr/ own voice completely or to wait for the obit of another Diaghilev. . . .

Also question of space and brevity. A list of the corpses now encumbering the U.S. cd. be got onto a page. BLAST did clear the air. . . .

I am forced every now and again to consider my own CASE.

The conclusion might seem to be EITHER

my work of the past 20 years in criticism and agitation (promotion) has been utterly negligible etc. Some things you will have to learn for yourself and nobody's telling you can possibly be any use. If you haven't a copy of my Trans. of *Ta Hao* [*sic*][2] I will cheerfully remit one. . . .

OR

I ought not be continually hamstrung and impeded as I now am.

A. by lack of small cash return

B. by impossibility of getting and keeping essential parts of my stuff in print and available for those that WANT to consult it. (them)

This is not a reflection on H & H, but four articles a year does not give the full measure of my potential. . . . Should America pay me say fifty dollars a month (as proportionate reward fer what it pays the Vandorens, Wilsons, Lippmanns etc.

Yr/ goddam publisher gets the three WRONG novels out of 550.

[1] Samuel Putnam, editor of the *New Review*, published from 1931 to 1932. The associate editors were Ezra Pound, Maxwell Bodenheim, and Richard Thoma. The magazine explored the effect of the machine upon aesthetics and creative expression.
[2] *Ta Hio*, The Great Learning, Pound's translation of a work by Confucius, was published by the University of Washington, Seattle, in 1928.

29   DUDLEY FITTS TO LINCOLN KIRSTEIN
[Undated]

Dear Lincoln

The translation of le "Mystère Laic" is so badly done as to be irremediable. I say this without having examined the original: the English version by O. E. Rudge is shabbily thrown together, hack-work in every line.[1] One wd. never know that Cocteau had the least distinction, and it wd. be an injustice to him to publish this translation. The whole MS wd. have to be thoroughly rewritten, and I advise a new translation, preferably by someone with a speaking-knowledge of English and a sense for English idiom and prose-style. Given any encouragement, I'll do it myself.—Of course, I'm not sure that a translation is necessary. Anyone sufficiently interested in Chirico, or sufficiently intelligent even to see what Cocteau is driving at, can read French as it is. (Wch is not necessarily the case with a book like Taupin's, of some value to the non-French-speaking student.) Who is Rudge? I understood you to say that the translation was by Pound—it looks like his typewriter and his handwriting: is it P, so aware of his shocking English that he blushed to use his own name? . . .

thursday

On 31 January 1931, Pound wrote Kirstein asking him to return "Terra Italica" if he did not want it, to which Kirstein replied, Feb. 11, apologizing for not having returned it before. He thought he had returned it but was horrified to find it in the files. He suggested *Pagany* as a suitable magazine for the article. On Feb. 17, Kirstein sent Dudley Fitts the manuscript of *Mystère Laic*, saying that it was not a good translation but that he didn't know what to do with it, and Kirstein suggested that Fitts make the obvious or necessary corrections or improvements. Letter 29 is the response to this suggestion.

[1] Olga Rudge, Pound's companion.

30   EZRA POUND TO
        LINCOLN KIRSTEIN
        20 March 1931

Dear Kirstein:

    . . . "Terra Italica" went on at once to Putnam (*New Review*) and is, I believe, destined for the next issue (following the one already in press). I shd. have preferred it to appear *in* America, but it is probably too late to disentangle it.

    The infelicitous Harriet has blown off again about my Propertius in the *English Journal*,[1] and I have sent them a reply. (They sent me proofs of her squib, but I haven't seen copies of the *Journal* either with her squib or my answer; so don't know whether they have yet appeared.

The appreciators of that effort have been very veree select. Hardy, Yeats, Mockel, Bunting, (Eliot in his first reaction ten years ago . . . but later drifting into ambiguity).

Fitts is from my point of view, very nearly hopeless.[2] Either Eliot or Zukofsky had already "said it" or else he goes dead wrong. IF by chance he understands ANYTHING he omits to manifest his understanding. Any l'il gal pleased with a bit of the bright decor or a bit of the sound, or any low-brow-pleased with one of the jokes wd., it seems to me, be nearer a fundamental comprehension.

Seems to me prime example of the kind of painstaking exposition that puts people off reading ANYTHING. (minus the occasional lapses where he explains it *wrong*).

The rest, as far as I can make out, a repetition either of Eliot (years ago in *Dial*) or Zuk. in *Èchanges*. . . .

For years I have in vain suggested to my confrères (Eliot, Bill Wms. etc.,) that they traduce. Eliot WAS to do Sanskrit; Bill, Spanish; Eliot the Agamemnon, etc.

Mr. Aldington has rambled in the fat pastureland. Mr. Waley[3] has profaned the Orient etc.

99% of all lit/ effort is wasted/ however, one must go on butting the brick wall of cent/pour/ and a LITTLE does ultimately get done/

for which one is kurrrsed at the time and blessed after one has forgotten it. . . .

In general, as to local scene / I shd/ advise you to dig out ole Bill Williams// not necessary to AGREE.

I shd/ also advise you to put up with being irritated by Zuk.

I personally shd/ always be interested in anybody else's attempt to rewrite one of my poems. Only one man ever has. He ended in the secret service . . . or rather is, I believe, still goin' on.

What constructive use is a critic unless the author can get what the crit. is driving at? No more concrete mode than revision.

<hr/>

[1] Originally, Harriet Monroe had selected four sections out of the twelve of "Homage to Sextus Propertius" for publication in *Poetry*, in March 1919. Other sections were published in the *New Age* between June and Aug. 1919. Prof. William Hale attacked the poem immediately, saying that it was an inaccurate translation and giving instances where the English diverged from the Latin. Pound denied that there

was ever any intent to translate directly. "My job," he told Orage, editor of the *New Age*, "was to bring a dead man to life, to present a living figure."

[2] Pound is referring to Fitts's review of *XXX Cantos* in vol. 4, no. 2 (Jan.–March 1931). He wrote, "Cantos XIV and XV are the *Inferno* of the poem, and are conceived in the manner of the traditional scatological invective. But for all their vigor (and they are certainly startling!) they carry very little conviction. They do not *assert*; they rant, they snarl. One is always conscious of Mr. Pound . . . with scores to pay off, with injuries to redress. . . . His attitude *is* the pedantic, unreal attitude. Throughout the poem he has substituted book-living for actual life." But, Fitts concludes, "Aside from what seems to me a fundamental error in attitude, it is a memorable work. Technically, it is nearly faultless; as a craftsman, Mr. Pound is so far in advance of all the rest of us that his book should be universally read, if only as a manual of poetic technic. But it is much more than splendid writing. It is a gallant proud attempt to assert the positive value of experience. It is very nearly the great music, 'fit for the Odes.'"

[3] Arthur Waley (1889–1966), sinologist and translator from the Chinese and Japanese.

31   EZRA POUND TO
             LINCOLN KIRSTEIN
             22 March 1931

Dear L/K/

Returning to yr/ letter. re/ advice. If you have kept the voluminous outpourings of the past year or more you might reread 'em. Seems to me I *must* have given about all the advice I have to give. I take it your note in general indicates that I am persona piu grata to the present monocratic government than to the late polycratic govt. of H. & H.

BUT I think, all the same I must have said nearly everything at least once.

re/ style in America. YES. and it is worth irritating people and sticking to that somewhat Toryish (tho' not fundamentally Tory position however unpopular.

BUT it is dangerous internally and ex- danger of Concord school omitting to notice Whitman. Historically, people in rough environment, if they have any sensibility or perceptions want "culture and refinement."

Whitman embodying nearly everything one disliked etc.

failure to see the wood for the trees.

/ / /

Secondly or thirdly

Danger of confusing your (for example) lyric impulse and yr/ editorial function.

As lyricist you can WANT (and shd/ want) whatever you damn please.

Editorial function something very different.

In that function one has to (at least) observe, admit the capacities of people who like what one does NOT like. Life wd. have been (in my case) much less interesting if I had waited till Joyce, Lewis, Eliot, D. H. Lawrence etc., complied with what my taste was in 1908.

/ / /

Oh HELL, how shall I put it. My son, elucidate thine own bloody damn point of view, by its contrast to others, not by trying to make the others conform.

All right/ you want a STYLE out of America. Stick at it. BUT when it comes it mayn't be where you are lookin' for it.

As editor all you can do is to get the best of what is done

A. from those you more or less agree with.

B. from those you DON'T.

and in latter case you can editorially profess to be conscious of an energy, which you believe to be wrongly directed.

32 EZRA POUND TO LINCOLN KIRSTEIN
8 July 1931

Dear Mr. Kirstein

I have recd. no letter saying you were not using "Mystère Laic"[1] in *H & H.*

I recd. a letter about difficulties of pamphlet publication.

I have not received the mss/ which you say you have returned. It shd. have been sent registered. I recd. no notice from you that the mss. had been sent back. It seems odd that neither mss/ nor notice of its return shd. have arrived. A coincidence that both items shd. have been lost in post.

You will probably discover that the ms/ has been mislaid in transferring your offices from one palatial office to another.

I am out of pocket the small advance made to translator.

The statement that the translation is inexact is an evasion; evidently originating in type of mind that considers it inexact to translate it "my uncle's hat" instead of preserving the French form "hat of my uncle."

I went through the whole translation and also consulted Cocteau on a number of points in order that there shd. be the proper exactness as to his *meaning* and its relation to what was at the back of his mind.

Even without these aggravations, the loss of year in placing the ms/ wd. be annoying.

It only remains for me to express sincere regret for the time wasted by me in correspondence with H & H and say that taken as a whole our relations have been thoroughly unsatisfactory to me.

I wish I had never heard of yr/ magazine and I think you a god damn fool not to have printed the M.L. both for its integral quality and for its value proportionally to what you do print.

[1] Cocteau's *Mystère Laic*, translated by Olga E. Rudge, was published in the Jan.– March 1932 issue of *Pagany*, edited by Richard Johns. Cocteau's thoughts are presented epigrammatically. From time to time the essay reverts to a discussion of the work of de Chirico. "Chirico is in fact a religious painter. A religious painter without faith. A painter of the laic mystery. He must have miracles. His realism keeps him from painting miracles which he couldn't believe in. He therefore has to produce them by setting objects and people in fortuitous circumstances. . . . A permitted thing cannot be pure."

33   LINCOLN KIRSTEIN TO EZRA POUND
6 August 1931

Dear Mr. Pound:

I was shocked and horrified to receive your last letter. It's all a ghastly mistake. I am sure I wrote to you about it but I can't find my letter, which patently proves your point. I was sure I sent back the manuscript three months ago, and I spent about two days looking through our files for records. None were there. Then we looked through all the old stenographic books and they weren't there. Everybody here remembered very well sending it back to you, including myself. I even remembered the letterhead, the color of the ink and how much it cost to register it. So it must have been lost. Suddenly Dudley Fitts appeared bringing the manuscript in. I don't blame you for feeling very sore about it and there is no point in my going on to apologize. I don't know how he got hold of it, but he seems to have.

I am very sorry you incurred any expense as far as the translation goes. I will, of course, pay whatever that is as soon as you let me know. Although I am quite naturally upset that all this inefficiency occurred, I cannot tell you how sorry I was to learn that it only remains for you to "express sincere regret for the time wasted by me in correspondence with *H. & H*., and to say that taken as a whole our relations have been thoroughly unsatisfactory." You further go on to say that you wish you had never heard of the magazine and think I am a "god damn fool," etc., etc. There's nothing to be said about this at all. If you feel that way about it, that's all there is to say. I would perfectly well admit any sort of hard feeling on the basis of our inefficiency in regard to the Cocteau, but I see no reason for the rest of your remarks. I have done my best to take your suggestions and advice for which I have been very grateful always. We have been very pleased to have printed the people you sent us. You cannot say that we haven't been interested in what you have had yourself to say from the extent of your "Correspondence" printed in the magazine. However, I am not particularly surprised that you should feel the way you do about us, since you generally behave this way about every magazine in which you have any initial interest. I am only glad that you held on to us as long as you did. If you ever have anything more that you want to say through us or change your mind in regard to us, it would be more than O.K.

P.S. I am sending back the "Mystère Laic" registered special handling.

CHAPTER II
T. S. Eliot

I   **LINCOLN KIRSTEIN
TO T. S. ELIOT**
September 1927

Dear Mr. Eliot,

I have hesitated in writing you about the matter of a bibliography but both Mr. Richard Wood[1] and Mr. Bonamy Dobrée[2] have partially convinced me such a letter as this would not trouble you too much.

Under separate cover I hope you will find a list of the first editions of your works—with what are—as far as I know—the correct collations. The note on the last sheet is self-explanatory. That material is already collected, but needs editing. My colleague Mr. Fry has forgotten to include a notice of variorum readings, while I've not had enough time to list *Journey of the Magi*.

The bibliography will appear in a quarterly magazine which is to be published at Harvard this year. I send you an advance copy, which was printed as an example of format, to show to advertisers. I am painfully aware of its literary shortcomings but should you happen to glance at it, would you please consider The Button story and the poem "He who gathers song" as omitted. The actual magazine is to be approximately sixty-seven pages and will contain besides magazine and book reviews, some photographs of Architecture and Paintings by Harvard men.[3] It is a new departure in Cambridge publications and will be received with some hostility.

65

We hope to print the bibliography at Christmas time as the first of a series which will also include Henry Adams, George Santayana, and probably Irving Babbitt.[4]

It would be very kind of you, if you could inform us,—without giving yourself too much trouble—whether or not we have omitted any of your books. Perhaps there have been small editions—not for sale, of which we could have found no record? I am conscious that you may be perhaps not in sympathy with the idea of such a bibliography, but I assure you, Mr. Fry and myself are only two of a great number where interest in your work, would, we believe warrant an almost immediate appearance of a careful list when it is published in the *Hound and Horn*—it will bring forth comment and correction so that later we hope to issue the completed and amplified work in book form. In the number of the *Hound and Horn* which carries the Bibliography will also be several critical articles concerning your poetry and criticism written by those of us at Harvard who are particularly grateful and cognizant of your stimulating influence.

The Christmas number goes to Press, November 28th, and we would very greatly appreciate hearing from you before that time.

The influence of .T. S. Eliot (1888–1965) on the *Hound and Horn* was felt in a number of ways. The magazine initially modeled itself after Eliot's London-based *Criterion*, notably in the depth and seriousness of its criticism and book reviews. In 1927 at the inception of the *Hound and Horn*, then subtitled "A Harvard Miscellany," editors Lincoln Kirstein and Varian Fry had planned a series of critical articles about eminent Harvard alumni such as T. S. Eliot, Henry James, George Santayana, and others. A two-part critical essay on Eliot by Richard Blackmur with bibliography by Varian Fry was published in vol. 1, and a three-part critical essay on Henry Adams by Louis Zukofsky was printed in vol. 3, nos. 3 and 4 (April–June and July–Sept. 1930) and vol. 4, no. 1 (Oct.–Dec. 1930), but after that the project was dropped, with the exception of the penultimate issue, vol. 7, no. 3 (April–June 1934), a homage to Henry James. Eliot's proposal that he write on Humanism, instead of on the expatriation of Henry James as the editors had suggested, propelled the *Hound and Horn* toward the first of its ideological programs, Humanism. His essay *Second Thoughts on Humanism* was published in vol. 2, no. 4 (June–Aug. 1929). Some years later his poem "Difficulties of a Statesman" was printed in vol. 6, no. 1 (Oct.–Dec. 1932). Subsequently, correspondence between Eliot and the *Hound and Horn* lapsed—the magazine having become independent and no longer seeking to emulate the *Criterion*.

Although I was not given permission to use Eliot's letters in the *Hound and Horn* Archive, the record of the letters from the editors to Eliot documents their relationship with the renowned poet, whom Kirstein remembered in a conversation with me as kind, encouraging, and fatherly "in the way men in their forties can be to men in their twenties."

On 14 September 1927 Eliot responded to Kirstein's first letter, saying that he would be honored to have a bibliography of his work published and suggesting that the editors add to it his lecture on Shakespeare and his *Seneca His Tenne Tragedies*, to be published shortly by Constable and Knopf, for which he had written the introduction and which he considered his most scholarly work to date. In reply to Kirstein's suggestion that he write on the expatriation of Henry James and its effect on his work, on 16 November 1928 Eliot wrote that he was not ready to write about James again but offered instead to write on the New Humanism and Babbitt and his disciples.

[1] Richardson King Wood (1904–1976), who worked for *Fortune* magazine as a writer and editor and later became an independent business consultant. He was "a brilliant young American who had gone to Cambridge after Harvard, and made a big impression on everyone there. My entrée to Eliot came through him," Kirstein wrote me, 16 Jan. 1976.

[2] At this time, Dobrée was an editor of *Criterion*.

[3] The table of contents for the first issue of the *Hound and Horn* (Sept. 1927) listed an essay by Newton Arvin on the pseudo-diary notes of "Henry Marston"; poetry by H. N. Doughty, Jr., Tom Mabry, John A. Abbott, and Lincoln Kirstein; reproductions of paintings by Maurice Grosser and of photographs by Jere Abbott; an article on architecture by Henry-Russell Hitchcock, Jr.; and book reviews by R. P. Blackmur and Lincoln Kirstein—all of whom, with the exception of Blackmur, had connections with Harvard as undergraduate students or alumni.

[4] A three-part critical essay on Henry Adams by Louis Zukofsky was printed in vol. 3, nos. 3 and 4 (April–June and July–Sept. 1930) and vol. 4, no. 1 (Oct.–Dec. 1930); Bernard Bandler wrote on "The Individualism of Irving Babbitt" in vol. 3, no. 1 (Oct.–Dec. 1929); but no essay on Santayana was published in the magazine.

2   LINCOLN KIRSTEIN
TO T. S. ELIOT
6 December 1928

Dear Mr. Eliot,

Thank you for your letter of 16 November. We should be very much honored to have you write for us on any subject that appeals to you. As Mr. Babbitt is contributing a series of articles on humanism to ensuing numbers of the *Hound and Horn*,[1] it would be extremely pertinent to have you write on "the New Humanism, and Babbitt and his disciples," as you suggest.

We should be very grateful to have your final decision as to subject within the month. The manuscript should be in our hands by the first of April, 1929.

With all best wishes for the *Criterion*,

[1] Kirstein was overly optimistic, for Babbitt did not write any articles on Humanism for the *Hound and Horn*.

3   RICHARD BLACKMUR
         TO T. S. ELIOT
         13 February 1929

Dear Mr. Eliot:

Thank you very much for your letter of the twenty-fifth of January, which I have kept by me so long merely because I wished to make my answer complete.

If we can have your essay by the first week in April, we will be easily able to get it into the June issue. The length of four thousand words is agreeable, and the title—"Second Thoughts on Humanism"[1]—could not, under the special circumstances, be better. In the next issue of the *Hound and Horn* there will be a paper—"The Humanism of W. C. Brownell"[2]—on which I am certain your paper will be a very apt comment. I suppose and hope that your "Second Thoughts" have some relation to your *Forum* article on Babbitt. I know from personal conversation that a great many people have been struck with a notion of humanism as a *substitute* for religion—myself especially.

About simultaneous publications. The other day in conversation with Mr. Montgomery Belgion[3] I learned that Ramon Fernandez[4] was in a very long process of giving you some sort of essay perhaps on George Eliot—I am not sure now. If you think it would be possible to arrange such an essay with M. Fernandez, this is precisely the sort of thing that we would like to be able to publish simultaneous with the *Criterion*, or in the subsequent issue. I understand that M. Fernandez is a very slow writer and cannot be depended upon so far as time is concerned. I also understand that it is very difficult to deal with the N.R.F.[5], which would leave yourself as the only possible medium of exchange. However, if you would rather not take the trouble it will be entirely agreeable to me to let Fernandez go. But I do hope that you will be able to make some other particular suggestions sometime between now and summer.

As to our rates, they are as uniform as yours, and as low—your own article will be the only exception that we have made. We pay seven dollars and a half a page for poetry, and three dollars and a half a page for prose. We pay ten dollars a piece for our longer reviews, and nothing at all for the shorter notices. This is not through choice, but through a very bitter necessity. (Which reminds me that Conrad Aiken misinformed you that our circulation was five thousand; it is only two thousand; which is neither here nor there, but still I should hardly wish to have you think too well of America in this respect.)

I am sending you a copy of the reprint of my article on yourself. Believe me, that I am rather ashamed of many paragraphs, both as to style and content, and I am in fact, rather sorry that the thing was reprinted at all. But I hope some time to go over it carefully making corrections, modifications; expanding it generally so as to include the mood, which I think I share, exposed in *Lancelot Andrewes*, and the program announced in its preface.[6] I should be enormously grateful if you would be willing to make particular comment on what I have written, either as to point of fact, or "interpretation."

If it were possible for us to have your manuscript some time in March we would be able to send you proofs. I think that the fifteenth of March would be the last date at which this would be feasible. If you cannot do this, you may be sure we will take every extraordinary care to see that nothing slips by.

Please take all our thanks for the high and kind things which you say of us; there is no good opinion with which we could be more pleased.

[1] Published in vol. 2, no. 4 (July–Sept. 1929), in which he sought a religious base for Humanism—"Man is man because he can recognize spiritual realities not because he can invent them."

[2] By Bernard Bandler, published in vol. 2, no. 3 (April–June 1929), in which he applied a painstaking scrutiny to what he considered to be vague assertions and unsupported claims. "Mr. Babbitt embraces all traditions and holds no point of view personally his own. . . . If one asks what it is that Mr. Babbitt values, what apart

from refuting the ever recurrent expressions of romanticism he would have man do, the answer is hard to find."

[3] Montgomery Belgion, a friend and associate of Eliot's, frequently published articles in the *Criterion*.

[4] Ramon Fernandez (1894–1944), a philosophic critic of literature.

[5] *Nouvelle Revue Francaise.*

[6] Here Eliot states that his "point of view may be described as classicist in literature, royalist in politics, and Anglo-Catholic in religion." *For Lancelot Andrewes* (Garden City, N.Y.: Doubleday, Doran, 1929), vii.

4   RICHARD P. BLACKMUR
       TO T. S. ELIOT
       20 March 1929

Dear Mr. Eliot:

We received "Second Thoughts on Humanism" last Saturday; and are now sending you a galley proof of it; and wish to give you our ever-lasting thanks for it. We all think it is a very fine paper and feel that it fits in amazingly well with what little we have of a "programme". I do wish, however, that you might be able sometime to answer the criticism which you say has been made to you, namely, the question "If you succeed in proving that humanism is insufficient without religion, what is left for those who cannot believe?" . . .

I am very sorry that I haven't yet been able to give *Lancelot Andrewes* enough attention to be any way near sure what I understand to be your present position, nor can I even at all definitely see what final attitude might spring from it. Nor am I sure, had I given it the attention, that I would quite dare to tell you what I think: so sure am I that I would remain, here in America, confronted with an essential puzzle in relation to Royalism, and Anglo-Catholicism, if not to Classicism. Nevertheless, it *seems* to add up to an attitude which I share, although necessarily not in identical terms.

I shall take the liberty within a week or so of sending you some notes on my own on E. E. Cummings;[1] not necessarily with an idea to publish. . . .

[1] An essay by Blackmur, "Notes on E. E. Cummings' Language," was published in vol. 4, no. 2 (Jan.–March 1931).

5   **BERNARD BANDLER**
TO T. S. ELIOT
3 November 1930

Dear Mr. Eliot:

I meant to write you before this and thank you for the luncheon you gave me. It was a great delight to see you, and I regret only that we did not see more of one another.

Would you care to review Ezra Pound's "Cantos" for us? Is there any likelihood of our being able to publish a poem of yours in the Winter issue? Could I ask—which I neglected to speak about in London— about the *Hound and Horn*'s publishing the prize short story simultaneously with the *Criterion*, the n.r.f., and so forth?[1] We corresponded about it, as you remember, last spring, but I have heard nothing further on the subject.

[1] The idea of publishing a prize short story simultaneously was a project that never emerged beyond the discussion stage.

6   **LINCOLN KIRSTEIN**
TO T. S. ELIOT
5 June 1931

Dear Mr. Eliot:

Last summer you spoke to Mr. Bandler about the possibility of publishing some of your poetry in the *Hound and Horn*. We hope that you have not changed your mind, for we would of course be most anxious to print anything you might care to send us. We next go to press on August 15th. I have no idea at all as to your attitude towards the possibility of printing, for example, such verses as "Marina" or "Animula," before they come out in the *Criterion* Miscellany.

It will be a great privilege for us to print anything as beautiful as this.

Eliot regretted that he had no poetry to offer them, for although he was working on a piece for the Ariel poems, it was stipulated that the poem should not have been previously published, but in 1932 he offered *Hound and Horn* part of an "unfinished poem" which had appeared previously in a French translation in the magazine *Commerce.* "Difficulties of a Statesman" was published in vol. 6, no. 1 (Oct.–Dec. 1932).

7   LINCOLN KIRSTEIN
TO T. S. ELIOT
17 July 1931

Dear Mr. Eliot:

I hesitate to write you, knowing how busy you must be and the probable extent of your commitments. However, Mr. Bandler and myself were talking yesterday about ideas for our future, and we wondered whether or not you would be interested in writing about Joyce. This almost might seem a rather obvious subject, but as far as I can remember, and in spite of the extensive literature in this country, there is hardly anything that isolates him with the authority of which he is deserving. Such an article could take any form that you might choose.

If you will consent to do this we would, of course, not press you for the time. There is no reason why it should have to be finished for another year. We do hope that you might give this your consideration at least.

We are always so very grateful for Mr. Bonamy Dobrée's great kindness to us in the pages of the *Criterion.*

> Eliot replied later in the month that though he did not wish to write critically on Joyce at that time, he was thinking of asking Stuart Gilbert for a piece on Joyce's later work for the *Criterion* and put forward the possibility of its being published at the same time in the *Hound and Horn.*

8   LINCOLN KIRSTEIN
TO T. S. ELIOT
10 November 1931

Dear Mr. Eliot:

I have no idea of whether or not you ever read any of the manuscripts that are submitted for publication to Faber & Faber, but, without infringing on your time I wondered whether or not you would be interested in looking over a book of mine which I believe my publishers have sent to Faber & Faber—this only on the chance that it will come under your jurisdiction or interest.

The name of the book is *Flesh is Heir*. I believe at present it has a sub-title of A Historical Romance, but the historical background is the decade 1920–1930.[1]

The correspondence between Eliot and *Hound and Horn* ends with a note from Eliot to Kirstein dated 16 Dec. 1932, written from Harvard University where he was Charles Eliot Norton Professor of Poetry; in the note he thanked Kirstein for a check in payment of his poem, saying he had been pleasantly surprised—he had not expected payment at all. He stated that he could not sell the rights to his Charles Eliot Norton lectures delivered at Harvard as they were the property of Harvard University. He wished they could meet more often and hoped that there would be "opportunities in the New Year."

[1] *Flesh is Heir* was published by Brewer, Warren and Putnam in 1932. In a letter to me 16 Sept. 1975 Lincoln Kirstein wrote, "I doubt if Eliot ever read *Flesh is Heir*; few did." Made up of a series of episodes in the life of Roger Baum, a boy and young man during the 1920s, the novel describes the life of its hero—"affluent, Jewish, sensitive, and shy"—at boarding school, on a trip to Europe where he inadvertently witnesses Diaghilev's funeral, to a job in a stained glass factory, through his first year at college. Reviewers attacked the hero's passivity and the static quality of the second half of the book but by and large commented favorably on the sensitivity of the writing and the freshness of the viewpoint—"one more voice in the rapidly swelling chorus of new writers who have grown dissatisfied with the novel of disillusionment and bitterness" (*Saturday Review of Literature*, 26 March 1932, p. 623). *Flesh is Heir* was reissued in 1975 by the Southern Illinois University Press. The second book of Kirstein's, *For My Brother: A True Story by José Martínez Berlanga as told to Lincoln Kirstein*, was published by Hogarth Press in London (1943).

CHAPTER III

Dudley Fitts and
A. Hyatt Mayor

I   DUDLEY FITTS TO
           LINCOLN KIRSTEIN
           [November 1929]

Dear Lincoln:

I enclose a short notice of *The Noise That Time Makes*.[1] Thank you very much for sending it: I enjoyed it hugely. It's my idea of what our poetry ought to try to be—not entirely successful, in Mr. Moore's case, but much more valid than most contemporary stuff. I think the Fugitives have more guts than any other "group" now writing: I admire Ransom and Davidson and Tate greatly,[2]—unpretentious, sinewy, sweetly acrid poems. . . .

Have you seen Yvor Winters' *Gyroscope*[3] affair? The current number is mostly Grant Code,[4] one or two pieces being good—the others hillyeran.[5] —I hope to jesus that now there's no danger of Dick's Cummings article[6] coming out. —Or any more of Wm C Wms' "poems".[7]

Dudley Fitts (1903–1968), poet, critic, and translator, credited the *Hound and Horn* with being the first to publish his poetry. A friend of Kirstein's, he acted as editor *ex officio* and contributed poetry, criticism, and book reviews to the magazine. All subsequent letters from Fitts, unless otherwise specified, are from Choate School, Wallingford, Conn., where Fitts served on the faculty.

[1] A book of poetry by Merrill Moore, reviewed in vol. 3, no. 2 (Jan.–March 1930).
[2] The *Fugitive*, a magazine started at Vanderbilt University by John Crowe Ransom, Allen Tate, Donald Davidson, Merrill Moore, and others. Published from

1922 to 1925, it printed some of the best poetry then written in America. The title of the magazine was explained by Davidson: they were fugitives fleeing from "poet laureating, the cheapness and triviality of public taste . . . the lack of serious devotion to literature, to the arts, to ideas."

[3] Yvor Winters (1900–1968), poet, teacher, and critic, was noted for his rigorous standards and tendentious views. He was western editor of *Hound and Horn* from 1932 to 1934. *Gyroscope*, a magazine published quarterly from 1929 to 1930 in Palo Alto, Cal., was edited by Winters, his wife, novelist and poet Janet Lewis, and Howard Baker; it featured the poetry and prose of the members of Winters's circle at Stanford University, which also included Caroline Gordon, Katherine Anne Porter, and Grant Code.

[4] Grant Code (1896–1974), author, poet, editor, and actor.

[5] Robert Hillyer (1895–1961), traditionalist poet who wrote on such eternal verities as love, death, and nature, had no use for the soul-searching of modern man and regarded modern poetry as obscure.

[6] Blackmur's article "Notes on E. E. Cummings' Language" appeared in vol. 4, no. 2 (Jan.–March 1931).

[7] *Hound and Horn* published William Carlos Williams's two poems "Rain," in vol. 3, no. 1 (Oct.–Dec. 1931), and "In a 'Sconset Bus," in vol. 5, no. 4 (July–Sept. 1932).

2   DUDLEY FITTS TO
LINCOLN KIRSTEIN
15 November [1929]

all right, guy—

Here's yr long review. . . .[1] I do hope this will at least not displease Mr. Bandler—I feel very violently about Moore, Ransom, & Cie, & the implications therefrom involving contemporary verse. (so wd you, dearie, if you had to read *Blues*[2] (Jesus Christ, did you ever see anything so vomitous as the latest *Blues*—especially the Williams ape's prefatory burblings?), Louis Untermeyer,[3] & had to answer the rabbits' eternal question: Well, why don't they write poetry today, if poetry is still a live art?). —As to yr fear that Moore isn't important enough: any man is important enough who stands on his own feet & says something validly and well. M is more important, I dare say, than Cowley—whose Juniata[4] is, after all, a pretty shadow cast by Eliot & Cummings. —I'm so sick of all the noise, the prefaces, the transitions,[5] the frenetics. Does it ever occur to these gents to cast away their Manuals of Prosody, & write poems as they want to write poems? (There are two Manuals of Prosody: the conventional, like Bobbie Hillyer's, & the anarchic, like Wm c Wm's). Old Age probably has me by the balls, anyhow. Not only do I want less stridor and more rhyme, but I want a wife & seventeen childer and a Connecticut home and Skeats's six-volume Chaucer. . . .

I'm having a swell time with *Look Homeward, Angel*.[6] A very fine book. I've not nearly finished it. . . . Lots of *Ulysses* in it, isn't there? And, strangely enough, the synchronology of *Babbitt*—Sinclair Lewis, I mean, not the Solemn Guy. —To hell, incidentally, with all this pother abt humanism. My god, let's stop theorizing & get down to work. . . .

excuse jumpiness as usual,

P.S. I sent back Small Susan—one serious error in the epigraph—'semynge', not 'servyse'.[7] Glad you like it. My God, the taste of *Blues* will haunt me for a month. And avoid Louise Bogan. . . .[8]

[1] Of Merrill Moore's book *The Noise that Time Makes*.
[2] *Blues*, a magazine "of new rhythms," was published from 1929 to 1930 and edited by Charles Henri Ford. Among contributing editors were William Carlos Williams, Jacques LeClercq, and Eugene Jolas. In the May 1929 issue, Williams wrote of the experimental idea behind *Blues*: "Poetry lives where life is hardest, hottest, most subject to jailing, infringements, and whatever it may be that groups of citizens oppose to danger."
[3] Louis Untermeyer (1885–1977), editor and author, contributing editor of the *Liberator* and the *Seven Arts*, and poetry editor of the *American Mercury* from 1934 to 1937.
[4] Malcolm Cowley's book of poems *Blue Juniata* was given a mixed review by Yvor Winters in vol. 3, no. 1 (Oct.–Dec. 1929).
[5] The reference is to the magazine *transition*, published monthly from 1928 to 1938 in Paris and The Hague, edited by Eugene Jolas and Elliot Paul and concerned with language that expressed the subconscious. It sought the writing of Gertrude Stein, James Joyce, and lesser-known writers interested in producing experimental writing that would not be published elsewhere.
[6] Cf. Chap. I, Letter 15, n. 2.
[7] "The Liturgy of Small Susan," a poem published in vol. 3, no. 2 (Jan.–March 1930).
[8] Louise Bogan (1897–1969), poet and translator, poetry critic for the *New Yorker* for thirty-eight years.

3   DUDLEY FITTS TO
           LINCOLN KIRSTEIN
                [1930]

                                            sunday AM

DEAR LINCOLN
   here it is, and I'm a wreck: haven't thought of anything but Pound
for weeks.[1] Change what you will: the conclusion is probably weak,
but that's the fault of time-lack (what a sentence!): I banged it out on
the train. Don't cut it; if you can add anything to the last few para-
graphs, by all means do so. We feel alike abt the poem, I think. And I
have felt that what was necessary was rather a sympathetic exposition,
especially with relation to technic, than a criticism for failure. Leave
that to the others. I do hope that if you think the summation is bad,
you'll inject a little of the noted Kirstein vigour into it. I simply have
no more time: after all, Child, I have a job to keep.
   Let me have proofs: there's a lot of Greek to be watched. Send spe-
cial delivery, and I'll return them direct to the printer (if you send me
his name and address).

[1] Fitts refers to his review of Pound's *XXX Cantos* in vol. 4, no. 2 (Jan.–March
1931). See Chap. I, Letter 30, n. 2.

4   DUDLEY FITTS TO
           LINCOLN KIRSTEIN
                [Undated]

             monologue before luncheon . . .
I think E P is right in using so much Provençal, Italian, and Latin. At
first, I thought it either conscious esotericism or fuck-you pedantry.
(I.e., the 'to-hell-with-the-public' tone of his note to the Cantos printed
in H&H wd suggest the latter criticism.) —But reading the Cantos for
the first time straight through, the emotional significance of even un-
allocated and frequently untranslatable phrases & fragments, is clearly
evident. It is like a not seen, but felt, accretion of weight in architecture
(badly said); & while translation, or clarification, wd lighten and il-
luminate, it wd at the same time be a lightening for the worse.

The first time I felt this was debating the alien phrases at the end of The Waste Land, with Doug Shepardson. 'Quando fiam ceu chelidôn,' for instance, if it were translated ('When shall I be as a swallow',) wd in a way clarify many things: 1) the emotion behind the phrase; 2) the transition to 'O Swallow, swallow'; and 3) it wd, by inducing overtones of emotional association (some obvious, as the reference to the Pervigilium—lost Springtide, lost youth, &c; some more tenuous, as the overtones of 'Swallow' equals 'Tennyson &c: a tired lovely technic) make it easier to tell yr classes what Eliot 'means'. (Not that these associations & relationships are lost in the Latin, by any means; they're not.) But the retention of the Latin *colours*, just as Dante's 'jeu suiz Arnaut' *colours*; the less Latin you know, sometimes, the more it gives, emotionally. (E.g., to be frivolous: liturgical associations, the usual romantic haze; & if I hadn't known 'chelidôn' as a greek word meaning 'swallow', I wd have connected it with 'chelys', the musical instrument; wch wd have added, if mistakenly, lots).

Ezra's use, then of similar devices is (I think) not only legitimate, but desirable. No less legitimate, though possibly less desirable, is his forcing of personal incident as a general symbol. It is less desirable only because Ezra lets his pictorial, or narrative-esoteric, sense run away with him. Compare the greek business-man in Waste-Land, for instance, with Sigismundo in the Cantos. One is a sketch, a mention-into-universality; the other an album-face, an expansion-into-individuality.

Do not send these between-class meditations to Ezra or anyone else.

The intuition of poetry is not the act of translation, but of synthetic comprehension. Intuition of a landscape is not the analysis & tagging of each leaf that compounds it. 'When I say "for ever" I think of the temple of Zeus, the road to Patras', says Robert[2] in one of his best poems. And cd have added 'To know "for ever" is not necessarily to know every drum in the temple, or to have brushed off & experimented with every stone in the road'.

Everything that has been experience is valid material.

[1] Ezra Pound.
[2] Robert Fitzgerald (*b.* 1910), poet and translator, and Boylston Professor of Rhetoric and Oratory at Harvard University.

5   DUDLEY FITTS TO
LINCOLN KIRSTEIN
Easter Monday [1931]

dear sir

thanks for Ezra's note. I didn't want to come back to school, any-
how; at the Meriden station I stumbled over a cat, fell: and, falling, one
of my suitcases crashed open, evolving pyjamas books dressinggowns
shirts and cufflinks into the plaza; then I arrived here and read Ezra's
note. . . . All in all, I think E is perfectly right: but maybe it's the god
damned depression; I think he's right: as a critic I'm a Gorham B.
Munson; and as a poet, a Babette D.[1] Looking back, I can't see why
you liked that article; & I shall never attempt anything so serious
again. E. isn't fair abt Zuk. and Eliot, though: I read Zuk. once, with
extreme distaste; and never read Eliot on Pound. —I wish to hell I
knew what Ezra says is WRONG (sic). If you ever write him, ask him. If
I get any more depressed, I'll write him myself.

I didn't get the Gug.[2] Ransom did; and that's grand—apparently
he needed it. Glad somebody like Zuk. or Bunting didn't. . . .

Did anyone of consequence, except yourself, like that review? (I
mean E P). . . .

christ Lincoln I'm going to stop it and confine myself to lectur-
ing and correction-of-themes and carnal sin. I feel like W S Knick-
erbocker.[3]

Fitzgerald casually won the Boylston Prize[4] the other night. Try to
keep him from Kings College until he has a degree from here. He'll get
so much more, two years from now: he's just beginning to get poise.

Please write immediately and say something vigorous or something
or something . . . .

yrs in sorrow,

[1] Babette Deutsch (*b.* 1895), American poet, editor, critic, and translator.
[2] Guggenheim Fellowship.
[3] W. S. Knickerbocker (1890–1970), at this time editor of the *Sewanee Review*.
[4] An annual prize given at Harvard for the best essay on a literary subject.

6   DUDLEY FITTS TO
      LINCOLN KIRSTEIN
      10 October 1931

Kirstein, you anguis-in-herbâ

. . . Naughty, to cut my review, after urging me into apoplectic haste.

I have met a guy who transcends Knickerbocker, & makes yr most blackest beast look like an intellectual & nivose lamb. I must tell you abt him some day. He wrote me a mash-note, after you rejected some of his doggerel, & came down intending (I piously believe) to make me (as the girls say). He said: I want to be a catholic but I don't believe in Jesus; what shall I do? He said: I want to learn to understand the H & H; what shall I read? He said: Do you know anything about Mr. Kirstein: tell me everything about Mr. Kirstein. [&. I said.: Take a cold bath. I said.: Under the Lilacs. I said.: Kirstein, being the bastard of Grover Cleveland out of Man-of-War, wears cellophane tights & winters in the Hebrides. He is a frivolous nation, given to light wines & fear. His speciality is Advice to the Lovelorn, and for twelve months he has been going with a man ten years his senior but has discovered that Llewellyn has a wife & the gleet & what shall he do?]

7   DUDLEY FITTS TO
      LINCOLN KIRSTEIN
      14 February 1932

Dear Lincoln:

. . . Yesterday a long, filthy, very friendly letter from Ezra, ultimus apostolorum. It seems that the whole thing he particularly objects to in me is my "holding up and obstructing" Rudge's trans. of le "Mystère Laic"—today published in *Pagany*. It seems that I am a malign influence upon you (he is very unpleasant on the subject of Kirstein— Stinkum Cherrystein, y'know). I don't remember that I had any considerable influence in holding up the "Mystère Laic"; I have read it over in *Pagany*, and still think it's shabby hack-translation; I suspect that Ezrita made the trans. himself. . . .

8   DUDLEY FITTS TO
         LINCOLN KIRSTEIN
         16 February [1932]

dear Lincoln—

You will excuse me for not finding in Mr. Cunningham[1] fit matter for enthusiasm. The Dogmatic Sequence is portentous, with occasional hopeful lines; in general, it's the same sort of 'poetry-club-ing' that made the twenties swoon over Ezra. It's in line with all the very conscious assumption of the classical attitude (cf. Winters' own couplets, anacreontics, &c): all very well as *ejercicios*, to serve as groundwork for the formation of a skill where native skill is lacking; but that's closet-work. Hymn for the Sixth Hour is the stupid sort of digitation that looks gnomic & ain't so. Inscription for a Wedding Gift is a very nice gesture, effective as all Sydney Carton's gestures were. One step up from 'Dancing c̄ tears in my eyes': renunciation-cum-gulp. (Mr. Cunningham also thinks that O is the same thing as Oh: but that's a pendantry for which Mr. Winters will blame me. . . .) The County Fair wd be agreeable if the necessity for a rhyme for 'caressed' (stanza 1) didn't lead the guy into being ridiculous abt chills in his 'chest'. 'Chest', good god!

The most intriguing poem of the lot is Winters' letter. There's the Apostolic Air, for you! Is the man being funny? Not that what he says lacks sense: on the contrary, it's true as truth; but what an ineffable Manner! (Yet this is the same man who, three years ago, raved about Code; sent him pictures, even, from the Family Album. . . .)

I should think you'd spend most of your time retching. These funny little men, with their puny shoulder-chips, their preciosities, their so very bad manners! I think the bad manners, especially, are the final twitch-at-the-chain. It is, I suppose, a vital matter to a certain type of mind; I can't imagine its being so vital as bread-and-butter: this ceaseless recrimination, this chatter of personalities, this scurrying about dark streets in rented suits. . . . The pleasure of being accosted by Ezra is a real pleasure; the pleasure to be derived from Winters on Kirstein *quâ* editor, or from Zuk. on Winters *quâ* "gentleman," is, for the reverse of this reason, non-existent.

                    I weary of all yr boyfriends, Sir.

¹ J. V. Cunningham (*b.* 1911), American poet and scholar, a member of Yvor Winters's literary group at Stanford University, where he taught from 1934 to 1945 and from which he received his doctorate in 1945. He was professor of English at Brandeis University, and is now retired. Cunningham's "Two Poems," were published in vol. 6, no. 1 (Oct.–Dec. 1932), and "Three Poems," in vol. 7, no. 1 (Oct.–Dec. 1933). His poetry chronicle *Envoi,* a critique of the poetry published in *Poetry* magazine, appeared in vol. 6, no. 1 (Oct.–Dec. 1932).

9   DUDLEY FITTS TO
           LINCOLN KIRSTEIN
           4 April 1932

Dear Lincoln:

*Conquistador*¹ is as profoundly moving as the Cantos; and seems to me a better emploi of the same form: it is tougher, coheres better, is more taut, more direct; also, it is clean, uncluttered, unposed. I think the march against Mexico, the Noche Triste, and the retreat to Tlaxcala, are unsurpassable. I was bored by the catalogues in various places: they seemed, like their Homeric models, too much on the order of among-those-present; but the evocation of the Captains, at the beginning, is grandeur at its grandest. I think much more might have been done with Montezuma, surely as powerful a symbol, in his weakness, as Hernán Cortès in his strength. And I think that A M might have spared some of the Poundery—the suspended endings of cantos, the incessant initial 'And', the frequently willful confusion of scenes and events. But what a technic; The variations of his terza-rima are sufficient study for endless winter evenings. . . . The tremendous nostalgic climaxes, like the last three lines; the violent illumination of scene and action by a word, a colour, a cadence.

Glad as hell to have your letter. Sorry the reviews² haven't been better. The book antagonizes and upsets little wits. It has upset some pretty good ones, for that matter. . . . Everybody in Boston is talking about it: the legends about you are almost evangelical: Your father offered you anything from fifty to five hundred thousand not to print the book; Mina³ evicted you; . . . you are; and you are; and you. I am sick of defending the first part of the book, which I think is swell; and deploring much of the rest, which I think is not. You will, if I may annoy you again, have to do something about your occasional style. It jitters too often. Hell. . . . No, you didn't send the book; or if you did, it hasn't arrived yet. —One of the most ardent admirers of *Flesh is Heir* is Mrs. Lowell: she's a swell press-agent.

Letters almost weekly from Pound, with the insolent information that I Can Be Saved—god Damn his soul, for I'm a damned sight nearer salvation than the model he quotes me: Zukofsky; yes, & than others.

Can you for Jesus sake do something to make H & H readable? It's almost as torpid as the *Criterion*.

If the peseta continues to drop, I shall go to Spain—Mallorca—rather than to Mexico this summer. . . .

I do not think I am strange. I regret yr silences because frequently I ask you things in letters, & by the time you get around to answering I've forgotten the questions.

Because of the economic eccentricities of the times, I am precisely penniless, and quite cheerful. . . . I don't know anything else about anybody else and like some of Seán's[4] stories.

[1] The epic poem by Archibald MacLeish for which he received the Pulitzer Prize was reviewed in vol. 5, no. 2 (April–June 1932) by Kirstein, who called MacLeish "one of the half dozen greatest poets in the world. To have written 'Conquistador' is to have erected a monument to the possibility of heroism. It is an act of faith in the belief of poetry and human action, on a grand scale, again."
[2] Of *Flesh is Heir*.
[3] Mina Curtiss, Kirstein's sister, on whose life some of the events chronicled in *Flesh is Heir* were allegedly patterned.
[4] Seán O'Faoláin.

10　　　LINCOLN KIRSTEIN
　　　　TO DUDLEY FITTS
　　　　6 April 1932

Dear Dudley:

. . . I am so glad you liked *Conquistador*. To me it is by far the greatest poem written in this country, which of course lets out the "Waste Land" and the Cantos. The catalogues don't bore me. I think that the evocation of the captains is absolutely Homeric. I have never read such powerful restraint anywhere. Archie is very interesting as far as Montezuma goes. I think he was rather chary of sentimentalizing him. I don't think he thinks he is very important. I don't think Cortès was put forward as a strong symbol particularly, and hence there was no necessity for opposition. The point of the book seems to me the march of the annonymous conquerors against the more or less unresisting west. I think Archie's technic is absolutely dazzling. Surely no one but Pound or Eliot can write as subtly or as musically.

The bad reviews of my book continue. The crowning stupidity was Dahlburg's, confusing even the names of the characters, which proves conclusively that he had not even read it.[1] I met Gorham Munson at dinner the other night and he profusely apologized for his notice. I lied and said that I hadn't seen it, and he told me that there was a general understanding around the town to take me down a peg if possible. I know very well that my style is lousy, but I tried so hard to write a book that was not literary. I'll show you my next manuscript before it appears, to have the full benefit of your opinion.

Do save all of Pound's letters so that I can see them. . . .

The next number of the *Hound and Horn* is really much more readable. I do hope to see you soon. . . .

---

[1] Edward Dahlberg's review in the April 1932 issue of the *Nation* stated, "Although in places Mr. Kirstein shows a talent for writing, one can hardly recommend *Flesh is Heir* either for its entertainment or its literary uniqueness."

I I   DUDLEY FITTS TO
LINCOLN KIRSTEIN
30 May 1932

dear Lincoln—

. . . do me this favour: I am sending you (either in proof, or, if in mag. form, marked) a poem called "Till Morning Light," and a story "You Dull Angels" by a really extraordinary boy, James Laughlin.[1] Will you read them and, making allowances for his seventeen years, tell me if you see anything in them? Whether it is because I know him so well, and have worked with him so long, I do not know; I may have got all the perspective twisted; but parts of the poem, and parts of the story (especially the little cat episode at the end) I find very moving.

Will you tell yr friend and 'regional editor,' Senor Tate, that, speaking strictly as a rhetorician, I must object that my verses are anything but aimless exercises, since no exercise can be aimless, can it? I suppose he's referring to the Mexican doggerels, as usual; and I think he's wrong, because I think he's humourless and unsympathetic. I don't know. But the Pound derivation is bosh, and he should know better. Source-hunting used to be a particular vice of mine, and I distrust it: definitely class-room. But I must revive it long enough to point out to Prof. Tate that if I am thinned-out Pound, I am even more thinned-out Bach and curdled Spohr, with a dash of Silius Italicus and a soupçon of Barnum. And it's not my fault that I have a finer melodic sense, and an infinitely more flexible technic, than Dr. Tate; any more than it's *his* fault that, with all his faults, he is one of our most poignantly expressive poets (I mean the ODE &c).

I thought you came off rather badly with the incredible playboy from Troy N.Y.,[2] and certainly his leisure-class preoccupation is inane enough. Lit'ry disputes and quarrels and dislikes and bitternesses are the silliest and most funest of all: for they all wear glasses and unbathe irregularly, Sir; and heat themselves up over what is, after all, decorative nothing: forgetting that the only dreamreality is thalamic.

Goodbye, Editor, and Increase yr
Kind—

---

[1] James Laughlin, now publisher of *New Directions*. Nothing by Laughlin was published in *Hound and Horn*.

[2] Granville Hicks, a contributor to the *New Republic*, had reviewed *Flesh is Heir* and incorporated into his review a criticism of the *Hound and Horn* as being a "leisure-class" publication run by those who prefer "not to face the grave social problems of the present day. . . . this peculiarly leisure-class form of pedantry also explains their preference for the more difficult of contemporary poets and novelists. The mastering of obscure works occupies their leisure time, convinces them of their intelligence, and distinguishes them from less fortunate members of society." The attack by Hicks was answered by a letter from Bernard Bandler, A. Hyatt Mayor, and Lincoln Kirstein in the 5 May 1932 issue of the *New Republic*. See Chap. V, Letter 20.

12   LINCOLN KIRSTEIN
TO DUDLEY FITTS
4 June 1932

Dear Fitts:

You said nothing about Francis Fergusson's poems.[1] But they are going to be printed anyway because I think he is a member of our grouppe. Have you heard of our grouppe? Well, we are a HOUND AND HORN GROUPPE now, all under the blue and the gray.[2]

As far as the quarrel in the *New Republic* goes, the general consensus of opinion is that we came out badly, but you forgot that we were not engaging in any controversy, but we were merely pointing out errors in fact of what Hicks said. All this is good publicity and it proves in a way that people do consider the magazine as something worth quarrelling with.

I am very eager to see this boy James Laughlin's stuff. It hasn't come in. . . . I think Tate is a fool, but I am not allowed to say so in public, as he is a member of our grouppe. He has written a very good thing on Crane,[3] however, so that lets him out of my particular wrath at the moment. It may assuage your sensitive whatever to know that Archie[4] liked very much some verse of yours he saw in the *Hound and Horn*—he said about Mexico—I think he probably meant the "Sheriff's Daughter."[5]

Yours, by no means for the new era

[1] Francis Fergusson's "Two Poems" were published in vol. 5, no. 4 (July–Sept. 1932).

[2] Kirstein is referring to Allen Tate's southern editorship of the *Hound and Horn* in 1932, with the resulting increasing emphasis on the publication of writing by southerners.

[3] "In Memoriam: Hart Crane, 1899–1932" in vol. 5, no. 4 (July–Sept. 1932).

[4] Archibald MacLeish.

[5] "Six Poems for the Sheriff's Daughter," vol. 5, no. 2 (Jan.–March 1932).

13   DUDLEY FITTS TO
           LINCOLN KIRSTEIN
           December [1932?]

Dear Marse Linco'n—

With full realization that Yvor the Terrible[1] prowls the shore seeking whom he may devour, I make so bold as to state that I think this to be my best to date.[2] And that is (I am paraphrasing St. Hilary of Poictiers) that. I warn you, however, that it should be read *aloud*, (for I have gone to obscene detail with the melos &c) and carefully. Will you therefore abrogate your usual period-of-reflexion (six months, isn't it?), and tell me how pound-eliot-yeats-crane-winters-shakespeare-damned bad it is as soon as yer can? . . .

I think that poetry shd say only platitudes, i.e.:

1. You & I
   Must die.
2. Christ above!
   I'm in love!
3. If you will only drink first,
   You can scarcely suffer thirst.

and say these things as cleanlily and as directly as prosaically possible. Therefore a certain obviousness, and a distinct childish flatness, abt this poem. Which is not, Sir, unsweated-for.

[1] Yvor Winters, who collaborated with Kirstein in decisions on poetry.
[2] It is not clear to which poem this refers, as nothing more by Fitts was published in the *Hound and Horn* after the winter issue of 1932.

14   DUDLEY FITTS TO
            LINCOLN KIRSTEIN
            15 September 1933

dear Lincoln—

. . . A story, or a poem, is not valid simply because of its feeling: it's too much like good intentions without operation. A prose style, or a poetic style, is not a decoration, not something to be added or omitted as the capabilities of the writer allow: it is simply an organic part of the whole. You try to put me in the position of one who should be so blinded by "grammar & rhetoric" as to disregard the content & feeling of a piece; when really I am saying only that the adequate expression of any emotion demands an adequate manipulation of the medium—and while "an adequate manipulation of the medium" implies the ability to manage language, or harmonies, or chiaroscuro, correctly (that is to say, inoffensively), it certainly does not imply a preoccupation with mechanics for its own sake. Except in a very few pieces, you must admit that Lawrence was an unsuccessful poet; yet the lack is not of feeling, of sincerity, but merely of technic. At his worst, Archie is as bad a poet, but for the opposite reason: his preoccupation with technic—with the "grammar" of assonances, echoing cadences, the whole precious lexicon of tropes & poetical tricks—blinds him & his more devoted critics to the fact that he's saying precisely nothing, in a very beautifully woolly manner. To the ear, the beautiful expression of nothing may be pleasanter than the faulty expression of "something": my point is, that in neither case is the expression really expression.

I said last Sunday that language reminds me of cheese. I was thinking of carving in cheese, which is an art I am not backing: but I meant that writing a sentence (when I'm not writing hurriedly, as I am at present) produces in me exactly that feeling of firm yielding that I get from cutting through a piece of cheese. I mean that, for me, language exists as a malleable mass; & that composition is as plastic a process as sculpture. When I said that in order to write well the writer must feel a certain *unfamiliarity* with the language, I was really saying the same thing. A block of stone is unfamiliar; a canvas is unfamiliar; they've got to be moulded, manipulated, worked: there's nothing automatic or unconscious about the process at all. My complaint with the teaching of English, as it is reflected in these contributions, is that it allows the students to write automatically: it is assumed that because English is John's native language, John can of course "write" English, & express what he has to express. Teaching tends to concentrate, then, on "ideas" and "feeling." But there is no such thing as a "native language," in composition. There are "native stones" lying about in the streets, and you can throw them at people & fracture their skulls very prettily, & you have "made an impact"; but there's no "native stone" for a sculptor, & any impact he may desire to make, must be the result of painful carving. If we say that translation is one good way of preparing a boy for composition in his own language, we mean, really, that by making him see his own language through another language—by comparative analysis of structure, by painful striving after an adequate transposition of expression—one is making him aware of the objectivity, of the almost tangible strangeness, of his own language. I can think of no other practical basis for a classical education.

In the course of a review for H & H some years ago, I spoke of the cult of Sententious Illiteracy—I was speaking of Dreiser, Lawrence, Lewis, Anderson,[1] & suggested that their position might be summed up, by a careless disciple, in the phrase "It don't make no difference how you say a thing, so long as you gotta thing to say." To me this is as meaningless as the beauty-hurts-muh school of James Branch Cabell, or Landor, or Tennyson. And when you say, "I place a certain consistency of feeling above everything. Whether they (*sic*) are grammatical or not doesn't always interest me," you seem to me to be saying substantially the same thing.

The stories you have approved here are an example. Guérard's story[2] is an awkwardly formless rehashing, on a somewhat higher plane, of McAlmon's childhood-memories manner. The incidents hang together only in time: there really isn't a correlation, a synthesis, either of "idea" or of "feeling." It is anything but "consistent feeling." But even if there were content, the inept, fumbling manipulation of the language, wd completely obscure it (I don't mean that you wouldn't know what Guérard was trying to say; you would; but the expression would not carry any valid impact. More infernal paving-stones). . . .

But I am not particularly interested in getting you to change the award. I don't care for the Conley story,[3] either; my judgment was simply that it was the least bad of the stories I had read. What I am trying to do is to get you to see my position on the ends & aims of writing as an art; to try to make you understand my feeling that the adequate transmission of an adequate emotion demands an adequate technic. And that emotion and technic are not separable. That so far from saying that the end of composition is elegant, grammatically correct, beautiful writing, I am saying that, with all the most passionate feeling in the world, you can't evoke a symphonic idea from an harmonium. That (I am not, God knows, trying to be nasty) what makes *Hound and Horn* so largely unreadable, and what makes *The New Masses* et al. completely unreadable, is not the fact that the contributors haven't excellent ideas, and oceans & oceans of emotion; but simply that in so many cases they haven't the art to transmit either. Or, shall I conclude the whole series of rather cockeyed metaphors by referring you to a gramophone: record, soundbox, needle, seem to be separable enough: you can cook eggs in the soundbox, you can use the record for a hoop for Baby, & you can clean your nails with the needle. But you can't move an audience with a gramophone unless all of these parts are in their places, functioning perfectly. The best record in the world is only a Good Intention if you try to play it with a worn-down needle, and it's simply Sententious Illiteracy to say that because the music is there in baked wax, the audience should experience orgasms & emit applause.

I have been working all week on a letter dealing with the competition, incorporating some of these observations. Your letter this morning has made me see how hopeless the thing is, and I have decided to give the job up. If you will think for a moment, you'll see that my position is ridiculous, anyhow. As a judge, I make recommendations; you promptly over-rule them, and award the prize to a story which incorporates almost every one of the ineptitudes that I have lambasted in my report. I am not complaining that you shouldn't do this: it's your competition, and not mine, and you have every right to do this; but you must see that I can't, without perpetrating either a colossal dishonesty or a deathly cynicism, subscribe to it in print. I pass over the fact that neither of the winning contributions was submitted to me until the prize was (apparently) awarded—last week-end! And the fact that I don't really see what all my reading of manuscripts this summer comes to—unless it be a series of headaches and lamentations over time that I might have spent more profitably otherwise. I know you too well to think that I was the goat appointed to eat up that amazing mass of literary offal, while youse guys sat at ease in foreign bar-rooms. My honest opinion has been, ever since finishing the job, that the only possible reason for awarding any prize is, that you have advertized that a prize is to be given. It wd be tedious to explain that nothing worth considering was submitted; and to the competitors, such an explanation wd look like a cheap evasion. For $150, the H & H could have bought thirty-three cases of 3.2 beer, and recovered $8.25 upon return of the bottles.

So, unless you order me to do otherwise, I suggest that (you being the largient one) you write your own note. I shd be grateful if in the course of it you would summarize enough of this letter to make it clear that, like Brandeis, I emphatically dissent. And even more grateful if you would read this letter patiently, not spasmodically as your manner is, and try to see that I have some honesty in my position, and that I am something more than a grammarian who happens to have read Joyce. I am not fond of myself, at all; I certainly don't fancy my ability either as a poet or a critic. I haven't your background, or your brain, or your passion for ideas. And I teach school, and, worse, I like it. But in my most bitter moments of self-analysis, I really can't see myself so utter an incompetent as you, with all the grace in the world, and Ezra, with all the incoherence in the world, seem to think me.

A note, entitled "The Undergraduate Competition," at the beginning of the issue vol. 7, no. 1 (Oct.–Dec. 1933) stated that the *Hound and Horn* took pleasure in awarding the prizes in its first national undergraduate competition for verse and the short story to J. V. Cunningham and Albert J. Guérard, Jr., both of Stanford University. It added that "Elizabeth Bishop of Vassar contributed such an extremely interesting story and poem that she deserves honorable mention. Over one thousand manuscripts were received from nearly every state in the union. The editors of *Hound and Horn* wish particularly to thank Mr. Dudley Fitts who read all the manuscripts and who dissented in the fiction award, voting for *Break-Day*, a story by J. Allan Conley of the University of California."

After the disagreement over the writing competition, Fitts broke off his relationship with the *Hound and Horn*. Lincoln Kirstein wrote me on 30 August 1981, "Dudley Fitts was so angry, he quit. After that, we never spoke."

[1] Fitts is referring here to the "moderns"—Theodore Dreiser, D. H. Lawrence, Sinclair Lewis, and Sherwood Anderson, of whose naturalistic writing he disapproved.
[2] "Davos in Winter," a prize-winning story by Albert J. Guérard, Jr. (*b.* 1914) was published in vol. 7, no. 1 (Oct.–Dec. 1933). He was then an eighteen-year-old Stanford University undergraduate and a student of Yvor Winters. Guérard went on to a distinguished career as professor of English at Stanford University and literary critic.
[3] "Break-Day," by J. Allan Conley (*b.* 1912) of the University of California. He is professor of English at the University of Illinois, Chicago center.

15   A. HYATT MAYOR TO
          LINCOLN KIRSTEIN
          1 November [1929]

. . .Your comments have started me on quite new lines of thought.[1] I have stuck too timidly to history, and I have not had the courage to attempt evaluation. I must indeed attempt a word on his[2] successes, and especially on his integrity. I don't know enough about Poussin's career to compare them, but the fresh eye of my ignorance seems to see more of a likeness between Picasso and Mantegna. They are both haunted by the total wreckage of the antique, they both start as painters and end with grisaille.[3] I feel in Picasso cubiste the same static agony I feel in some Mantegna St. Sebastian. With Poussin I see less relation. Picasso has none of Poussin's most native feeling, that for the classic landscape, the feeling that makes Cézanne very like Poussin, save that he saw the columns of the Campagna in factory smokestacks. And besides, Picasso starts out with loneliness and an effusion of pity, while Poussin starts out fierce: (that stairful of people who are hand-over-handing St. Erasmus' warm entrails, like firemen passing the hose.)

I will get the MS back to you as much before the first of Nov. as I can.

A. Hyatt Mayor (1901–1980), an editor of *Hound and Horn* from 1929 to 1932, wrote essays on Picasso, Gaston Lachaise, Gordon Craig, and on translations for the *Hound and Horn*, as well as numerous book reviews and the Art Chronicle. He described the *Hound and Horn* office to me in an interview in 1975 as "utter chaos. Hours? There were no regular hours. You came in when you could and worked as long as you had to." He left the magazine in 1932 for the Print Department of the Metropolitan Museum, of which he was curator from 1946 until his retirement in 1966.

[1] This letter refers to Mayor's article on Picasso's method vol. 3, no. 2 (Jan.–March 1930).
[2] Picasso's.
[3] Decorative painting in grey monochrome.

16   A. HYATT MAYOR TO
          LINCOLN KIRSTEIN
          1 November [1929]

Dear Lincoln:

. . . Derain and Matisse is an interesting subject—about which I know very little.[1] I cannot make up my mind about Derain. The only one I like is the big "Cornemuse" that Valentine says he is sending you. I see nothing in Matisse but the most beautiful and daring color, color to get drunk on, and sometimes a queer slimy streak of psychology. Neither of them is humanly relevant, as Picasso so intensely is. When I see your show, that may give me ideas for an article. I certainly hope so.

[1] This letter is the reply to Lincoln Kirstein's suggestion that Mayor write on André Derain and Henri Matisse.

17   A. HYATT MAYOR TO
        LINCOLN KIRSTEIN
        [Undated]

Dear Lincoln:

I am ashamed to have kept this so long,[1] but it arrived as I was
going to the train for Woodstock. I like it very much, but it repeats
itself unnecessarily. The last ten pages or so seem the best—or maybe I
had by then gotten into Cocteau's rhythm. Anyway, it certainly does
repeat itself and if it is not cut, few readers will last until those splendid
things at the end—the view of Rome and the glimpses of people un-
masked. Many of the things explain Cocteau's works or defend them,
and few people have read them. I think it would be a good thing for the
H & H to print, illustrated, of course, with some good de Chiricos.

Of course I do feel that Cocteau is whooplala for all his friends and
grrrrrrr for all the rest, and is to that extent a twisted perceiver. Also
much of what he writes is unclear simply because it is hasty and
undigested. And yet for all that there are real jewels, perhaps not eter-
nal jewels, but with flash enough to last us our time. At least he is of
the moment, and alarmingly pertinent, and so worth printing by all
means.

Julien Levy just wrote me about the Atget photos.[2] Would it be
humanly possible to get one or two in this issue of the H & H? It
would be a great stroke to be the first on the lot with them, and I could
put in a note on them in my Chronicle. He wrote me that Cowley was
unable to get an article on them ready by the 15.[3] I wish to Hell he had
told me about them, for I would have run to see them when I was in
New York last week with nothing to do. My Chronicle is on the 2 Mu-
seums, with a loud BOO on the Met.[4] Quis custodiet istos custodes?[5]

I do hope it is possible to get some Atgets.

I never told you how much I liked your Ballet article.[6] I was de-
lighted to see your élan come across into print, for it is a rarely difficult
freshness to project. And then your ability for being on the spot, that
always makes me feel the lame-halt-and-blind last of the procession.
Wonderful. How I admire it, and admire it all the more when I see its
velocity fixed in print.

¹ An essay by Jean Cocteau, probably *Mystère Laic*, with references to Giorgio de Chirico, the artist.
² Eugène Atget (1855–1927), French photographer, whose extraordinary eye for detail and sense of design combined to produce unusually revelatory photographs of Paris and its people.
³ Possibly for the *New Republic*, of which Malcolm Cowley was an editor.
⁴ Art Chronicle: "Museums Modern and Metropolitan," vol. 4, no. 1 (Oct.–Dec. 1930).
⁵ From Juvenal: "Who is watching the watchmen?"
⁶ On the Diaghilev period in vol. 3, no. 4 (July–Sept. 1930).

18   A. HYATT MAYOR
TO ALAN STROOCK
Thursday [Undated]

Dear Bill:

I am sorry about the Atget, about my trying to get them into the H & H, I mean. I had no idea that Lincoln was against having them and that he was going to do nothing but American things, or I never would have spoken. I above all things would avoid butting in on the functions of the editors. I thought that of course Cowley must be writing on Atget at Lincoln's express wish. By far best let the matter drop, for a confusion of councils would land the H & H into a mess. I have been around the theatre enough to realise that nothing can be accomplished without the strictest subordination, and that nothing is worth the price of disobedience. *One* head must direct and have the final say. St. Thomas himself could not speak louder on that point.

If you have any suggestions about the Chronicle, do share them with me, for your criticism last time was most valuable.

I'll probably see you around Labor Day. Francis, by the way is in my apartment, with my phone number, voLunteer 7761. (Francis Fergusson, I mean.) He is hunting a job acting, probably in some revue or maybe one of the classic revivals planned for this winter.

19   ALAN STROOCK TO
              A. HYATT MAYOR
                9 August 1930

Dear Hyatt:

. . . The matter of the Atget photos is getting more and more com-
plicated every day. I cabled Bernie,[1] asking him whether he had any
objections to publishing them on the grounds that they were not
American, and he cabled back that we should "positively publish"
them, and told me to ask Lincoln if Diaghilev was American. So now
the Pope and Henry VIII are having another fight, and I hardly know
where to apply my subordination. Personally, I am so much in favor of
seeing the Atgets reproduced, that I am going to do my best to bring
Lincoln around. That is no easy job, but it is the only course I can see.
I agree with you that *one* head should direct and have the final say, but
just try asking both Lincoln and Bernie at the same time, which that
should be! Will let you know developments. . . .

[1] Bernard Bandler.

20   LINCOLN KIRSTEIN
              TO A. HYATT MAYOR
                21 October 1931

Dear Hyatt:

I am going to do the Art Chronicle on the subject of figure painting
and its reference to mural decoration, taking my examples from Sert,
Benton, Orozco, Rivera and Léger.[1] Léger, I think, will be here part of
the winter. He is a very sweet character and that curious fish of a cubist
who seems as old-fashioned as a symbolist. For him there is no painting
after 1400, except with curious exceptions for Bellini and Carpac-
cio. Walker Evans has done some magnificent photographs of circus
posters on barns and drug stores, ripped by the wind and rain, so that
they look like some horrible accident.[2] There are two circus ones and
two movie ones and I think they would be admirable in conjunction

with Dudley Fitts' poem about the Southwest. God knows they are American.

¹José Maria Sert (1876–1945), Spanish painter, who designed murals for the Waldorf-Astoria in 1930–1931 and for Rockefeller Center in 1933 (Sert's panels for the Waldorf-Astoria were removed, sold several years ago, and sent to Spain); Thomas Hart Benton (*b*. 1889), American artist and muralist; José Clemente Orozco (1883–1949), Mexican artist whose work depicts revolutionary and historical scenes and themes; Diego Rivera (1886–1957), Mexican artist, whose murals depict peasants and workers; Fernand Léger (1881–1955), French painter, whose characteristic style was inspired by machine and industrial motifs.

²Walker Evans's photographs of the circus posters on barns and drug stores were not printed. Two other sets of Evans's photographs were published in vol. 6, no. 1 (Oct.–Dec. 1932), photographs of marchers and strikers, and down-and-outers sleeping in doorways on South Street; and in vol. 6, no. 3 (April–June 1933), photographs of a farm family, restaurant countermen, and a man working on a truck, loading animals.

21   A. HYATT MAYOR TO
LINCOLN KIRSTEIN
25 October [1931]

Dear Lincoln:

. . . I went out and saw Blackmur about his Wallace Stevens article the other day, I suggested a number of minor changes which he very readily agreed to, and also some condensations, which he was less prompt about accepting, but may after he looks them over. I think the article is just the sort of thing that we should print, even though it is a bit long, and if he shortens it, it ought to be about perfect.

What do you think about Foster Damon doing something for the Henry James number? He is an excellent critic, our one really first class literary critic, and ought not to be allowed to slip out from under us the way he is doing.¹ If Eliot will do nothing, as I fear, he might do James and Hawthorne looking at Europe.

Pound refuses to do anything for H. J. number. He suggests that when we have finished commemorating the illustrious.dead, we might make a memorial number for *him*. He does, however, suggest that we get Zukofsky to make extracts from Pound's long notes on H J in *Instigations*. A poor idea, I think, because Zukofsky is, to my thinking, rotten. However, what about Foster Damon's doing something about those notes of Pound's? You might suggest that to him. Perhaps his ideal subject might be *Europe viewed by Hawthorne, James and Pound*. I know Foster could do that well, if you can put the thumb screws on him hard enough to make him. Do see what Bernard and Francis think about it.

I am delighted Stark Young is willing to write for us. He ought to be an excellent addition.[2]

[1] Foster Damon (1893–1971), poet, literary biographer, and university professor, who taught English at Harvard, later becoming a professor of English at Brown University. He had written an essay on Joyce's *Ulysses*, "Odyssey in Dublin," in vol. 2, no. 1 (Oct.–Dec. 1929), that was acclaimed widely; but he did not contribute to the Henry James number.

[2] Stark Young (1882–1963), novelist, drama editor of the *New Republic*, and theater critic for the *New York Times*.

22   A. HYATT MAYOR TO
          LINCOLN KIRSTEIN
                [1931]

Dear Lincoln:

About O'Faoláin's story. It is too *long*, whatever it might be (67 pp!) for a quarterly. Every story of such length should be rejected at once, no matter what.[1] And besides, I don't want to be chauvinistic, but the H & H is an *American* magazine. Its criticism may legitimately look abroad, indeed ought to, but not its poems and stories. Certainly it ought not to give an Irish story such a preponderant place in a number—not unless you were going to do an homage to Ireland number. I don't mind giving so much space to stories, but not to one single story, and certainly not if that one is Irish. . . . I don't think a long story holds a number together by its mere length, and an Irish long story would throw *everything* else out of focus. This story certainly has great charm, but has also great emptiness in it. Is the other story of which he speaks shorter? If much shorter it *might* not distract and throw the number out of gear. What about showing this story to the *Bookman*? They might take it off your hands and relieve you of all moral responsibility, also paying him much more than we would.

Stark Young would probably do good Theatre chronicles, and I think he ought to appreciate a magazine where he could say what he damn pleased.

[1] Mayor's comment refers to "Fugue, Op. 2," a story that was rejected. "Fugue" was O'Faoláin's only story printed in *Hound and Horn* in vol. 2, no. 1 (Oct.–Dec. 1929).

CHAPTER IV

E. E. Cummings, Caroline Gordon, Archibald MacLeish, Marianne Moore, Seán O'Faoláin, Katherine Anne Porter, William Carlos Williams

I   DORIS LEVINE TO
                E. E. CUMMINGS
                  8 April 1932

Dear Mr. Cummings:
    Enclosed is your check for $150.00 in payment for your article "From a Russian Diary."[1]

> E. E. Cummings (1894–1962), the poet, was the friend whom Kirstein intended to use as "poet-instigator" for his fledgling ballet company, as Diaghilev had used Cocteau for his Ballets Russes. Poetry and two essays from his prose work *Eimi* (1933), the story of his trip to Russia, were published in the *Hound and Horn*.
>
>   Doris Levine was secretary of the *Hound and Horn* from 1932 to 1934, and of the School of American Ballet from 1934 to 1941.

> [1] Published in vol. 5, no. 3 (April–June 1932). An excerpt of this essay, which was to become the first chapter of Cummings's book *Eimi* (Greek for "I am"), expressed the essence of the individualist confronting "the system." Here is Cummings's discussion with the "sandyhaired spokesman for the Soviet Embassy in Paris":
>
>   The redfox leans toward me. Why do you wish to go to Russia?
>
>   Because I've never been there.
>
>   (He slumps, recovers.) You are interested in economic and sociological problems?
>
>   No.
>
>   Perhaps you are aware that there has been a change of government in recent years?
>
>   Yes, I say without being able to suppress a smile.

And your sympathies are not with socialism?

May I be perfectly frank?

Please!

I know almost nothing about these important matters and care even less.

(His eyes appreciate my answer.) For what do you care?

My work.

Which is writing?

And painting.

What kind of writing?

Chiefly verse; some prose.

Then you wish to go to Russia as a writer and painter? Is that it?

No; I wish to go as myself.

(An almost smile.) Do you realise that to go as what you call Yourself will cost a great deal? . . . Visiting Russia as you intend would be futile from every point of view. The best way for you to go would be as a member of some organization—

But, so far as I know, I'm not a member of any organization.

In that case, you should go as a tourist. . . .

2   E. E. CUMMINGS TO
      LINCOLN KIRSTEIN
      1933

                              axle's grease
                              sprocket-on-hub
                                    twink
                                 1933

Missed (& missing) Link
              we, the undersigned, do hearbuy heartily
              expect await and attend your socalled
              arrival with imminent hopes for proximate
              con games undrums tacts
Lays Keedees
              deesweet shweeay trahntwah

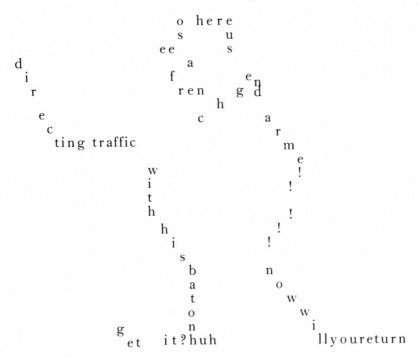

E. E. CUMMINGS TO LINCOLN KIRSTEIN

3

Friday [Undated]

Dear Lincoln—

am now ready to work on TOM;[1] shall need $100 a week for 5 weeks: if you want me to do the ballet, please enclose one century by what somebody loosely called return mail

—yours (for the extermination of insipidities)

[1] Kirstein had commissioned Cummings to write a libretto for a choreodrama based on *Uncle Tom's Cabin*, which he thought would be ideal for an American ballet. Edward Warburg, Kirstein's college friend and early partner in establishing the New York City Ballet, paid Ben Shahn to make sketches for scenery and costumes, but Balanchine could find no material in *Tom* for creating dance. Cummings's

prose-poem was hence rejected as choreodrama but was later published, accom-
panied by some of Shahn's designs. One is saddened at having missed the oppor-
tunity to witness a Balanchine ballet choreographing a passage such as this by
Cummings: "Ecstatically twiststraightening Tom, and all the blacks squirmspurt
whirlsurgingly outward and at the footlights high together leaping stand. . . .
Dance of the benevolent Master and Mistress. . . . they constipate the frontstage
with platitudes of terpsichore."

4   E. E. CUMMINGS TO
           LINCOLN KIRSTEIN
           10 July [1934?]

dere grond par
          Wee have bin soe hap pee 2 ree sieve yor lettur grond par
wee r soe hap pee u r n joyinge u selve grond par please grond
par doant stopp have ay gude tym
          marion & i wee have bin soe gude itt hairtz grond par inn fakt
wee r n joyinge thee soe cawld fawl off thee frensh frong yess ree-
lee grond par & truelie itt isz soe
          u cann arsk theee nay boors thay wil awl sa yess wel 2 re tuurn 2
plesund thinggs grond par howw r u grond par?r u reelee & truelie
runnnnnnninggggggg rown ass yor lettur seamz 2 inn dick itt?r u
grond par?o howw neyescz itt mus tb
          marion & i wee hav bin hereingk awl abowt lun dun grond par &
wee thingk lun dun mus tb simpulie swil isz itt soe grond par isz itt
truelie & reelee soe?& doo pee pull pla ay geyme cawld ten isz & raide
inn ay cabb wairingk ay hatt cawld ay hai had grond par isz itt soe
grond par sa 2 us pleas
          well i mus tb clothes ing ass i amb ay bout 2 b eet ingk din nur &
toe da bee ingk lan-d wee doo nort eet meet noo grond par b corzs awl
thee boos hur shupz r clothesed reelee
          i gues thadt sup rise du i gues u thorghut i wood sa b corzs wee
marion & i wus katholickz or sumpn
          thangs forh thee prezun u gaiv uss grond par i wil trie harrrd 2
rite sumpn 4 yor mugsin grond par i truelie wil grond par i amb unn
hunurbil mahn soe r tha awl grond par awl hunurbil mahns reelie
grond par u db sup rised u wood

wee sor Lee Far[1] own lee lasst nite att thee soe cawld tow nhawl att thee soe cawld town noff san chere main grond par wass hee pew trid grond par o grond par didd heee stinkkkk!

vairie soone iss thee cat i meen thee cators shwee ay xkooz mee grond par mai frensh iss nott kwite laik mr. leee farrr ' es dan sing wel anie wa grond par vairie soone iss thee nashnil hulluday wee wil dan s inn thee streeeeeeet & dring 2 yoor helth grond par marion ses 2 pleas gif u 1 bigggggggggggggg kkkkkkkkkkis grond par reelie & truelie shee didd own leee shee didnte saie pleeas shee iss lookink v.w. meenink too skee leyah dun man yee feek

wel O. Vwaw & pleas doo gif owr beste 2 awl inn choirink frenz yoor d vote id lit til ad my rairs grond par,

veuillez grond par agreer

Lays Kiddiz

[1] Serge Lifar (*b.* 1905), Russian-born choreographer and dancer.

---

5   **LINCOLN KIRSTEIN**
                TO E. E. CUMMINGS
                1 August 1934

Dear Estlin:

I apologize for being so behind-handed. Please forgive me. A serious catastrophe has arrived and I have just had time to collect myself. I know you will be sorry to hear that Balanchine[1] has been extremely ill, and I have been all through the reverse birth pangs of considering the school as finished and done for.[2] Luckily things have cleared up somewhat, and we intend to go on, with or without him—and now, I think hopefully and blessedly with him. It's been a very hellish experience from a number of points of view. But we have decided on one thing, which is to do TOM at once—that is, as soon as the music gets written. We will, of course, need your constant collaboration, and Balanchine is particularly interested in using words, although he knows you have made no indication for any. This of course depends upon you, and you must talk with him about it. I still think that the possibility of using parallel passages out of the book, selected by yourself, or rearranged, could be chanted or spoken or sung, with enormous effect. *Tom* is a big thing, a real choreodrama, and we must afford to use everything possible that is necessary.

Balanchine's idea is to treat the whole cast of dancers as a group or troupe of actor-tragedians who dance. They are all to be dressed the same way, in simple, classical costume. They have extremely beautiful accessories, however, in the form of brilliant masks, whips, boots, etc., gilded and highly stylized like ritual weapons. The effect is one almost of poverty, except by the luxury of the extremities of the body. People will think that we are skimping, until Heaven opens. Then, with a terrific bang, everyone is dressed in the utmost significance. . . . Costumes without any period, but suggestive of the Highest Fashion the world has ever seen—for example, the men might be in white and gold, suggesting the regency or high renaissance, and the women superbly accoutred in Louis XV. It would not give the impression of any period or epoch, but merely the most worldly, romantic and extravagant, and of course noble heaven.

I'll pay you the rest regularly. Give my best love to Marian.

[1] George Balanchine (*b.* 1904), Russian-born choreographer and artistic director of the New York City Ballet.
[2] School of American Ballet, which opened in January 1934 and of which Kirstein is president.

6   LINCOLN KIRSTEIN
TO E. E. CUMMINGS
30 August 1934

Dear Estlin:

I apologize for not sending you the money before, and for sending you only fifty. I've been away. We have had a very hectic time here. Balanchine has been ill again, and he did his usual rapid recovery. But it was extremely hectic and unpleasant, and it has filled me with a sense of insecurity which is almost intolerable. The·School opened, however, and we are very pleased at the number of kids. But they are all horribly hard up, and there wasn't any money in the School on account of enlargements we made, so I had to pay out of my own pocket and consequently I am this hard up.

Balanchine has a wonderful idea for a kind of prologue to TOM. He wants a huge black curtain stretched across the stage. It will hang perfectly flat, then it will seem as if somebody hit it from behind, and presently the whole surface is struck rhythmically with hands and feet. The material is clutched and twisted and beaten, and great waves of motion go across it. It might be a good overture.

I am having the whole thing translated into Russian for him. It will take about two weeks long. The translator said that I probably realized the English was not very good.

Quite a few things are happening which I can't write to you about but which I will tell you.

My best love to Marian.

7   LINCOLN KIRSTEIN
TO E. E. CUMMINGS
18 December 1934

Dear Estlin:

I have been very long about sending you this check, which completes our agreement about TOM. It seems unlikely that it will be produced for a number of reasons, at least at the present.

Of course you are at perfect liberty to print this at any time or place that you want, or to give it to any other theatrical producer who might use it.

I am, of course, sorry that things have turned out as they have, but they have.

8   CAROLINE GORDON TO
LINCOLN KIRSTEIN
[February 1931]

My dear Mr. Kirstein:

I am very glad that you like "The Ice House,"[1] and glad that you can publish it in the *Hound and Horn*. The story is an incident connected with the battle of Fredericksburg. I felt rather superstitious when I discovered that I had finished it on the anniversary of the battle!

If you see Tom Mabry[2] tell him we have a fine Jersey cow named Daisy Miller.

Caroline Gordon (1895–1981), southern novelist, short-story writer, and literary critic, was married for a time to writer and critic Allen Tate. Much of her fiction reflects her conservative, Agrarian viewpoint, which sees stability in a hierarchical society of landowners and workers rather than in a liberal, urban, industrial society. Two of her short stories were published in *Hound and Horn*—"The Ice House" and "The Captive."

[1] "The Ice House," a story depicting the trickery and greed of a Yankee commissioned to encoffin the bones of slain Union soldiers for shipment to the North, was published in vol. 4, no. 4 (July–Sept. 1931).

[2] Thomas Dabney Mabry, cousin of Caroline Gordon and friend of Kirstein, was a writer who had book reviews published in the *Hound and Horn*. He was executive director of the Museum of Modern Art from 1935 to 1939.

9   CAROLINE GORDON TO
       LINCOLN KIRSTEIN
       [Undated]

My dear Mr. Kirstein:

I cannot tell you how much moved I am by your letter. I am sure that it is rare for a writer to receive such a letter. I had been feeling pretty low about my book,[1] fearing that it suffered by being too compressed and wishing that I could have had another year and so on. You seem to know what I had in mind to do and what you say about the book makes me feel that perhaps I have succeeded better than I thought. You can imagine how I am heartened by the things you have said.

The things you have said about the technical problems involved in that kind of book interest me, but there are other things in your letter that please me as much. I have no very clearly formulated ideas about the America of today, but I write, of course from a definite attitude. When I read your letter I realize that we have the same attitude. What you say about the promises that are being perjured—I have been reading in the Civil War period and the period just before it for some years

LINCOLN KIRSTEIN

EZRA POUND

E. E. CUMMINGS

WILLIAM CARLOS
WILLIAMS

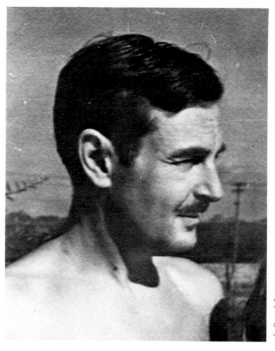

A. HYATT MAYOR

ARCHIBALD
MacLEISH

DLEY FITTS

ALLEN TATE

YVOR WINTERS

CAROLINE GORDON

STEPHEN SPENDER

Fontana Paperbacks

KATHERINE ANNE
PORTER

SEÁN O'FAOLÁIN

Family photograph

now and the more I read the more I am convinced that what you say is true. The splendid promise is there, in old letters, old diaries, the memories of old people. I picked up a book the other day, a volume of reminiscences. The writer was a man of no formal education, not particularly distinguished in his community, but his reminiscences might serve as a model for the prose style of a generation. This man lived a rough pioneer life in a log cabin whose site was cut out of a solid wall of the wild cane that then covered all this country, his prose style reflects the conversation that he heard on the porches of log dwellings. He was *civilized*. His grandsons, University of Virginia products, successful professional men, are so uncouth that they can hardly sustain a conversation.

The focus of my feelings, of course, is regret for the lost cause. It would have been better, I think, if our grandfathers had been carried off the field dead. The South that exists today has little of the Old South in it—we have sold out, certainly. An Englishman wrote to Allen[2] the other day that the thing he could not understand was the tame acquiescence of the South in her defeat. "The barbarities of Cromwell," he said, "are still bitterly remembered." I believe that people find nourishment in the remembrance of such things. It is better than to say, "It is all over now and what difference did it make?"

It is natural that I, being Southern should feel as I do, but you who probably have a different kind of ancestry—I doubt if either of your grandfathers fought for the Confederacy—you feel the same thing. A Frenchman felt it before either of us was born. You remember Baudelaire's terrible picture of a world Americanized?

Let me thank you again for your fine and generous letter—and for publishing "The Ice House." I am sure you are the only editor in the country who would have done it.

About this letter, Caroline Gordon wrote me on 25 July 1975, "Among the ardors of youth the letter makes clear the fact that I have always been politically sound—when most of my contemporaries were either carrying Communist cards or turning into 'Parlor Pinks' (handy ammunition for one who does not believe women should be allowed to vote!). Mr. Kirstein rendered 'the cause of American Letters' valuable services when he and Bernard Bandler were editing *Hound and Horn*. Too bad he 'defected.' He might have rendered still more. Sponsorship of the American ballet seems a little like applying a band-aid to an open wound. . . . It is obvious to an Unreconstructed Confederate that the world is now suppurating. Our big cities, as a result of culture poured on from the top, are now almost uninhabitable and all over the country smaller cities are imitating their savageries."

[1] *Penhally*, a novel by Caroline Gordon, published in 1931, was about the decline of the house of Penhally and the Llewelyn family, suffering from defeat in the Civil War. *Penhally* was characterized by Ford Madox Ford as the best novel produced in America.
[2] Allen Tate.

10   CAROLINE GORDON TO BERNARD BANDLER
[March 1932]

Dear Bernard:

We are sailing, alas, from Baltimore in July and so won't see you in New York. I am quite disappointed not to go through New York. We have been away so long it would be nice to see our friends before starting off another year abroad but things have been so complicated here lately that it seems best to get off as soon as we can.

Our discussion about *Penhally* is as you say hardly one to be continued in writing. It seems to me that we just have a slightly different slant on this question of tradition. I remember when Lawrence made the point of America's being the great death continent. Something in me said deeply that was true. Baudelaire's picture of the world when it is Americanized (you remember when the child in his cradle dreams of marrying a great heiress and so on) has also impressed me deeply.

We disagree only on a minor point. It seems to me that they did not, all of them, leave tradition behind but that tradition itself took a downward, a deathward slant. The child was strangled in the cradle.

I might illustrate that point by the Meriwethers, the family I know most about. They came over here because Charles II owed Nicholas Meriwether money and paid it with a grant of land. Old Nicholas did not come himself but he sent three of his five sons; that is, he cut them off from the life of their fathers and all that it held for the sake of material goods. (Of course that is a strict way of looking at it; the young men, of course, had no idea of what they were relinquishing.)

One of two of these young men went back and got English wives.

All of them made a strenuous effort to continue the English way of life. The manners and ways of life of their fathers persisted for several generations but were gradually transformed and buried finally under newer ways. One of my loutish cousins, if he ever reads any history, would know dimly that his sympathies should be with the Jacobites, but he wouldn't know why. Similarly he pronounces certain words certain ways and gives certain names to his children without knowing why. He might tell you that it was because his father did thus and so but it is just as much because one of his great grandfathers did thus and so. That is how tradition operates through people who are not even conscious of its existence.

But certainly we do say NO to many, to most of the vital things that Europe somehow manages to preserve through poverty, war and every other disaster. I would like to think it is because we are young and raw and exuberant, but I don't. I think it is the blighting influence of the Anglo-Saxon. I heard a Dutchman complaining the other night that even the laboring classes in Europe heard good music, went to museums to see good pictures. But the English lower classes never enjoyed any such pleasures. And the upper classes in England have always considered any display of intelligence bad form. And the English, like the modern Americans, have always made the continent their playground simply because they couldn't have that kind of fun at home. It is the great death continent all right and the Anglo-Saxon is the nigger in the wood pile.

No more of this. We will argue about it indefinitely at a future date, though, I am sure. Is there any chance of your going abroad in the next year? We play to stay several weeks (it will turn out months) in Paris, then go to Toulon and stay put until we get an awful lot of work done. Paris would be better, in a way, on account of libraries, but I am afraid to risk a Paris winter with Allen. He is so susceptible to influenza. I believe a winter somewhere in the south will do a lot for him. In the last few days he has begun to feel more like himself than he has for months.

I *wish* you were going to be at Toulon with us—I realize that you have other things to do besides sitting around talking to the Tates (who ought to be working). Still, it *would* be nice.

Scribner's still holds my Indian story.[1] Poor Perkins is trying to ram it down Crichton's throat but Crichton evidently doesn't take to it much—he's had it months now. I'd ask for it back but I entered it in the contest.

[1] Scribner's did not accept "The Captive," which was published in vol. 6, no. 1 (Oct.–Dec. 1932). Maxwell Perkins (1885–1947) was the noted editor and later vice-president of Charles Scribner's Sons, where Kyle Crichton (1896–1960) was editor.

11   ARCHIBALD MACLEISH
        TO LINCOLN KIRSTEIN
        17 December [1928]

Dear Lincoln:

I have read the review you asked me to read. I apparently misunderstood your letter entirely. However that may be I accept of course your statement that your letter was intended to express the opinions of the review.

I cannot however agree with your contention that the review was written in good faith. It constitutes an attack upon my personal life, my literary honesty and my integrity which has nothing of the usually expected critical detachment, and its tone is personal and spiteful. The statement, to quote no other, that my title is a boast of mastery over life, is either based upon a complete ignorance of the play of Hamlet or upon malice.[1] Since I do not know who your reviewer is I am unable to account for his animus but I think you will hardly care to deny that it exists.

My regret is that your letter accompanying your magazine, or preceding it rather, deprives me of one of my few defenses against the general journalistic hostility which my poem has aroused. I approve however your candor and wisdom.

Archibald MacLeish (1892–1982), was a friend of Kirstein's and contributed an essay, "Stephen Spender and the Critics," although none of his poetry appeared in the *Hound and Horn*.

[1] This letter refers to the review of *The Hamlet of A. MacLeish* by Richard Blackmur in vol. 2, no. 2 (Jan.–March 1929).

12   ARCHIBALD MACLEISH
TO LINCOLN KIRSTEIN
[Undated]

Dear Lincoln:

I had hoped to wait to see the fragment in proof before I allowed my present conviction about it to coagulate.[1] But it would be a very poor return for your extraordinary generosity in throwing the magazine open to me to let the thing hang. I don't know what trouble and expense you may not already have gone to, and I certainly owe you too much for the encouragement you have already given me to put you to further annoyance.

All of which sounds very pretentious but is most deeply felt.

The truth is that I cannot feel the fragment has any kind of completeness. I am sure it would be opaque to your readers. And I am even surer that it gives no idea whatever of the poem from which it has been yanked. The poem moves in one long stride and it was so written. The division into books is merely a kind of punctuation. And no note I could write, short of a rewriting of the poem itself, would *place* these lines. Therefore I am asking your indulgence, your forgiveness of my all too evident instability of judgment, and your exclusion of the piece. I can only hope to almighty God you haven't already gotten into a printing mess about it.

I think I should add, in view of my previous experience of the *Hound and Horn*—or rather my previous experience of that curious young man whatever his name was,[2] that the failure of this affair to carry through is a source of real disappointment to me. I should have been very very proud indeed to appear under your editorship and on your pages and I hope soon I may. The fault is entirely mine in thinking a group of lines could be cut like a steak from the piece.

I send you again my humiliated apologies and my vrai hommage.

---

[1] The "fragment in proof" was a passage from *Conquistador*, MacLeish's epic poem about Cortez's conquest of Mexico, told from the point of view of one of the conquistadores who, in his old age, is dissatisfied with the glosses of history and wants to tell his personal version of what happened. The poem was reviewed by Lincoln Kirstein in vol. 5, no. 3 (April–June 1932). (Cf. Chap. III, Letter 9, n. 1.)

[2] Richard Blackmur.

13   ARCHIBALD MACLEISH
        TO LINCOLN KIRSTEIN
        [Undated]

Dear Lincoln:

I do most deeply appreciate the kind things you say about *Conquistador*. The rest of the poem is to be in the same form. It will take all my life at the present rate—though I shall live a long time.

What you have written almost, but not quite, emboldens me to say to you that my experience with magazines since I came to New York makes me hope most earnestly that you will go on with the *Hound and Horn* as a magazine devoted to the arts of writing and painting. All the rest of them are running after the philosophs—the Babbitts and the rest whose only effect on writing (whatever their good effect on thinking) is to kill it. By Christ we need a place where nothing but WORK is published. There is too goddammmmmmuch thinking.

14   ARCHIBALD MACLEISH
        TO LINCOLN KIRSTEIN
        August 1931

Dear Lincoln:

I am most grateful for your letter. I'd like to talk to you sometime about you and the H&H. Kind of thing one can't write about but I've thought of it a great deal.

I have an Invective for the Writing of a Poem which is in the *Conquistador* form and is about sixty or eighty lines long and which you might not like because it is very angry and has proper names (Rockefeller Jr. and Mellon) in it.[1] If you would care to see it I will send it down but *Conquistador* is now in such a precarious balance that I don't want to send it unless you feel pretty sure the *genre* is not out of the question. Refusals are extremely upsetting when you are at work on the piece still. Afterwards they don't matter.

Thanks again for asking me and for your letter. The gist of my you-and-the-H-and-H point of view is that you are a writer and a painter and you ought not to be an editor because it is a contortionist act to be an editor when you are an artist. Do you want to talk about it.

> In a letter to me on 22 May 1975, Archibald MacLeish wrote, "Lincoln's father used to ask me in to lunch to talk about whether he should go on funding the *Hound and Horn*. It put me on the spot because I wanted Lincoln to devote himself to his own work and because I didn't like the increasingly prissy pedantic tone of the magazine—Blackmur and all that. I thought Lincoln was the prisoner of his crew and had better scuttle the ship. But though I told Lincoln I never told his father."

¹ *Frescoes for Mr. Rockefeller's City*, published in 1933.

15   LINCOLN KIRSTEIN TO ARCHIBALD MACLEISH
2 September 1932

Dear Archie:

I got the following today from Mr. Hemingway. The magazine has gone to press and will cost us quite a lot of money to reset and include this note. Do you think it is worth it? If so, I'll do it.

I am sorry to bother you about this, but I am really at a loss to know what to do and you would know his feeling about the matter more than myself.

> The brief exchange between Lincoln Kirstein and Archibald MacLeish in Letters 15 and 16 had to do with an essay published in vol. 5, no. 4 (July–Sept. 1932) by Lawrence Leighton, a lecturer at Dartmouth, entitled "An Autopsy and a Prescription." Leighton felt that the work of Ernest Hemingway, John Dos Passos, and F. Scott Fitzgerald . . . was "repulsive, sterile, and dead." He wrote that by following the master, Flaubert, they had written works that were purely reportorial and Philistine in nature. They were "blind to the finer things in life," and he cited the writing of the French author Raymond Radiguet as the work of an author who made use of a tradition and a convention which insures that their characters "do not come from nowhere and . . . when they depart from the book" have a possible future existence. The essay ended with the sentences, "One feels behind Radiguet, Mme. de Lafayette, Benjamin Constant, Proust, even Racine. In this country we have Cooper, Hawthorne, Melville, James, Mark Twain. But this past is not used."
>
> Radiguet was regarded as a young genius by Cocteau and his group, and his advocacy of a simplicity of style and a return to classicism in writing greatly influenced their thinking. His novel *Le Diable au Corps* (1922) was highly regarded, and a second novel, *Le Bal du Comte d'Orgel* (1923), was a popular success; what promised to be a brilliant career was cut short by his death of typhoid at the age of twenty.
>
> Hemingway's response to Leighton's article was published in vol. 6, no. 1 (Oct.–Dec. 1932), and reads, in part:
>
> "I take exception to one sentence:

'One feels behind Radiguet, Mme. de Lafayette, Benjamin Constant, Proust, even Racine.'

Surely this should read, 'Radiguet behind Mme. de Lafayette.' The rest of the sentence might stand although it would be more just to place Cocteau behind Radiguet and give Racine the benefit of the doubt. But perhaps Mr. Leighton has a feeling for Racine and would not wish to deprive him of his place."

16   ARCHIBALD MACLEISH
TO LINCOLN KIRSTEIN
September 1932

And how shall I answer you? To me the letter is a masterpiece. I lay on the floor to laugh. I'd put it on p. 1 col. 1 with a floral border. Doubtless it will enrage Mr. Leighton but it was meant to do that. And since you admire E. H. why should you protect Mr. Leighton against him? You must bear in mind that though you admire E. H. the *Hound and Horn* has so far published Mr. Leighton's attack and Mr. Galantière's attack[1] and nothing else. It must be E. H.'s innings. But you are the editor and should act accordingly and anything I may say is of course vitiated by the fact that although I thought Mr. Leighton's article very clever and well written I thought it deserved precisely this form of contempt, for it is obviously the work of an impotent mind unable to endure the vitality of a creative mind. If he had stuck to his [*sic*] destruction he would have made sense although bad sense. But when he hauled out Radiguet as an example of what H & D & F should be he scuttled his own ship. For Radiguet is merely Thornton Wilder manqué. A perverse Thornton Wilder. He was a fad in Paris five years ago. He will be a fad in Dartmouth next year. But he is not to be compared with any one of the three American writers from any point of view save that of smartness. So I should be delighted to see these few brilliant sentences applied to Mr. Leighton's derrière.

I have answered your request as well as I can. The other letter seems to me incredible, dull, and not worth publishing on any account.[2] Unless it be the comments on Radiguet. God but I hate professors.

[1] In a review of Hemingway's *A Farewell to Arms* in vol. 3, no. 2 (Jan.–March 1930).
[2] It is not known what letter MacLeish is referring to.

17   ARCHIBALD MACLEISH
      TO LINCOLN KIRSTEIN
           [Undated]

Dear Lincoln:
     This is a poem I wrote last summer and wanted at once to send you for possible publication in the H and H. I was unable to part with it then or indeed until now. At last I have cleared up my difficulties with one of the lines and am satisfied.
     Apparently my remarks on criticism in the Spender review went home.[1] As nearly as I can make out the boys are now reviewing that review and not the book. It's not without its humor.
     Please give me a ring if you are ever free for lunch. I'd love to hear how the ballet school is going. Nabokoff wants to write Union Pacific. Hope he does. There is a lot of life and a hell of a lot of good music in Nabokoff.[2]

     P.S. Please, even if you like the poem, don't take it unless you can publish it soon. I hate to have stuff on ice. Makes me feel split inside.

[1] "Stephen Spender and the Critics," a review of Spender's poetry in vol. 7, no. 1 (Oct.–Dec. 1933).
[2] Archibald MacLeish wrote the ballet-libretto with Nicholas Nabokov for *Union Pacific*, a verse ballet, written for Federal Theatre Project (WPA), produced on Broadway in April 1934. It was later performed by the Monte Carlo Ballet Russe in Philadelphia in 1934.

18   LINCOLN KIRSTEIN TO
      ARCHIBALD MACLEISH
           2 January 1934

Dear Archie:
     I like your poem on Lawrence very much, and would of course like to print it. But since you don't want to leave it go very long, I can't take it. The January number of *Hound and Horn* is about to appear. The March number is entirely devoted to Henry James. So I can't print it until June, and that's too long for you, I know, because you can

get it printed wherever you want to. However, I hope you will have something in June that you will like to send me.

The enclosed document might entertain you. It's not a very good poem, I know. I wrote it as the last scene of a play, the first of which was fortunately not ever written. I want very much to see you very soon, and I'll call you up in a day or two.

19   MARIANNE MOORE TO
         LINCOLN KIRSTEIN
         31 May 1932

Dear Mr. Kirstein:

To know that you liked my pages in *Poetry* well enough to think you might care to publish something by me in the *Hound & Horn* is a pleasure, and I value the support given me for my review of Conrad Aiken,[1] by your letter at that time. I shall be glad to offer you a poem. I have something in mind but have not got very far with it.

I doubt that I thanked the *Hound & Horn* for two copies sent me of the January–March issue. I welcomed in that issue what you said of Eugene O'Neill,[2] and may I say that I enjoyed a commentary on motion pictures by you that I saw in *The Art Weekly*—one in which *Tarzan of the Apes* was mentioned.

Marianne Moore (1887–1972) was editor of the *Dial* from 1925 until its end in 1929. Lincoln Kirstein admired her poetry and wrote, asking Moore to contribute to the *Hound and Horn*. Two poems, "The Jerboa" and "The Plumet Basilisk," as well as book reviews and an essay in the Henry James Issue, "Henry James as a Characteristic American," were printed in the magazine.

[1] Miss Moore reviewed two books of Aiken's poetry in vol. 5, no. 2 (Jan.–March 1932), *The Coming Forth by Day of Osiris Jones* and *Prelude for Memnon*.
[2] In *Theatre Chronicle*, vol. 5, no. 2 (Jan.–March 1932), Lincoln Kirstein reviewed O'Neill's *Mourning Becomes Electra* and wrote, "The emotions of O'Neill's New Englanders are inconsiderable, comparing them with Greeks or Elizabethans. . . . There is no tragedy, no loss in their successive horrors. . . . the play lacks any real motivation. . . . We are trapped in an ingenious web of a twentieth-century 'psychological' pattern which has become more intensely literary than the tradition of the Cloak and Sword. . . . Please, Mr. Producer, give us excitement, romantic excitement, heroes and heroines. We don't want to see ourselves any longer."

20   ## MARIANNE MOORE TO
        ## LINCOLN KIRSTEIN
        28 March 1933

Dear Mr. Kirstein:

Thank you for permission to Mr. Leippert to reprint "The Jerboa";[1] also, more than I can say, for suggesting that I offer the *Hound and Horn* other verse. I seem always to be in arrears respecting various obligations; but your invitation will assist my momentum, for nothing tempts me so much as verse.

When living in New York we never came to Brooklyn but you may have more courage, and if you should be going to the Brooklyn Museum or the Brooklyn Institute perhaps you would not be too hurried sometime to call on my mother and me? We are not a great way from the Nevins Street subway station and should be happy to see you. If you should have time to come, however, I hope you will make sure, by telephoning, that we are in; the number is Sterling 3-1123 and I could then tell you the best way of getting here.

[1] The reference is to permission given to the Macmillan Co. to reprint "The Jerboa" in *Selected Poems*, 1935. Published in vol. 4, no. 1 (Oct.–Dec. 1932).

21   ## MARIANNE MOORE TO
        ## LINCOLN KIRSTEIN
        20 October 1933

Dear Mr. Kirstein:

In your questioning of possibilities, altering the *Hound and Horn*'s format has resulted I think, in something very fine. This is an exception to the rule that changing one's format is bad luck. I do not like mannered printing and feel that you have safely evaded the lower case iron-railing trend of fashionable typography and have secured a lively contemporary severity. The margins and space under titles are just right to my mind and the glazed white, though fashionable, is ideal. There is a sacrifice of identity in the transmuted hound; but such a sacrifice where an unfeeling world is concerned may be worth the cost.[1]

Speaking of comment, so gallant a summary as this, of Harry Alan Potamkin, should benefit the living as well as honor the dead.[2] "It is with the indescribable, useless ache that one wishes he were alive" is a tribute Mr. Potamkin would have liked. And in your praise he has my coinciding heartiness, despite the fact that since seeing *Lot In Sodom* I am out to prove that Dr. Watson "knows more about the art of the film than anyone in this country."[3] I have some pieces of his verse that I should like you to see, and that I am unauthorized to show them should make editorial self-interest easy. It was Mrs. Watson who showed the things to me. I might have fitted them to some other publication than the *Hound and Horn* but that Dr. Watson has seemed to have a predilection for you. However, if I am just puzzling you with conundrums you must excuse yourself without excusing yourself. Dr. Watson does not know I am exposing him.

I do thank you for the heartiness of your letter respecting the Henry James; it furnishes a large incentive.

I am grateful for your generous cheque—thirty dollars—just now received.

[1] A faithful representation of a hound and horn was transmuted to a somewhat austere and stylized logo of hound and horn.

[2] H. A. Potamkin (1900–1933) wrote essays on the great film directors René Clair, Georg Wilhelm Pabst, Vsevolod Pudovkin, and Sergei Eisenstein, which appeared in vol. 6, nos. 1–4 (1932–1933). A tribute to him in vol. 7, no. 1 (Oct.–Dec. 1933), after his death of leukemia, stated that "it is safe to say he knew more about the art of the film than any one in this country, and except for the great Russian directors who were his friends and advisers, as much as any one in the world."

[3] Dr. J. S. Watson, along with Scofield Thayer, was editor and publisher of the *Dial*; he produced *Lot in Sodom*, an experimental film.

22   LINCOLN KIRSTEIN TO
MARIANNE MOORE
25 October 1933

Dear Miss Moore:

I want to read the poems by Dr. Watson over again more carefully. I haven't had a chance as yet to see his film, and I want very much to do so. If it is ever going to be shown again perhaps we could go together.

Your own experience as an editor makes any comment from you twice as valuable as from anybody else, and I do hope you will give us the benefit of your advice in the future.

23   LINCOLN KIRSTEIN TO MARIANNE MOORE
6 November 1933

Dear Miss Moore:
I am very sorry to have to finally send back to you Dr. Watson's poems, but I don't like them very much.

24   MARIANNE MOORE TO LINCOLN KIRSTEIN
7 November 1933

Dear Mr. Kirstein,
It is too bad that you have been burdened with a perplexity and Doctor Watson taken at a disadvantage by my enthusiasm for his real writing. What a person does in a drawing-room with half a dozen improvising verses, can easily captivate if from nothing else, from its very perversity as compared with the writer's serious work. I owe Doctor Watson apology as well as you, for he has been told what I did and is somewhat disconcerted by my temerity.

25   SEÁN O'FAOLÁIN TO LINCOLN KIRSTEIN
3 July 1930

Dear Lincoln,
While the fit is on me I must tell you that the Summer number of the H and H is one of the most interesting yet by reason of your essay and Shafer's.[1] The opening COMMENT is amazing in its irrelevance.[2] The writer might realise that great art etc. is produced by great artists,

and not by currents of thought. If all things are to be referred after the manner of the Comment to art—what an aesthetic atmosphere you will all soon be breathing! America is a strange place—too bloody civilised altogether, too rarefied. Is there no man there who dare live quietly and write well without falling into the many camps of those who live like an Alpha-Romeo on a track and write like the poets of the *Hound*; or of those who live like scented silk-underwear and write gutsily as a breeze in the Irish Sea, and as foully? I always felt you Americans need a tradition of leisure—more than anything else—not merely time to do nothing, but a tradition of doing nothing for nothing's sake. There you had a grand argument about Humanism and the Commentator of the *Hound* proceeds to wash his hands and consider what's left now boys that it's all over! Good Christ why do you drop a good thing like that? Jesus, the bloody argument hasn't begun yet. What a nation! I had hoped for more solid things from the H. than this news-sheet impatience for something new, fresh, etc. and so on. Take your time for art's sake. And Life's sake. The H. is, may I be insulting enough to tell it, just as bad as the stage-American doing the Louvre. Not always, I confess gladly: it gives me pleasure to have been promised an article by Dana Durand on Vico it must be a year ago and to be still kept waiting.[3] But then Harvard is or was, the ballast of the magazine. If you become a New York publication you may as well shut up the shop.

Mencken is the tin can on America's tail.[4] One's enough! No number should be published which does not contain—as the *Criterion* aspires to—at least one article of *permanent* value as a contribution to knowledge. But good God you Americans don't know what *permanent* means. Didn't you invent the phrase semi-permanent? Pardon my rudeness. In my heart I love you all. When shall I see you again? I won't be here August–September. After that a new address. "Semi-Permanent" address:—

> J. R. Whelan
> St. Mary's College
> Strawberry Hill
> Middlesex
> England

N.B.

But keep it *Whelan*—I keep my more unconventional side to myself *there*.

Seán O'Faoláin (*b.* 1900) received his M.A. degree from Harvard University, where he met the *Hound and Horn* group in 1927. In his autobiography, *Vive Moi!* (Boston: Little, Brown, 1964), he describes vividly their impact on him. "My connection with [Lincoln Kirstein, Richard Blackmur, Varian Fry, and Bernard Bandler] and other young men associated with the *Hound and Horn*, had one delightful effect on me. Listening to them gossiping about their day-by-day lives whenever they came to drink a cup of tea with us [O'Faoláin and his wife, Eileen] in our chicken coop at Number 10A Appian Way; or arguing hotly about literature in the office of the *H & H* in Harvard Square, with its bright red-framed reproductions of cover designs and photographs; or going off with Dick [Blackmur] for a coffee or a bootleg beer, I found my image of Harvard changing completely. It was not alone that the eager zest of all these young men counterbalanced the dullness of the Teutons; or that their interests were so wide and contemporaneous; or that, through listening to them, I first really became interested in the modern metaphysicals, in E. E. Cummings, Hart Crane, Wallace Stevens, Marianne Moore, the Southern Fugitive group, Ezra Pound and many more, who, for various reasons, had hitherto passed over my head. It was that through them I made the elementary but fundamental discovery . . . that it is really the undergraduate who makes a university, gives it its lasting character, smell, feel, quality, tradition" (p. 315).

His first published short story, "Fugue," appeared in the *Hound and Horn.*

[1] Kirstein's essay, "The Diaghilev Period" and "The Definition of Humanism" by Robert Shafer, professor of philosophy at the University of Cincinnati. Both in vol. 3, no. 4 (July–Sept. 1930).

[2] The opening Commentary in vol. 3, no. 4 stated, "Any further discussion of Humanism is fruitless, since Humanism is vague and unfocussed. . . . it solves no dilemmas . . . because it faced none concretely; it led nowhere because it never started for a definite destination."

[3] No article on Vico by Dana Durand appeared in *Hound and Horn.*

[4] H. L. Mencken (1880–1956), acerbic and highly opinionated critic of manners and mores, editor and essayist, who had particular influence in the 1920s, author of *The American Language* (1919 and 1936).

26   SEÁN O'FAOLÁIN TO
LINCOLN KIRSTEIN
[Undated]

L,

Why the blazes don't you write to me? Only a few people yet recognise me for a writer and you are one and when the few get lost I feel so lonely. I have finished a lovely story—another "Fugue, op. 2."[1] It is 60 pages long, doublespaced type—shall I send it to the *Hound*? It is almost all I did since returning, for this blasted schoolmastering is such a time catch, and deadens me. I must get rid of it soon or die. Reading Karsavina reminded me of you.[2] What are you doing. Don't say you are going in for business or any form of commercial art. F comm. art. Drop me a line, do. Thanks for putting Simon and Schuster on to me. This second Fugue is portion of a novel on my brain. Often I envy you Boston and often I long for Irish bogwater. You are too good for commerce. That poem of yours remains in my mind always.

¹ O'Faoláin's first published short story, "Fugue," appeared in vol. 2, no. 1 (Oct.–Dec. 1928). "Fugue, op. 2" was not considered for publication because of its length and because of its Irish theme, at a time when the *Hound and Horn* wanted to print primarily American writing. (Cf. Chap. III, Letter 22).
² Tamara Karsavina (1885–1978) the outstanding ballerina of the Diaghilev Ballets Russes. The book O'Faoláin was reading was probably *Theatre Street* (1932) her book on ballet.

27   SEÁN O'FAOLÁIN TO
         LINCOLN KIRSTEIN
         20 April 1931

My Dear Lincoln,

Indeed I am all with you in hating with the hatred of weariness, of boredom, the business of second-hand criticism. Yet what is criticism. (It is not geography, of course, or a guide-book. We mean something else.) How does it happen? A man has an attitude. Unexpressed. Therefore unformulated. He reads a book that brings him to his own surface. He utilises this as his plaster to model out his attitude. But he must—and he usually does not—go on and carve it into the marble. We have too many who don't realise the adventure as I have described it—they being un-selfconscious. They go on to another and yet another book. They become Cook's guides, cheap geographers. They perform a necessary function. But we are thereupon not concerned with them. They never formulate their own attitude.

The most original criticism is the man himself—his own bit of art is the thing. Only one book do I know that is both—the loveliest book in the world. *Marius the Epicurean.*¹ If I were to want to translate any book it would be something by that Aristippus of Cyrene that Marius spoke of. Does such a book exist—I don't think so. Just some utterances handed down traditionally. But Pater didn't translate anyone. Autobiography is criticism, when it is intelligent. There is nothing conscious in Irish, no philosophy, no sophistication, no enquiry. Critics have too many points of view—chameleons.

I swore to have my book of short stories ready this Easter.[2] I went to Ireland to look for a job and spent a month canvassing for it and so wrote not a word. The job is a chair of English at the National in Cork. Provincialism facing me. The job will be decided June 1st or so. But I must get the stories ready by then anyway so you should print Fugue Two in June or it will be stale on you. You will be printing from a book published several months if you wait till August. As to cheque send it when you can—by all means before June when I will be packing up and going somewhere. If it doesn't come by then I'll be dunning you.

I hope the Hound keeps on chasing the stag ad infinity, like the folk on Keats Grecian Urn. Too bad Bandler went out. Are there no youths to come in his place? You describe Cambridge lugubriously. Don't let the magazine down if you can help it though it's devilish if you are running it all alone. It's the best America has and nothing else to re-place it. An open arena in an intolerant enough country is a gift of God. Only so long as it doesn't get like the *Dial* did, all hurly-burly like a lady's work-basket after the kitten had chewed it up—full of pretty things but no verve to the ensemble. But is there anything harder than a magazine to keep together? To keep in rein. To *direct*? There was not yet the impresario to do it. Too many individuals all at their own game. Can you think of any way to harness all? Is it impossible? To synthesise, to present the ballet every quarter? The American ballet alias the *Hound and Horn*.

[1] By Walter Pater. Published in 1885, it is the philosophical biography of an imaginary Roman.
[2] *Midsummer Night Madness* (1932).

28   SEÁN O'FAOLÁIN TO
             LINCOLN KIRSTEIN
             2 October 1931

Dear Lincoln:

The works seem to have gone wrong, don't they? You still have time to print my story. I hope you are going to do so. The Viking Press is publishing my book not until the Spring of '32—presumably in order to have the novel soon after at any rate not too long after. They have my ms. opus Fugue II (since called "The Small Lady").

I don't know what you are doing about it but by Xmas at any rate would you please send them the ms. of that story so that my book will be in their hands then—complete.

This year is my last teaching. Next I 'go native' in the mountains of Ireland for the rest of my life, writing only. How much of my life I have wasted as a prostitute—as all teachers and lecturers are!

The novel is halfwritten already but—oh! bloody lectures and bloody pupils and bloody Spenser and Chaucer. Ugh!

Please write and confirm this. You *are* very annoying. But I hope you are keeping your pecker up.

Eileen is very well and happy and wishes you to know she thinks often of you. I can't write angrily to you because you are rather a dear and I am afraid you are a bit too good for the U.S. But if I thought you were fat and feeling uncomfortable I wouldn't half tell you things.......!!!!!!!

29   SEÁN O'FAOLÁIN
TO LINCOLN KIRSTEIN
18 October 1931

Dear Lincoln,

This story has caused me more annoyance than I can say. Actually it is you who have been responsible. If it has caused you any worry don't blame me. Your magazine must be running on temperament—that's all I can say. I sympathise, believe me. *I* also expect sympathy.

It now appears that this book of stories of mine may conceivably appear this side of Christmas. Would you ring or call on Mr. B. W. Huebsch of the Viking Press. 18 E. 48th St. N.Y.C.—I have written to say you may do so—and explain the situation. He will tell you when the book is to appear and whether you have time to print it in your Winter number—IF YOU STILL WANT TO. Please understand that I am not forcing you to print the story. But I must say I have not the slightest urge to send a story again to the *Hound and Horn*. Needless to say after the book appears you cannot, without infringing copyright, print it.

Your dilatoriness seems to be costing me in and around $150. Next Spring I am going native in the Irish mountains and living on my pen. I shan't risk losing £30 again.

30   LINCOLN KIRSTEIN TO
            SEÁN O'FAOLÁIN
            4 January 1932

Dear Sean:

This is merely a note to tell you that we will either publish your story in the Spring number of the *Hound and Horn* or pay you one hundred dollars for it if we don't publish it. There is no use saying I feel badly about it because your irritation is so justified that I only fear it would further rankle to make excuses. I have tried to place it at what would be far better rates, in Scribner's and the Atlantic Monthly, without success, on account of its length.

Things are very bad here. The future of everything is extremely confused and I have no idea of what will happen.

31   SEÁN O'FAOLÁIN TO
            LINCOLN KIRSTEIN
            [Undated]

Lincoln, a chara,

Thanks for H. and H. and cheque. (Depression obviously with you.) I was ill when the mag. came so I read every word of it from cover to cover inc. the ads. It's years since I saw it now and it has got much finer in the meantime. The typography is symptomatic of that—less arty and more utilitarian. Is that the depression or just you; i.e. you thought the real hound too pretty? I regret him—he was lovely, though perhaps too much of him there. Remember though that never will your ideals shine so brightly as in your undergrad days. The US is utilitarian enough without helping it any. I suggest the old hound was Boston—and the hieroglyphic is New York. Glad to see a James number announced. Or I should fear that New York had done you wrong. You gather I prefer the less "firm" mag.? I maybe do. I dunno.

Entre nous Dick B. takes them all too damn seriously. But then all Americans are too serious. Imagine analysing Pound as if he were Keats! He does it very well, does Dick. But Jesus! Pound?[1]

Novel reviews good—stimulating, again too bloody solemn. Buggur all novels. (Not enough life in the world, in me, or anywhere, not excluding the H and H. (i.e. let's have an article on current politics. Give literature and art a miss. All art is bollocks. Unless like the Rosen Kavalier it just drunks your reason silly.)

Verse—polished surfaces.

Stories—no reality (I suspect Curtis Brown sent you a story of mine about an old nun. And I suspect you turned it back because it was too simple. Ah, Lincoln, whether or no—beware of Hollywood, slickness, newness, novelty, and all the rest of the enemies of "simple folk.")

Music notes—good. All music notes are good.

Space House. (No, Most certainly not. The worst vulgarity on your part to print that slosh—the young man in search of a jolt.)[2]

I forget the rest. McLeod should be hung.[3]

Plucky man to keep that mag. going. And through an awful time— I mean not financially.

Love. You people were very kind to the *Nest of Simple Folk.*[4] It's a true book but by an unbeliever in men. Next time I'll hit the sky.

POST THIS FOR ME, Love from Eileen.

P.S. All this is insolent and I hope you will forgive me. I know you will take it cum grano salis. Simple things, real things, no novelties, *old* writers, current life, *ideas.* —these I want in a mag.

---

[1] O'Faoláin is referring to "Masks of Ezra Pound," an essay by R. P. Blackmur in vol. 7, no. 2 (Jan.–March 1934). This whole letter refers to this issue of *Hound and Horn.*

[2] "The Space-House" in Notes on Architecture by Frederick Kiesler.

[3] Norman MacLeod wrote a long poem, "Letter from Russia," describing his reaction to a visit there. O'Faoláin also had a "Letter from Ireland" on the political situation in his country, and René Daumal, in a "Letter from France," gave an overview of the cultural, literary, and political scene in France.

[4] *A Nest of Simple Folk*, a collection of O'Faoláin's short stories, published in 1933.

32 KATHERINE ANNE PORTER TO RICHARD BLACKMUR
29 November 1929

My Dear Mr. Blackmur:

Mr. Matthew Josephson suggested that I send you a short story,[1] believing you might be interested in the kind of thing I do. This story is one of a half dozen somewhat in the same vein, with Mexico as the background, which I purpose to finish this winter. This is the first I have completed.

The title I owe to a passage in T. S. Eliot's "Gerontion"

"In depraved May, dogwood and chestnut,
        flowering judas,
To be eaten, to be divided, to be drunk
Among whispers: . . . ."

and I am wondering if I should have set this quotation below the title. But if you don't like the story, I imagine this will not be important.

Katherine Anne Porter (1890–1980), writer, born in Texas, who was known for her sensitive and finely crafted short stories and for her novel *Ship of Fools*, lived the dedicated life of the artist. In a letter to me, 1 July 1975, she wrote, "I have given my whole life to writing and my whole life without it would have been worth nothing." And in answer to my request for biographical details, she continued, "The absurdly wearisome life of the artist is of no importance—the only thing that counts is what he was able to bring out of this chaos." *Flowering Judas*, Porter's first book of collected short stories, was published in 1930.

Miss Porter's short story "Flowering Judas" was published in *Hound and Horn*, as well as an essay on Cotton Mather, "A Bright Particular Faith, A.D. 1700."

[1] "Flowering Judas," vol. 3, no. 3 (April–June 1930).

33   BERNARD BANDLER TO
       KATHERINE ANNE PORTER
          3 December 1929

Dear Miss Porter:

Thank you so much for sending us your story "Flowering Judas," I think it is splendid and we shall publish it in an early issue. Personally, I am not in favor of setting the quotation from "Gerontion" below the title; your story is so thoroughly valid on its own account that any suggestion of Eliot would imply a faint derivation which would be unfair.

I hope we shall have the privilege of receiving more stories from you in the future.

34   KATHERINE ANNE PORTER
       TO BERNARD BANDLER
          8 December 1929

Dear Mr. Bandler:

Thank you for acceptance and praise of "Flowering Judas!" It is all very heartening.

I do a fair amount of hack work, and am revising a long-delayed book,[1] so my short stories must be written during an irregular series of snatched intervals. I have another going on slowly at present, called "Adios, La Primavera."[2] It belongs to the Mexican group, and is a kind of love story, I suppose. I shall be happy for you to see it first.

The "Flowering Judas" stands, then, without reference to "Gerontion," since you approve of it. It seemed to me appropriate yet I feared a quotation at the head would be clumsy.

Do you send author's proofs for corrections? The one or two magazines that have published my stories lately do not have this custom, and it leads to some hair-raising errors! May I see the story before it goes up?

---

[1] In a letter to me 1 July 1975, Miss Porter wrote that the book, called *Many Redeemers*, was about Mexico and Mexican politics, but after about four chapters, she "decided that it was not any good and destroyed it."

[2] Miss Porter does not remember what story that may have been but wrote to me

1 July 1975 that she had yet to weed out and destroy or try to finish any number of unfinished stories that "I relinquished because I was not doing them as I wished to. I started three novels and I have relinquished and destroyed all of them."

35   KATHERINE ANNE PORTER
TO BERNARD BANDLER
12 December 1929

Dear Mr. Bandler:

It occurs to me that you probably pay on publication,[1] and if you do, this would be so sad for me; I shall ask you to suspend your rule this once in my favor. Existence, in a purely material sense, is for me, I assure you, precarious.

Even so, I should probably hesitate to mention this matter, if I did not feel that it is—it must be!—a familiar complaint to you!

[1] Rather than earlier, on acceptance of a manuscript:

36   KATHERINE ANNE PORTER
TO LINCOLN KIRSTEIN
20 March 1933

My dear Mr. Kirstein:

If you have not promised them to some one else, I should like very much to review two novels for *Hound and Horn*: *The Rash Act*, by Ford Madox Ford and *Pity is not Enough*, by Josephine Herbst.[1]

I have read them both in advance copies, and find them so interesting, each for quite different reasons, it would please me immensely to comment on them. If you wish me to do this, would you let me know about space you allow for individual novels?

Would you be interested in a chapter of my study of Cotton Mather? It is a documented account of his experience with the Goodwin children of Charleston, Bridget Glover, a witch, and the whole train of events that led to the Salem episode. As to my methods in this study, I agree with Mr. Bernard De Voto's[2] theory of the function of the biographer: I have no thesis to expound, and I have added no fictions of my own to the possible fictions of Mr. Mather and his contemporaries. One can do no more with the material in hand, and the episode has its own kind of fantasy to which I can add nothing but a careful and logical re-telling.

[1] Ford Madox Ford (1873–1939), British novelist, critic, poet, and editor of *Transatlantic Review* and other little magazines. *Pity Is Not Enough* was the first of a trilogy (followed by *The Executioner Waits* and *Rope of Gold*) to cover "not only the decay of capitalist society but also the upthrust of a new group society." None of these books was reviewed in *Hound and Horn*.

[2] Bernard De Voto (1897–1955), critic, historian, and novelist. In his article "The Skeptical Biographer," *Harper's*, 166 (Jan. 1933), pp. 181–92, De Voto wrote that the literary mind with its intuitiveness, sensibility, and imagination was not given to the hard analysis of facts necessary to report what had actually occurred in a man's life. The techniques then currently in vogue among literary biographers, such as the psychoanalysis, exegesis, and invention of scenes and conversations, were highly imaginative but based on guesswork and were not true biography, which called for "an unremitting skepticism."

37   KATHERINE ANNE PORTER
TO LINCOLN KIRSTEIN
29 April 1933

Dear Mr. Kirstein:

Since you write that you would like to see any part of my biography of Cotton Mather, I am sending one of my favorite chapters. It is shorter and more compact than the episode of the Goodwin children, and is an important event in the life of Mather which no other biographer has noticed particularly. . . .

I do not agree with Mr. de Voto in everything, but I think he is right in saying that a biographer should stick by the records, and this I had done long before I ever heard of Mr. de Voto. . . . Please don't be alarmed. I think it is fairly useless to explain why one works as one does. Here is the chapter, let that be my argument.

P.S. You will notice that even in the final copy, I was still hesitant about the title. The original title was "Death and Abigail." If you don't care for these, I shall try to think of another.

38   KATHERINE ANNE PORTER
TO LINCOLN KIRSTEIN
[Undated]

Dear Mr. Kirstein:

It delights me to know you are so pleased with "A Bright Particu-
lar Faith, A.D. 1700."[1] Several friends have seen parts of the manu-
script, but this is the first time I have offered a chapter for publication.
If you would still like the Martha Goodwin episode—the story of the
first possessed girl that Mather influenced and directed—I might still
send it. It is interesting because it prepared the way for the Salem epi-
sode. Mather's dealings with women were most horribly oblique and
curious, so tangled I can offer no theory, but merely tell the story as
clearly as I can. The Goodwin chapter would be better published first,
since it occurred several years before the death of Abigail. . . .

There is no danger that the book will appear this year, or even the
next. It was contracted for and I began work on it in 1927. I spent
two years on research in Salem, Worcester, Boston and New York,
and wrote the first eleven chapters in Bermuda, 1929, in about seven
months. For lack of money I was then interrupted and have never been
able to return to it until now. I have done about a year's reading around
the subject and the period to refresh myself, and am more interested in
the book than ever, and have begun the second half. I work on it alter-
nately with my novel, *Many Redeemers* which also goes slowly.

There is no prospect of my seeing New York again until next
spring, but then I have great hopes of being there, and surely we must
meet. Four years absence from America is too much for me, I am
frankly homesick.

P.S. Do let me say I believe deeply you should not ignore Josephine
Herbst's novel, *Pity is not Enough*. The more I read it and think about
it, the more I am convinced it is a most important novel. It is a strong
and serious and beautiful piece of work, *the* novel about American life
that so many others have been trying to write—but she has done it. I
don't know when I have been so touched and impressed by an Ameri-
can novel. You will understand that she belongs to another way of
thinking and feeling, not at all mine, her view point is different,

her style and language are strange, but everything is superbly rock-bottom, true to her own conscience. . . .

<hr />

[1] Published in vol. 6, no. 2 (Jan. –March 1933). Miss Porter used the final illness of Mrs. Abigail Mather as the framework for her study of the Reverend Mather's faith and morals. The biography of Cotton Mather was listed regularly as Miss Porter's "Work in Progress," but in a letter to me in 1975, she wrote that "although it really has not been [in progress] for several years, I still have at this late date a kind of hope that I will be able to finish it."

39   KATHERINE ANNE PORTER TO LINCOLN KIRSTEIN
19 October 1933

Dear Lincoln:

I'm slow in answering your letter because I am up to the ears in a mixture of short story, novel AND Cotton Mather. . . .

I still want fearfully to write a review of Josie Herbst's fine novel. It seems to me too good to overlook. I wish you could find me a little space. I have a long short story going on fairly, a very important story for me, something I have tried for years to write, but the time did not come until now. If you like, I will send it to you to look at, when it is really ready. It marches very well, I have great hopes of it.

There are writers here I think you might like, but I will make a serious selection of names and works and write you specially about this in, I hope, a few days. I really have something but I want to consider it a little.

I plan now to be in New York in April, with *Doomsday*[1] and other works under my arm. You will receive shortly a copy of my song book,[2] which I hope you will sing straight through to your own pleasure and mine. Monroe[3] of course thinks first of bindings and type and the look of the pages, and he has made a lovely job of it, but I really want the poems to be sung, for they can be, they were made for that. I am wondering why you could not make a medieval ballet using the music of Adam de la Halle (about 1250), who wrote operas and ballets for the court at Naples. . . .[4] Maybe it is worth thinking about. . . . I should like trying that sort of libretto after *Doomsday*. . . . But for *Le*

Jeu I should be making after all only an adaptation. . . . I would have to fish the whole score out of the deep, official archives here.

It will be very pleasant to see you again, to see also how your plans are coming out. If you have anything in mind you think I might be able to do for the *Hound and Horn*, let me know. There are many fast boats, it does not take long to send word. And think again about *Pity is not Enough* by Herbst. I believe you would see what I mean if you read it a little more. . . .

[P.S.] Fernande Olivier, Picasso's first and most famous mistress, has published *her* version of Picasso and his friends. It is being much praised by critics for its sensibility and intelligence, and knowledge of painting. It is most interesting to compare her really lovely and acute record with the portrait of her by Gertrude Stein, who makes her out a beautiful nitwit. . . . I doubt the veracity of *all* Gertrude's portraits, judgements, and conclusions about *everything*.

---

[1] Miss Porter had no recollection of a ballet called *Doomsday*. *Le Jeu* possibly referred to a medieval French ballad-opera *Le Jeu de Robin et Marion*, with music by Adam de la Halle. She wrote one libretto for a ballet, for which the sets—modeled after the gardens of Xochimilco—were designed by the Mexican artist Alberto Best-Maugard. The ballet was performed in Mexico and in Paris (not in New York because the paper stage-sets were a fire hazard), but Miss Porter never saw it. "I only know that Miss Pavlova [accepted it and] was delighted with it. I saw a letter from her to Mr. Best." (Letter to me, 1 July 1975.)

[2] *The French Song Book* (1933), for which Katherine Anne Porter compiled and translated French songs.

[3] Monroe Wheeler (*b.* 1900), administrator, trustee of the Museum of Modern Art, and author of various books on the arts.

[4] In reply to my question about "the mediaeval ballet using the music of Adam de la Halle," Miss Porter wrote to me in July 1975: "The libretto that I liked and wished seriously to see in the flesh . . . was the battle between David and Goliath with music by a mediaeval—or perhaps 16th century—composer whose record I had once in Paris about 1934 in a volume of old music I bought at that time . . . the first music from the 12th to the 16th century that I had ever known as recorded. I seem to remember that I mentioned this to Lincoln, but I may not have. In any case, nothing came of it, and I have gone on being a balletomane from then until now, sitting happily watching the performance, which is where I probably belong anyhow."

40　　KATHERINE ANNE PORTER TO
LINCOLN KIRSTEIN
11 November 1933

Dear Lincoln:

First something important to Adrienne's feelings about the translation being published in December. . . . She wants badly for the story to be signed by her familiar pen-name—J. M. SOLLIER.[1] I don't remember that she said anything about this before, but she may have, as she was upset as only authors can be about such things, and besides, her real name was slightly misspelled in the announcement. So:

Do be good enough to have the story signed by J. M. Sollier, and add in your notes on authors that this is the pen-name of Adrienne Monnier (two n's) who founded and runs a book shop and lending library, "La Maison des Amis des Livres"; is compiling a very complete Critical Catalogue of her lending library which she has assembled between 1915 and 1932. The first volume has appeared. She also founded and edited and published a literary review, *Le Navire d'Argent*, between June 1925 and May 1926. I have seen a complete file on this, and I think it very fine, altogether worth mentioning and remembering. . . . And besides there is her little set of short stories, of which you chose "Foolish Virgins." I send you all this for you to choose what you want for your notes. . . .

I wasn't thinking about the medieval French ballet for the next season or maybe not even the next. You are never in any danger of getting anything instantly from me. It's just something to think about through the ages, and if we ever come to it, it might be very beautiful. . . . *Doomsday* has been put aside in favor of Cotton Mather, prophet of Doomsday; that book must now be done and published and no more nonsense. But can you give me an idea of the latest date you might seriously want that libretto? And I'll send it. . . .[2]

Your copy of the songbook should arrive sometime this month. I *believe*. It's being sent direct from Holland. Your idea of my getting up a concert is magnificent, but how does one do that sort of thing from Paris to New York? I once admired Greta Torpadie's way of singing very old and very new music above any singer I ever heard; she was born for these extremes: but where is she now?[3] And besides her I know of no one: do you? Glenway[4] and Monroe[5] will be in New York soon. I shall tell them about this, and maybe something very pleasant can be done.

I hear you made a fine commotion at the showing of the Eisenstein film,[6] and of course you know I think this is admirable of you. Do sometimes write that letter, by longhand, if you must, I can't, and tell me what happens.

[1] Adrienne Monnier's pen-name came from her mother's surname, Sollier. Her bookstore at 7 rue de l'Odéon was across the street from Sylvia Beach's "Shakespeare and Co.," at 12 rue de l'Odéon. Both were popular meeting places for French and American writers of the day.

[2] Kirstein had written that he could not produce the medieval ballet "for a long time because I want to restrict all our historical revivals to American subject matter" but hoped Miss Porter was going ahead with *Doomsday*.

[3] In a letter to me of 1 July 1975, Miss Porter explained that Greta Torpadie was "a very sophisticated and interesting [Swedish] singer of extremely modern music in that day and at that time I was so enslaved to everything modern that I could not listen to any music unless it was warm on the page and either directed or performed by the composer."

[4] Glenway Wescott (*b.* 1901), poet and writer.

[5] Monroe Wheeler.

[6] There was a great furor over Upton Sinclair's editing of Sergei Eisenstein's movie *Qué Viva Mexico!* At the preview of the film, retitled *Thunder over Mexico*, held at the New School of Social Research, Lincoln Kirstein made a speech of protest and was forcibly ejected from the showing.

41 KATHERINE ANNE PORTER TO LINCOLN KIRSTEIN
19 February 1934

Dear Lincoln:

The copies of the January *Hound and Horn* arrived, and it is a very fine number. But that was rather a long time since, and I must make a complaint. I have not received my check for the Cotton Mather chapter. You may think that $50 more or less makes no difference to me. I assure you it does, and that I have been hoping for it with some anxiety. After all, creative writers must live as well as critics and printers, and I still wonder —I always have—why the people whose work is the reason for being of all magazines, theatres, picture galleries, and the like, should be forever the last and the worst paid. . . . I think poverty, which comfortably situated persons always think is good for the artist, is no better for him than for any other. . . . It is not one of the limitations we find profitable.

It is, though I can't think why—possibly the weight of opinion against the artist in this matter affects me—always distressing to me to have to discuss the question of payment for my work. Yet it is my sole source of personal income. I cannot say living because it is not that, and it is important that I be paid something for it. I hope, if you like the ballet libretto, you will be prepared to pay me $500 for it. For this the ballet would be yours outright for good, but I think so well of the idea I should like to keep the right to work it over into a full length opera. . . . The title, of course, is yours anyhow. But there are several others which would do almost as well. I hope you will make some place in your budget for the libretto writers and composers, as well as for your dancers and technical experts. Do let me know about this for it is of the utmost importance, if I am to be able to go on with my work. But I think I need not explain this to you, whose whole material is drawn from the work of artists. You cannot possibly be either unaware or unsympathetic.

I have been waiting to write until I had something definite to say about the libretto. The idea came in one fine stroke after my mind had described wavering circles around it for months. But now I need some very practical information from you. The ballet has become somewhat longer and more complicated than I thought at first. I could wish for a singing chorus, a special score—I do not in fact see how this can be avoided—and a number of such exacting projects.

How many dancers will you have? Besides the two leading roles, there are a number of secondary roles that will require good dancers. Do you mean to make a single feature of this ballet, or is it to be half of a program, or only one number among several? As it stands now in my mind, it is in three scenes, all in the New England woods; the first in broad afternoon and a full landscape, the second merging into twilight in a thin, delicate wooded place, the third at midnight in deep forest. The music requires guitars, zithers, lutes, reed flutes, church bells, and Indian drums. There should be themes from the 16th and 17th century love songs and drinking songs, the oldest Puritan hymns, the mingled tones and rhythms of bells and drums. . . . So you see it will take some doing.

I have made a synthesis of three historical episodes, surprisingly dramatic and lending themselves to your purpose: and it really is a ballet. It must be danced. Do let me know just what you had planned, so that in my fervor I shall not exceed whatever limitations you have which cannot be overcome. I wish you would cable me, for I am quite serious about it, believe we shall have a superb ballet out of it, and I wish I might be free to finish and send it to you at once. . . .

Europe is in a marvellous uproar. It does not surprise me, really; it gives me a painful but rather energizing sense of utter insecurity. I wish terribly to finish now all that I have begun so long ago, because the time is coming when I must be doing quite other things, I fear. . . . Your letter pleased me very much; as for the Puritanism you speak of with hope, I think its new name for the present is Communism. Like all Puritan movements, it carries a heavy charge of political and economical, as well as ethical and moral, implications. . . . It is a way of life or nothing. A true re-birth or a meaningless posture. . . . It's no good trying to make the best of both worlds.

This letter is already too long, because I delay so in writing I have then always too much to say; but I remember now your disgust with literary criticism, your feeling that maybe the *Hound and Horn* should disappear. I do not agree that there are enough small magazines—or large ones either—to publish good work. I should not like to see the failure of this one which has never failed in a special kind of virtue. But I do think the situation is evil when there are a hundred thousand words of critical estimate to ten thousand of original literature. But if you believe at all in any branch of the arts, then you must really believe in them all, for one cannot thrive without the others. It is very well to devote yourself almost exclusively to one, of course. That is a secret of strength. My interest is in the written word. Otherwise I should never write another line. But this deprives me of nothing. I have also music, dancing, painting. If I excluded one of them from my sympathies, I should be throwing away something I need, which I mean to use.

This city is calm and gray after the battles, the Place de la Concorde is already restored, the factions are sobered and thoughtful, the government is for the moment impressed, the dead are buried. These deaths are the only things that really happened. Otherwise things are not much changed.

Do act upon the various requests and recommendations of this letter as immediately as you can. I shall be waiting to hear.

In her letter to me of 18 July 1975, Miss Porter described her home in Paris at this time as "the sixth floor of a nice ramshackle old apartment house overlooking a lovely convent garden where I could see the young novice nuns up in the apple trees picking apples and putting them in a basket they had on their left arms, their left hands giving them their hold on the branches by them and their right hands picking out in all directions. Nightingales sang there and the sisters came out regularly with large baskets and cut bushels of green things to eat. I had to climb five long straight flights of stairs to get there but I still think it was one of the nicest places I ever lived in."

42   WILLIAM CARLOS WILLIAMS TO LINCOLN KIRSTEIN
8 December 1929

My dear Kirstein:

In reply to your letter of Dec. 5: I am delighted that you are pleased with the poem "Love in a Truck etc.", it will give me great pleasure to appear in H. & H. a second time.[1]

As to the last four lines: I believe you have spotted a weakness in my middle English! What I wanted to say was simply that Spring had arrived or had come in. I was speaking in a mildly ironic vein, as much as to say: Boy, it ain't half the dainty, sweet little affair of butterflies and daisies you think it. What I should have said was simply "ycommen" mocking the old songs by using an Old English form of speech.

Weeeel, let's make a change in the last line, let's say—

the bounty
of . . . and spring
they say—
spring is here

Please make the change, indicated, in the script. Many thanks.

William Carlos Williams (1883–1963) contributed widely to avant-garde magazines. His poems "Rain" and "In a 'Sconset Bus" were published in the *Hound and*

Horn, vol. 3, no. 1 (Oct.–Dec. 1929) and vol. 5, no. 4 (July–Sept. 1932).
¹ "Love in a Truck" or "The Sea Elephant" was not published in *Hound and Horn*.
It appeared first in *The Miscellany*, vol. 1, no. 5 (Nov. 1930), pp. 14–18.

43 LINCOLN KIRSTEIN TO
WILLIAM CARLOS WILLIAMS
4 September 1931

Dear Dr. Williams:

Thank you so very much for your very welcome letter. I am sorry that you think our book reviews are too goddamned cocksure. I had hoped on the contrary that we did offer data and not opinions, although the personal element is almost impossible to keep out of a review. I think you are perfectly right in that we ought to be more informative, and we are putting more stress on our chronicles from now on. The only trouble with "a reporter who does not himself give a damn about writing but has a lust for a certain literary sort of news" is that he usually doesn't know what good writing is, and we really haven't got space to chronicle every scribbler in the country.

I know of course that there are a lot of people who dislike us very much. My only regret is that they are not centered in their attack. Good opposition is absolutely priceless. We don't think at all that we are righteous. We have to have some kind of definition and positiveness even to irritate, or else the whole thing sounds flat. If we are obstinate and seem to be snobbish that is our error in technique and we are always grateful to anyone who will point this out to us.

44 WILLIAM CARLOS WILLIAMS TO
LINCOLN KIRSTEIN
23 July 1932

Dear Mr. Kirstein:

Certainly I shall be glad to wait for the check until you find it convenient to send it. Though few of us are able to do it, those of us who are publishing new work I mean, it should always be recognized that everything we print should be paid for. Which is to say that though *Hound and Horn* could get much of the material it prints today from its writers and not pay for it, your continuing to pay is particularly to your credit.

Your last issue gave me good reading. I heartily dislike the Leighton criticism which is ill tempered and short sighted from the viewpoint of a modern technique which we, Americans, are in the act of creating for ourselves.[1] There is a fundamental misapprehension in most opinions emanating from men who occupy teaching positions in the universities and who attempt to criticise new work, work created by conditions with which they do not have an opportunity to come inexorably into contact. They must fall back on something, something "universal", an ideal criticism which is somehow more related to what might be wished than to anything that is. I can't see that Radiguet's work has any bearing on our difficulties—But the issue as a whole attracted me, particularly the translation from the French.[2] My poem was beautifully printed.[3]

[1] Cf. MacLeish correspondence, Letters 15–16, above.
[2] "Christian Personality" by Etienne Gilson, translated by A. C. Pegis. Published in vol. 5, no. 4 (July –Sept. 1932).
[3] "In a 'Sconset Bus."

CHAPTER V

Harry Crosby, Jean Cocteau, Dwight MacDonald, Eugene Jolas, Michael Gold, T. E. Lawrence, and others

I
HARRY CROSBY TO LINCOLN KIRSTEIN
10 May 1929

I enclose four photographs I took last week should they be of interest to the *Hound and Horn*. I have entitled this group Birds: 1929.[1]

I hope you received the Kay Boyle book we sent you.[2]

The Black Sun Press will also send you the Three Fragments from Work in Progress by James Joyce as soon as it is ready (about a month). I hope you will give it a review.[3]

Harry Crosby (1898–1929), writer and editor, founder with his wife, Caresse, of the Black Sun Press in Paris. He was assistant editor of the magazine *transition*.

[1] Three photographs entitled "Still Life" (the Parisian drug-store window referred to by Ezra Pound in his Letter 13), "Racing Car," and "Jockey" appeared in vol. 3, no. 2 (Jan.–March 1930). The photograph "Birds" was not printed.

[2] Kay Boyle's book *Wedding Day and Other Stories* was not reviewed by the *Hound and Horn*.

[3] Joyce's *Work in Progress* (the title of *Finnegans Wake* until its publication in 1939) was not reviewed in *Hound and Horn*.

2   JEAN COCTEAU TO
LINCOLN KIRSTEIN
1929

Cher Monsieur
ou cher ami
C'est en ami que je veux vous répondre. Le ton de votre lettre me
renseigne sur la gravité de votre travail. Sachez donc que j'approuve
d'avance tout ce que vous jugerez bien et que je vous aiderai dans la
mesure de mes forces.

Votre
Je n'aiderai jamais une entreprise qui me croirait un homme mo-
derne, fréquetant les bars etc. . . .

Jean Cocteau (1889–1963), French poet, playwright, artist, designer, and pro-
ducer for stage and screen.

3   LINCOLN KIRSTEIN TO
JEAN COCTEAU
24 December 1929

Dear M. Cocteau:
It was so kind of you to answer my letter. We are so very anxious to
publish "Orphée" as soon as we can that we want to rush through
whatever business details are necessary. . . .
What are your ideas on the subject? Could you let us know as soon
as you possibly could. We are sending you the translation, written by a
young man whose knowledge of vernacular French is such that ensures
a close but vivid transcription of your original ideas. Of course, there
will be several details to which I am sure you will object. I don't know
how you feel about retaining the original French in the matter of the
pun "merde." As far as I can see, the way he has done it is the only way
that will give any idea of the original without explaining it away.
I suppose you have too little time for writing letters, but should you
ever feel like it, perhaps you would tell me what has become of the
dancers in the Russian Ballet. Of Nemtchinova, Lifar, Woizikowsky,

and Doubrovska. I happened to wander in to the Church of St. Georgio dei Greci last summer on the day of Diaghileff's funeral, and in the days following strayed by chance out to Malcontenta. Finding myself in that beautiful empty palladian house looking at the frescos, suddenly appeared out of nowhere a whole troupe of the dancers, silent and grave and completely remote from reality. I have often wondered who owned the house and what brought them there. Massine,[1] as you probably know, dances in the largest movie theatre in New York. He has an enormous and competent ballet but is completely suffocated in the wretched taste of his directors.

[1] Leonid Massine (1895–1979), Russian-born choreographer.

4   DWIGHT MACDONALD TO
     LINCOLN KIRSTEIN
     29 December 1929

Dear Lincoln:

I am enjoying THE HOUND & HORN, especially such fine things as Foster Damon's essay on "Ulysses" and William Carlos Williams' "Rain".[1] Your essays on humanism leave me yawning, nor can I see much vitality in the poetry of Dudley Fitts. But on the whole, you put out a good sheet. As you can see by the letterhead, I am emulating you in a modest way. I'm sending you a copy of the first number, from which you can form your own opinions.[2] If you have any advice as to how to run a magazine, please let me have it by all means. Our big problem is what to do with subscriptions: buy a file or keep them, as at present, in an old cake box?

I hope you'll like the magazine well enough to take out a subscription. If you're interested in my own writings, you will see plenty of them in the pages of THE MISCELLANY. And when you come to New York, my invitation for lunch is still open.

Dwight MacDonald (*b.* 1906) worked as a staff writer for *Fortune* magazine from 1929 to 1936 and as an editor for *Partisan Review*, 1938–1943. He was editor and writer of his own magazine, *Politics*, from 1944 to 1949, wrote for the *New Yorker* magazine, and was film critic and political columnist for *Esquire* magazine.

[1] These works were published in vol. 3, no. 1 (Oct.–Dec. 1929).
[2] Published bimonthly from March 1930 to March 1931, *Miscellany* was edited by Frederick Dupee, Geoffrey T. Hellman, Dwight MacDonald, and George L. Kingsland Morris. It published the poetry of Yvor Winters, William Carlos Williams, Conrad Aiken, and others; and criticism by Dwight MacDonald, Frederick Dupee, and George L. Kingsland Morris.

5   EUGENE JOLAS TO ALAN STROOCK
5 July 1930

Dear Mr. Stroock:

I was very happy to receive your letter, and I thank you sincerely for the kind things you say about Transition. If I had had an inkling that you were interested in our subscription list, it would have given me great pleasure to let you have it. Unfortunately, however, I have already promised it, and naturally I cannot now go back on my word.

I followed the *Hound and Horn* with deep interest and the excellence of its ideological direction and its presentation is most stimulating. The death of *transition* leaves me relieved of a terrific burden, to be sure; whether the effect of its offensive will show itself I don't know, but the very high quality of your own explorations gives me hope that the battle is not lost in America. I wish you success. I shall continue to follow your magazine which seems to me to attack problems maturely and—though I certainly disagree with certain of your contributors—sanely.

Eugene Jolas, with Elliot Paul, was editor and founder of *transition*, published monthly from April 1927 to Spring 1938 with a two-year suspension between Summer 1930 and March 1932.

6   BERNARD BANDLER TO LOUIS ZUKOFSKY
8 December 1930

Dear Mr. Zukofsky,

I am returning your review of Pound's "Cantos" because I think it is, for the purposes of The HOUND & HORN, only a partial review. You

have obviously accomplished all you proposed doing; you have eluci-
dated Pound and interpreted him; you have seen him completely from
within; you have not, so far as I can see, attempted to estimate him
from without, and to judge him from what I understand of your theory,
you would probably contend that the judgement is impossible since
"Of a world no synopsis is possible except if it be connected with a
theologian's superimposed story upon it," and if one cannot describe a
world it is obviously impossible to judge it.[1]

We are publishing your "Note on Williams" and your poem, "Au-
bade 1925" in the Winter issue.[2]

Louis Zukofsky (1904–1978), poet and author.

[1] Published in vol. 4, no. 2 (Jan.–March 1931).

7   LINCOLN KIRSTEIN TO
JAMES JOYCE
5 June 1931

Dear Mr. Joyce:
When Mr. Bandler was in Paris last summer, you told him, I be-
lieve, that you would let us have whatever further installments of WORK
IN PROGRESS that you would now care to see in print. I hope you are
still of that mind as naturally we are most anxious to publish anything
you care to send us. Our rates are $3.50 a page. Whatever you send
will certainly be printed, nor will there be any trouble about the cen-
sor. All proofs will be sent back for your correction as often as you
wish. August fifteenth is our next date for going to press, but that is
probably too soon for you to make arrangements for this issue. We are
writing Miss Beach by the same mail.

While of course the WORK IN PROGRESS has appeared more or less
widely in England and on the Continent, I feel sure that so many
American readers will greatly value its publication in America, and I
hope I am not too forward in saying that the *Hound and Horn* offers as
fair a public as any other on this side of the water.

The only piece by James Joyce (1882–1941) to appear in *Hound and Horn* was
"From a Banned Writer to a Banned Singer," vol. 5, no. 4 (Oct.–Dec. 1932). In the

form of a letter to Mr. Sullivan of the Paris Opera, Mr. Joyce gives his impression of his friend in several of his leading roles: "Many competent critics regard Mr. Sullivan as the most extraordinary dramatic tenor that Europe has listened to for the last half century." The letter had first appeared in *New Statesman and Nation* (London) with an introductory note on 27 Feb. 1932. The note stated, "Mr. Joyce complains that Mr. Sullivan is 'banned' or at least unknown in England. The reflections written here were sent in a letter to Mr. Sullivan by Mr. Joyce after an occasion on which the singer was carried shoulder high by his Marseilles admirers after an astonishing performance in *Guillaume Tell*. 'Just out of kerryosity howlike is a Sullivan? It has the forte-faccia of a Markus Brutas, the wingthud of a spreadeagle, the body uniformed of a metro-policeman with the brass feet of a collared grand. It cresces up in Aquilone but diminuends austrowards. It was last seen and heard of by some macgilliccuddies above a lonely cloud of their reeks, duskening the greylight as it flew, its cry echechohoing among the anfractuosities: *pour la derniere fois!* The blackbulled ones, stampeding, drew in their horns, all appailed and much upset, which explaints the guttermilk on their overcoats.'"

8   LINCOLN KIRSTEIN TO LEWIS MUMFORD
30 June 1931

Dear Mr. Mumford:

I am taking the liberty of writing to you because I feel that we have certain interests in common. I have noticed in publishers' announcements that you are about to publish a book on *Brown Decades*. For the last year I have been collecting photographs of American architecture in the period 1830–1865. I believe that this comes before the times of your investigation, but perhaps you would be interested in seeing my photographs. The work itself has been done by a very able photographer, Mr. Walker Evans. The examples, generally speaking, are from Boston, Salem, West Massachusetts, and Connecticut. If you will be interested in seeing any of these Victorian houses, I'll be very pleased to show them to you.

Lewis Mumford (*b.* 1895), author. Although Mumford replied favorably to Kirstein's letter, there is no record of any further correspondence between the two.

9   LINCOLN KIRSTEIN TO
     JOHN BROOKS WHEELWRIGHT
     7 October 1931

Dear Jack:

I am sending you under separate cover *The Brown Decades*. I don't
want you to make a chronicle out of this. I want it to be a book review.
I think that he had a magnificent chance and muffed it. The whole
book is really an outline. I think he bungles his generalities very badly.

He gives no coherent picture and he includes a kind of bastardized
history of art in this country up to the present day, which seems to me
completely irrelevant. I think you might have a detailed review of it at
not too great a length because I don't think the book warrants it, but I
would mention all our initial period stuff which laid the background
for the Brown Decades which he [*illegible*], I would leave the chronicle
material for the general essays on our period.[1]

Walker Evans has got some amazing new photographs of New
Bedford, Martha's Vineyard and New York State. We are going to get
some more soon. I'm to be up in Boston the weekend of the twentieth.

John Brooks Wheelwright (1897–1940), poet and architect, was a great influence
on Kirstein, who described him to me as an "Anglo-Catholic-crypto-Communist."

[1] Wheelwright reviewed *Brown Decades* by Lewis Mumford in vol. 5, no. 2 (Jan.–
March 1932), and although he credited Mumford with amassing a general history
of architecture, he stated that he made many incorrect assertions in his book and
was therefore misleading to students of the subject. "He resembles a traveller to
London who would visit a public collection of pictures with divided mind and dis-
tracted interest, torn between the precious colored surfaces and the reflections on
the protecting glass which covered them, of other visitors to the gallery."

10   LINCOLN KIRSTEIN TO
      JOHN WALKER
      14 December 1931

Dear Johnny:

Thank you very much for your series of post cards. We are going
ahead with our plans for our memorial to Henry James and we would
greatly appreciate whatever cooperation you give us. I do hope Mrs.

Wharton will be interested in doing something. I am sure that after seeing our next number even Berenson will revise his opinion of the magazine. Please do continue to speak to him about how much he disliked Henry James. I'd like to know for what reasons, how James affected him.

The Harvard Society for Contemporary Art may go on for another year what with sudden enthusiasm from everybody on its threatened demise. The times are inconceivably bad here. Most of our rich friends had a great deal of stock in the New York Central which passed their dividends this year for the first time in the history of the road.

I seriously warn you that I will curse with bell, book and candle and every borrowed paraphernalia of hell that I can appropriate if you don't fulfill your moral obligations to posterity in the position in which you find yourself. It is inconceivably selfish, unimaginative and stupid of you to do nothing with the material that you have at hand. Not only will it be an enormous source of personal regret to you that you will have wasted your time when you could have spent it to such brilliant advantage, but it will also incapacitate you for any real future activity or use. There is no use to joke about it. Please, please, for your own sake at least, pick the brains of everyone and particularly B. B. This is really a sacred trust.

Rivera is here in New York. I went up and spent a morning with him. He strikes me as an able follower of the Giotteschi,[1] and rather little else. I think his big one-man show will give him far too much eminence. Noguchi[2] came back from Japan with a lot of Kakemonos that he had drawn in india ink on silk, a combination of Picasso and the East, and very good, too, beautifully framed with ivory stretchers and mounted on brocade. He has also done a lot of terra cotta figures and wants to return to the East to live for good. My novel appears in February. The Mellon purchases were announced formally.[3] Rockefeller has given a huge mediaeval museum to the City of New York. He is going to rebuild The Cloisters in the shape of an abbey. They are getting a lot of second-rate people, like Manship and Milles[4] to do the sculpture of Radio City, which I suppose was inevitable. I am lecturing for John Brown in Providence on Matisse, and I will compare him to Boucher[5] which ought to irritate everybody. The Fogg Museum seems to be pretty well off, considering the bad year. At least there is no cutting down of wages. Phil Hofer[6] is being mentioned as the successor of Belle Green.[7] Harry Francis[8] wanted Agnes[9] to get the job. She would be perfect for it except for social reasons I suppose, alas. Hershey[10] is supposedly the new director of the Metropolitan, although he swears he has not heard from them at all. People say P. J.[11] was asked, knowing very well he would refuse, as a compliment. Hendy[12] was severely attacked for his catalogue and for buying those modern pictures. Did I tell you that his Matisse and his Braque are very fine although he doesn't dare hang them. I saw a very fine late Titian that Steinmayer had here, St. Jerome in a red cloak. There is also a magnificent 17th century picture at Brummer's? called Orazio Gentileschi, the finest and largest thing like it, I know.[13] I hope Chick Austin[14] will buy it for Hartford. Please write me at once and let me know you are not going to hell, which you surely will if you are not careful.

John Walker (*b.* 1906) was director of the National Gallery of Art in Washington, D.C., and is now retired. After graduating from Harvard in 1930, he became assistant to Bernard Berenson in Italy for two years. Berenson (1865–1959) was the noted art critic and authority on Renaissance art.

[1] The followers of Giotto di Bondoni (1276?–1337?), considered by many to be the greatest Italian painter of the early Renaissance, best known for his frescoes of the lives of Saint Francis, the Virgin Mary, and Jesus.

[2] Isamu Noguchi (*b.* 1904), American sculptor.

[3] The Mellon purchases could have been purchases from the Hermitage in Leningrad, as mentioned in a story in the *New York Times* of that date.

[4] Paul Manship (1885–1966), American sculptor. One of his best known works is "Prometheus" in Rockefeller Center, New York. Carl Milles (1875–1955), Swedish-American sculptor.

[5] Francois Boucher (1703–1770), the most prominent painter of Rococo.

[6] Phillip Hofer (*b.* 1898) was advisor to the Spencer collection of the New York Public Library from 1929 to 1934, assistant director of the Morgan Library from 1934 to 1937, and founder and curator of the department of printing and graphic arts at the Harvard Library from 1938 to 1967. He was also assistant dean of the Harvard Business School from 1942 to 1944.

[7] Belle da Costa Greene (1883–1950), library director and bibliographer, was director of the Morgan Library from 1924 to 1948.

[8] Henry Sayles Francis (*b.* 1902) was curator of paintings, prints, and drawings at the Cleveland Museum of Art from 1931 to 1967.

[9] Agnes Mongan (*b.* 1905) is curator-emerita of prints and drawings at the Fogg Art Museum, Harvard University.

[10] Possibly Samuel F. Hershey (*b.* 1904), educator, designer, and painter.

[11] Professor Paul J. Sachs, of Harvard University.

[12] Sir Philip Hendy (*b.* 1900), curator of paintings at the Museum of Fine Arts in

Boston from 1930 to 1933 and director of the National Gallery in London from 1946 to 1967.

[13] Steinmayer, Brummer's—Manhattan art dealers.

[14] A. Everett Austin, director of the Wadsworth Atheneum in Hartford, Conn., and later director of the Ringling Museum in Sarasota, Fla.

11   LINCOLN KIRSTEIN
TO LUCY PORTER
21 December 1931

Dear Mrs. Porter:

Thank you very much for your letter of December 4th, from Glenveagh Castle, answering my letter about the *Hound and Horn*. You say that you feel "that if a magazine has money to sustain an office on the most expensive street in the world, it can easily continue without feeling the loss of my withdrawal." I apologize for the tone of my letter to you, I did not mean to imply that my letter should read as an appeal for charity. I merely had thought you would continue to be interested in the work of many people whom you have known.

Since your letter suggests that you are interested in what we are trying to do and are only ceasing your subscription because you wish to curtail your expenses, will you allow us to continue our extravagance in offering you a complimentary subscription?

12   BERNARD BANDLER TO
J. ROBERT OPPENHEIMER
10 February 1930

Dear Robert:

I hope you are well. I haven't heard from you in reply to my last two or three notes and I trust it hasn't been because of illness.

As a querulous editor, may I ask when I can expect your paper on Whitehead.[1] I, myself, haven't tackled "Process and Reality"; it looks so very formidable that I am rather frightened at the task.

The subject of this letter is to know whether you are interested in reviewing two volumes called "The Cult of Beauty in Charles Baude-laire," by a man called S. Rhodes, published in this country. I haven't done more than glance through the two volumes but the author not only has read Baudelaire but Renouvier, Gide, Proust, Maurras, Du-Bois, et cetera, so the books should be exceedingly good. I should like immensely to have you review them, and if you are pressed for work, you could let the two volumes carry over for three or four months, if you wish. Do let me hear from you soon.

J. Robert Oppenheimer (1904–1967), the nuclear physicist, was also a cultivated scholar, a humanist, and a linguist of eight tongues.

[1] The article referred to in this letter was to be on the philosopher Alfred Whitehead but was not published, nor was the review of Father D'Arcy, mentioned in Letter 15. Oppenheimer contributed a poem, "Crossing," to vol. 1, no. 4 (July–Sept. 1930), and his review of S. Rhodes's book *The Cult of Beauty in Charles Baudelaire* appeared in vol. 3, no. 4 (July–Sept. 1930).

13 J. ROBERT OPPENHEIMER
TO BERNARD BANDLER
29 [?] February [1930]

Dear Bernard

Thanks very much for the good and sweetly long-suffering note. I had hoped to get the article to you for the current issue; my father's illness, my own, and innumerable chores have made me postpone it. But it will get to you; it will get to you surely by July first, and if possible before that; it should be called a "Note on Physical Science." I grow, I am afraid, more and more distrustful of the highbrow review (tan d'emprakton antlei mechanan); and the contemplation of this very small note that I have promised to you inspires an unmistakable nausea; but I shall husband the high moments, and get it done; and I beg you only to extend your miraculous indulgence.

Father D'Arcy's book I shall be delighted to review. You will have the review for your next issue.

Do you know Sanskrit, Bernard? It is a fine language, easily eclipsing even Greek in formal beauty. The literature promises unending and wonderful rewards. At least for the Bhagavad Gita the translations are shadows.

If ever you should come west, do let me see you. I shall be in Pasadena until the middle of June; and for the summer at Cowles.

Every greeting

14   BERNARD BANDLER TO
      J. ROBERT OPPENHEIMER
      29 March 1932

Dear Robert,

. . . Do you think by any chance you can get to Clarkesville, Tenn. for the first week in June? Tate, Warren, Davidson and Company are inviting a number of people, Fergusson, Mayor, Kirstein, Parkes, Winters, Karlin and myself, to visit them. We will be devoted to no greater cause than that of seeing each other and having a chance to talk together. It will be no American Pontigny, no prepared topics and papers, and no great high seriousness. But it might prove, if sufficiently informal, great fun and it might be the beginning of similar meetings in the future. If you think you can make it, or if you cannot, will you please let me know at once? Tate, as host, has naturally preparations to make and the meeting will not come off at all unless enough of us are willing to go down.

I envy you Sanskrit. At present I am confined to Hebrew. Reading the Prophets closely only increases the distance between us and them, until they seem a new and not over interesting species. I have been reading Aristotle and St. Thomas' Commentaries on him, which is far more instructive. It is rather late in the day to discover that St. Thomas had a great mind. Next week I shall write you about the beauties of Shakespeare and of the Acropolis.

I hope your father is well and your own health better.

About this letter, Bernard Bandler wrote me 10 March 1976: "In 1929 Charles DuBos took me to Pontigny for a week where European intellectuals had been meeting yearly. Among those present were Curtius from Germany, Roger Martin duGard who had recently won the Nobel Prize, and a young man . . . by the name of André Malraux. I was greatly impressed by the brilliance of the performances (and they were performances) and thought wouldn't it be wonderful if we had something like that in the United States."

15 JOHN BROOKS WHEELWRIGHT
    TO LINCOLN KIRSTEIN
    18 April 1932

Dear Lincoln:

I finished *Flesh is Heir* some time ago and have been thinking it
over. I think it shows rather more than "promise" for a first novel. As
each episode gets under way, you make the situation unusually clear,
but I think the trick of ending on an unresolved chord is repeated too
often, and each time it is repeated it tends to cloud the clarity of what
has come before. At least in retrospect. I have not read the book a sec-
ond time. Of course it is not a novel, which is no fault of its form. The
fault lies in your portrayal of Roger Baum. The author and the hero are
not sufficiently identified or sufficiently separated. The author is a very
keen young man. The hero is rather a stupid one. The author is very
active, the hero is supine. Yet it is all shown from the hero's point of
view. Proust makes something of the same mistake. Dickens in David
Copperfield did not. This is the sort of thing which I dare say happens
in first novels. It would have been wiser for you, therefore, to have
omitted the character of Roger completely by giving him a different
name in each chapter with the consequent adjustments. I don't think
you made much out of "the Venice episode," at least not in comparison
to D'Annunzio's *Il Fuoco*. All the other incidents are most amusing
with a comic-strip brutality. It's a pity Mina was disturbed by her
chapter but I dare say she is over it now.[1] It seems to me Pinckney
was an unfortunate name to choose for the Bostonian. Pinckney is a
Charleston, South Carolina name. Pinckney Street was named for a
southerner who was Minister to Great Britain and did the Yankees
a trade favor. It seems to me that you give the impression that boys are
elected to the Dicky in their freshmen year. These two points are mere
carelessness on your part. The other faults in the book have at least the
virtue of resulting from your effort to do something more than write a
collection of short stories. I don't think you have succeeded, but for
many consecutive pages together the book is very good reading in-
deed. Thank you very much for sending it to me.

What happened to my review of Hitchcock and Johnson?[2] Are you

running it next time? If so, please send it back to me first as I must
shorten the part about Howe's tenement house. Do you like the article
on American Primitives?

P.S. Philip Johnson wants an article by me for *Shelter*. I have sent
him my dope about the Fuller House and suggested to him that you
might let him have Walker Evans' photographs for illustration. The
snap-shots that you took are very much better than this. Please let him
reproduce them if he likes my article enough to publish it. *Shelter* is a
very good name. I look forward to seeing the first number and to writ-
ing for it.

[1] Mina Curtiss, Lincoln Kirstein's sister, on whose life some of the events chronicled
in *Flesh is Heir* were allegedly patterned.
[2] An essay "The International Style Architecture since 1922" (Henry-Russell
Hitchcock and Philip Johnson), vol. 5, no. 2 (Jan.–March 1932).

16   LINCOLN KIRSTEIN
TO JAMES CAGNEY
26 August 1932

Dear Jim Cagney,

I finally sent you that book called *The Real McCoy*, which I keep
constantly talking about. Maybe I am all wrong, but I think there is a
lot of swell stuff in it. If by any remote chance you have any further
interest in the subject, I have got a whole library of rum-running
documents.

By this time I hope to God you are in front of a camera. It was swell
seeing you in New York. I hope some time we can have some beer.

About the actor, James Cagney (*b.* 1904), in *The New York City Ballet*, Lincoln
Kirstein writes, "Excited by Cagney's films, I wrote an essay for *Hound and Horn*,
Cagney responded by coming to watch a ballet class; he had been trained as a
dancer. I had notions as to which roles he should appropriate—John Paul Jones
(following Melville's *Israel Potter*), Billy the Kid, Benvenuto Cellini, Studs Loni-
gan" (p. 41).

17   LINCOLN KIRSTEIN
                TO JAMES CAGNEY
                27 December 1932

Dear Mr. Cagney:
    I am sending you something which might interest you. You ex-
pressed an interest in the life of John Paul Jones. I have recently had
reason to be working on some material on Herman Melville, the au-
thor of *Moby Dick*. He wrote a book called *Israel Potter*, which deals a
good deal with Jones, and the enclosed pages combine a considerable
amount of source material. *Israel Potter* itself contains a lot of fine back-
ground for possible scenarios, and if you ever think seriously of doing
anything about it, I'd recommend it.

18   EDITORS OF *HOUND & HORN*
                TO EDITORS OF *NEW REPUBLIC*
                9 June 1932

Dear Sirs:
    Surely there is no need to point out that Comrade Hicks' remarks
about the leisure class apply to Homer, Dante, Racine, Shakespeare,
Goethe, etc. We have no objection to being exiled in such company,
but the question arises: Where does that leave Mr. Hicks? The ques-
tion is of no interest, except that Mr. Hicks represents a widely held
point of view, (perhaps the notion that reading Marx is a more practi-
cal thing for an American to do than reading Aristotle) shared by
many of the contributors to The *New Republic*, such as Mr. Wilson
and Mr. Arvin and by The *New Masses*, and by American Communist
well-wishers. If Mr. Hicks were able to think out the implications of
his point of view this is what he would say.
    "I have college degrees, I must earn my living, and I have a job as a
teacher of literature. But literature means nothing to me, nor does
painting, music, science, philosophy, or any disinterested study. All
these activities which civilized people throughout all history pursued
for their own sake and for enjoyment have no justification. Life is se-
rious: it is filled with other people's pain, poverty and misfortunes. It is

pure self-indulgence for anyone to do any work which is not directed to alleviating the hardships of mankind, i.e., the proletariat. It is *worse* than self-indulgence; people who believe that they should live their own lives and strive for what goods and perfection are open to them are 'parasites or worse'. All work must stop, all individuality must perish, and all pleasures must be renounced until Mr. Hicks has made the miners in Kentucky, the coolies in China and the 'untouchables' in India contented. We and the miners are naturally good and comradely; the evil of human nature is concentrated in capitalists; and once their society is destroyed earth will be a paradise. Then arts and letters and science will flourish, and the wolf and the lamb will lie down together."

It is quite intelligible that people who have nothing and see no prospect of improving their fortunes should want to destroy a society. (We are unwilling to believe that Mr. Hicks is a member of this class). But let him reflect that it would be as foolish for himself to welcome communism, who has by his own admission an interest in culture, as it would be for a *Roman* school teacher to hail Attila at his approach as the heir and restorer of the glories of Greece.

But more seriously, we should like to point out that an alternative point of view is possible: We have two reasons for keeping clear of the class struggle:— 1. Intellectual freedom has as much to suffer from extreme fascism as from extreme communism. 2. We stick to what we know a little about, which is philosophy, art and literature. We do not go into politics and suggest tearing down present abuses because we have no ideas for better substitutes. Knowing our ignorance, we have studied the *New Masses* and the *New Republic* in order to discover what plan the liberal thought of this country has evolved to replace the present muddle, and we have so far discovered nothing thoroughly thought out or constructive in anything more than minor details. We believe that minding one's own business can often be of more use than missionary preaching, and that a man like Homer, who loved and pursued nothing but his art, brought deeper consolation to old and young, rich man and poor man, than a man like Rousseau, who professed to serve humanity directly.

This letter was the final rejoinder in the exchange between Granville Hicks and the *Hound and Horn* editors—Bernard Bandler, Lincoln Kirstein, and A. Hyatt Mayor—which had begun as an attack on the magazine as a publication of "leisure-class editors for leisure-class readers" ("Art and the Leisure Class," *New Republic*, 13 July 1932, p. 238). Hicks incorporated his attack in a review of Kirstein's novel *Flesh is Heir*. See the Introduction as well as Chap. III, Letter 11, n. 2.

19 MICHAEL GOLD TO LINCOLN KIRSTEIN
[Undated]

Dear Kirstein:

I thought I'd try out this roughhouse piece on your sedate quarterly—It's part of a novel on unemployment I'm doing.

If you don't think it suitable send it back c/o *New Masses*—63 W. 15th. If by accident you like it let me know at Ervinna, Pa.—will you?

—I liked yr. last issue—you are getting on to some living issues—glad to see you agree on Steffens.[1]

Michael Gold (1893–1967) was editor of *New Masses* from 1928 to 1932 and writer of proletarian literature. This letter refers to a story, "'Arfa Maroo'; from Shantytown Sketches," which first appeared in a *Daily Worker* column (17 Oct. 1933) and was later reprinted in Gold's anthology *Change the World* under the title "Night in a Hooverville." In *Mike Gold: A Literary Anthology* (New York: International Publishers, 1972), editor Michael Folsom writes that the "shantytown sketches were to have been a novel about life among the desperately unemployed in the impromptu squatter communities they established in the early Depression" (p. 216). Nothing by Gold was published in the *Hound and Horn*.

[1] In his review of the *Autobiography of Lincoln Steffens*, vol. 5, no. 1 (Oct.–Dec. 1931), Kirstein had written of the sense of confusion present in "The American Liberal Soul," attributing its cause ultimately to progressive education. See Chap. VI, Letter 5, n. 2.

20 MICHAEL GOLD TO LINCOLN KIRSTEIN
[Undated]

Dear Lincoln Kirstein:

I was afraid the other story was a little too rough or something for *Hound and Horn*. I know you are not anti-proletarian, and I know editors have a right to their taste. But I disagree when you say I can get this stuff printed anywhere. The fact is, I have been experimenting with the old proletarian will-o-the-wisp—the mass novel, and it's damn hard to do. Some of your esthetes ought to examine this problem of technique, which even the Russian critics have not yet settled. "Even a Shakespeare would find it impossible to describe the masses." Dos Passos has made about the only start in this country, and it's not quite successful.

—I enclose another story that started out to do the same job. Hope you like it better.

There really is no place to print such things except four or five magazines in this country, of which yours is one. *transition* was interesting because it left the doors wide open for new if crude and groping attempts in some new world.

However, have decided to drop the mass novel for a while—it's too tough—and try for a good-old fashioned story about two specific people—Communists, but individuals. Which is easier.

Good Luck

21   A. HYATT MAYOR TO LINCOLN KIRSTEIN
[Undated]

Parts of this are quite good enough to be printed, good enough in style, that is,—simple and concrete. But the point is not that, but this; do you want to give the H&H a party political bias? Do you want to enter the field already covered by the *New Masses*, the *New Republic* etc.? I, personally, would be very sorry to see the H&H lose its present character, but that is not for me to decide. This story is for the *New Masses* or for the *New Republic*, but so long as we keep our literary and philosophical character (and I think our detachment is our real virtue and value to this time when detachment has almost perished from the world) if we are to keep all this, then Michael Gold is not for us, and should be told so, with the above reasons. He writes like a very sensible man, and I am sure would understand. It is all a matter of what field we must rule out in order to concentrate on others, without which concentration we are nothing.

Through all this of course you will see my dislike for propaganda when it masquerades as fiction, for it produces usually, as here, mere anecdotes, even if they are well told anecdotes.

22   T. E. LAWRENCE
         TO LINCOLN KIRSTEIN
            12 April 1934

Dear Kirstein

Your letter of last December has been troubling me, for you made it hard to answer, and yet I have to answer it. See now, there are, I think, in the world no men very different from ourselves. I walk the streets of an evening, or work in our R.A.F. camps all day, and by measuring myself against these airmen or passers-by I know that I am just an average chap. You write as though there were degrees, or distinctions. I see likenesses, instead.

You get your idea from having read the *Seven Pillars* and the *Mint*, apparently. Few people have read the *Mint*, but many the *Seven Pillars*.[1] If they all got this same disproportioned view of myself I would believe that there was some falsity of scale or attitude of what I had put down. But these others only find the books natural. I did not mean them to transcend myself, to shout. I hope they do not. Probably they happen upon an unguarded angle of yourself, and seem to you more significant than is their truth. I have found that in myself. Sometimes a book that is not exceptional to others will mean a great deal to me. From which you should deduce not any superabundance in its writer, but a poverty (in that point) within yourself.

How pompous a paragraph I have written; but you scare me, rather, with your over-impression. Please come and see me, if you get to England again; and then you will see I am your own size—and everybody else's. A very big man will be six feet six; a very small one five feet. Human differences are negligible, except in human eyes.

Pompous again. I am glad you like Melville. He is not enough praised by Americans. Nijinski I saw dance once only, across the whole width of a full London theatre. It was more than beauty, but not like a man. I suppose if I had seen him off the stage he would have been normal. If we meet let us talk a little upon why some people are greater than their work, and others less. I puzzle myself often over that. And why did you so much like the *Mint*, which is a close photograph of our life in camp?

Now for Gurdjieff.[2] I had read some of his work (in French) a long while ago; not this which you have sent me, but stuff as real. It was closer-knit, too, as prose and as argument. I like it—as I like this *Herald of Coming Good*—but find myself a little to one side, facing perhaps the same question, but from another angle. Perhaps I am English or European, whereas Gurdjieff and yourself are not. Yet Katherine Mansfield. . . . but wasn't she a New Zealander? I do not know, but Russia, and its books and movements fail to strike me directly. Strange, interesting, moving—but there is no impact, no actuality. I find a common tint or tone or texture in all Russian work, and it all misses me in the end, however I like it for the moment.

"Man of action" you call me, in the last words of your letter "who has done what he chose to his full extent." Do, for heaven's sake, travel down to where I am next time you reach England, and put these ideas straight. We are all poor silly things trying to keep our feet in the swirl. Even if we succeed, it is not more than a static performance, nor deserving more applause. So I beg you to see me, and disabuse yourself of an illusion. Or do I take a single letter too seriously?

Yours somewhat bewildered,[3]

T. E. Lawrence (1888–1935), British soldier and author, known throughout the world as Lawrence of Arabia, was one of the most idolized of heroes in the twenties and thirties. In *The New York City Ballet* Lincoln Kirstein wrote, "Much moved by the British tradition of illegitimate or extralegal activity and feudal responsibility, I wrote a short essay on Lawrence's life following the Arab revolt [18 April 1934, the *New Republic*] and received a reply from him in his retirement." Embittered by the political stance taken by England and France toward the Arab countries after the war, Lawrence preferred to live in obscurity, assuming the name T. E. Shaw in 1927.

[1] *Seven Pillars of Wisdom* (privately printed in 1925, published in 1935) is Lawrence's classic account of his wartime experiences. *The Mint*, an account of his service in the Royal Air Force, at his request was not published until 1955.

[2] George Ivanovitch Gurdjieff (1866–1949), Armenian founder of a movement

aimed to bring peace of mind and self-control to its followers. Profoundly affected by
the teachings of Gurdjieff, Lincoln Kirstein wrote in the introduction to his book
Nijinsky Dancing (1975), "As in everything I do whatever is valid springs from the
person and ideas of G. I. Gurdjieff."
³ This letter and the following one are signed with Lawrence's assumed name,
T. E. Shaw.

23   **T. E. LAWRENCE TO
         LINCOLN KIRSTEIN**
            11 May 1934

Dear L. K.

Two letters each, I think. So I'll reply to yours at once.

I suppose I shouldn't have considered Gurdjieff as a writer at all:
but fellows who try to write get into that awful habit of running their
professional slide-rule over everything printed that comes in their way.
When I pick up a book the final consideration is how it's done. Con-
tents only come second! Sorry. Of course the man is dreadfully in ear-
nest, and only cared for the meaning of what he said.

Your review of Liddell-Hart's book¹ does, as you said, succinctly
convey your position. I'm rather regretting L-H's surrender to my
"charm." Had he maintained his critical distance and examined my
war-time strategy and tactics with a cool head, the results would have
been interesting—to me, at any rate! He is a good military thinker.
But instead there comes only Panegyric III, and I'm rather sick of my
virtues. The worst of being oneself is that one knows all one's vices,
too! And honestly it isn't fair to keep on harping on the credit side.

I suggested a meeting out of sheer altruism. If we ever come to-
gether you will see that I am human. There ain't any such supercrea-
tures as you would fain see: or if there are, I haven't been lucky enough
to meet one.

Your favorable judgment of the *Mint* would give me unqualified de-
light, had you flavoured your remarks upon me with some salt. I took a
lot of trouble, in writing the *Mint*, to ram it full of all the feeling I could
muster. The R.A.F. was a huge and gorgeous subject. Oh, I meant to
make a whale of a book. What came into being was hardly its introduc-
tion—and now I don't feel that I'll ever write anything again. It is hard

to have learnt so hard how to write—and then to have nothing to write about.

Don't forget to let me know if you do ever get across. Ede or Garnett[2] will know my address. A meeting will be good for you.

[1] *Colonel Lawrence: The Man behind the Legend* by Basil Henry Liddell-Hart (New York: Dodd, Mead, 1934), reviewed by Kirstein in the *New Republic*, 18 April 1934.
[2] H. S. Ede, author of *Savage Messiah*, a biography of the sculptor Henri Gaudier-Brzeska; David Garnett, British writer and the editor of the *Collected Letters of T. E. Lawrence*.

24   LINCOLN KIRSTEIN
TO VIRGIL THOMSON
17 May 1933

Dear Virgil:

Thank you ever so much for your letter. Don't hurry too much about your French letter or your Paris letter for the *Hound and Horn*. We have already gone to press, and the letter can't be published until next Fall. I expect to get to Paris around the tenth. If by any chance you hear that the Ballet is to be postponed again until the fifteenth, I wish you could drop me a note, because I have a lot of business here that I ought to stick to, but which I would throw up to come over. I went up to Hartford and had a long serious talk with Chick about the possibility of a ballet next year, that is, about the ballet demonstration that I spoke to you about and which I will talk to you more about when I see you.[1]

We are giving *Le Sang d'un Poète* tonight with gratifying enthusiasm. Haggin liked you too.[2]

Chick's little auditorium will really be sweet and very neat for the opera.[3] I wish you could get Kochno[4] to let you do an American Ballet for their tour, perhaps called *The Release of Richmond*—you know, negresses making preparations for a ball, the ball, trumpet calls to battle, farewells, and then the return of the soldiers more or less dead. It could be very pretty and not too damned American. That is, it seems to me an idiom which Russians can understand. I should imagine

Maurice⁵ doing a lovely Richmond ballroom, or an Alabama ballroom, or what have you.

I hope to see you very soon.

Virgil Thomson (*b.* 1896), American composer, critic, instrumentalist, and conductor, whose collaboration with Gertrude Stein on *Four Saints in Three Acts* (1932) made him famous. Although nothing by Thomson was printed in *Hound and Horn*, he composed the score for *Filling Station*, a ballet commissioned in 1937 for Lincoln Kirstein's Ballet Caravan.

¹ A. Everett (Chick) Austin and Kirstein conceived the notion that the Wadsworth Atheneum museum would be the ideal home for a ballet company and a ballet school. However, Balanchine was not in America to "immure himself in Hartford," Conn., and the School of American Ballet opened in January 1934 at 637 Madison Avenue, New York City.
² B. H. Haggin, the music critic for the *New Republic*, wrote a music chronicle for *Hound and Horn* from January 1932, to the final issue, Summer 1934.
³ Gertrude Stein's *Four Saints in Three Acts*, for which Thomson wrote the music, was produced in Hartford in 1934.
⁴ Boris Kochno (*b.* 1903), régisseur of Diaghilev's Ballets Russes and later the Monte Carlo Ballet Russe.
⁵ Maurice Grosser (*b.* 1903), artist, author of the libretto for Gertrude Stein's *Four Saints in Three Acts* (1934).

25   JAMES LAUGHLIN IV
      TO A. HYATT MAYOR
      [Undated]

Dear Mr. Mayor:

My subscription has of course been forwarded; no one who knows what your work has been toward the mythical? "American Renaissance" could desert Bitch and Bugle. Some of us, who are very young ones, regret the policy of expansion; we felt at home with the aesthetic note. We like dividends but an NRA H & H is less welcome. *Story*¹ now must inevitably get the fine prose that once you printed. . . .

But beyond this, which is really little, we back H & H as it, the best, deserves.

                              Yr's

Further: could you without breach of anything tell me what Pound charges for a canto? I want to buy one—thanks.

James Laughlin (*b.* 1914) was at the time a Harvard undergraduate. He is today the publisher of New Directions Press.

[1] *Story*, a magazine that published only short stories. Begun in 1931 and edited by Whit Burnett (with Martha Foley from 1931 to 1941), it was important for encouraging the publication of talented unknown writers and fostering innovation in the short-story form.

26   LINCOLN KIRSTEIN TO
JAMES LAUGHLIN IV
5 *October 1933*

Dear Mr. Laughlin:

It's nice of you to resubscribe. God knows we need it.

Do you want to buy a new canto from Pound, or do you want to buy a copy of the old cantos? I daresay you could get a very nice medium-sized canto for about $49.50. Pound is terribly hard up and I seriously mean that should you really want to commission one, you could get it for nothing, except postage. Should you mean that you want to buy a copy of these cantos, they are published in this country for $3.50.

27   JAMES LAUGHLIN IV
TO LINCOLN KIRSTEIN
24 *October [1933]*

Dear Mr. Kirstein:

Thanks for your note which comes roundabout. I asked about the Pound cantos, as I wish to buy some of the juicier new ones: J P Morgan, Zaharoff, Mitteleuropa, etc., if they are not all tied up. I know he wants to sell them but I don't want to be stuck; he thinks I have money, which isn't so. The project is a part of the rejuvenation program for the old Harvard Advocate which has never recovered from what you did to it some years back; we hoped to get some circulation by importing talent from without-the-walls. I gather indirectly that you paid 350 for (was it?) three; I shouldn't want to give nearly as much. Si vedra. I shall have something for you to look at in the course of the winter. I liked ever so much Guérard's prose: I say the hell with Fitts; it is good writing.[1] My prose is fluid, as you know, but I seem to see the watch-works rather than the time-it-is.

Hope I shall see you in Boston this year. I have been sad to miss you several times.

[1] Laughlin refers to the *Hound and Horn* short-story contest, won by Albert Guérard for his story "Davos in Winter." Fitts preferred a story, "Break-Day," by J. Allan Conley.

28   LINCOLN KIRSTEIN TO JAMES LAUGHLIN IV
27 October 1933

Dear Mr. Laughlin:

As I remember, I paid Pound for three cantos, one hundred dollars. He would take the same now, or probably less. I am sorry to say that I don't think the last things are very good, but maybe you would be surprised. I hope so.

I'm glad you like Guérard, and if you are ever in New York, please come and see me.

29   KENNETH PATCHEN TO LINCOLN KIRSTEIN
[Undated]

Dear Lincoln Kirstein:

I am working in the Cambridge Rubber Co. my job is to unload drums and crude rubber from a conveyor two men to a drum; drums weigh 500 pounds. Thirty-five cents an hour 7:30 until 5.

What do you wish changed in the review.[1] Neil Wright objected to certain sections of it on the grounds that they were obscure. I shall write it accordingly to your suggestions. I am utterly done in at the close of each working day but in spite of this I shall write.

I am grateful to you for your kindness and interest; it helps like the devil at a time like this. Do you have any suggestions.

P.S. Later I shall repay you the ten. At the moment I cannot.

Kenneth Patchen (1911–1972), the poet and artist who pioneered the reading of poetry to the accompaniment of jazz in the 1950s.

[1] It is not known what review this refers to. None of Patchen's work was published in *Hound and Horn*.

30   KENNETH PATCHEN TO
       LINCOLN KIRSTEIN
       [Undated]

Dear Lincoln Kirstein:

I have a little attic room ($2.00 the week) and I am working away against time.

I like Boston very much. Harry Murray[1] hopes to get me placed somewhere soon.

I worked Monday of this week on a construction job in Belmont. The carpenters were to have begun work on the following day. Conrad Aiken encouraged me to go on in the development of the review-idea. He thought it good.

Please let me hear from you concerning it.

[1] Henry Alexander Murray (*b.* 1893), distinguished psychologist. He was a friend of Theodore Spencer, F. O. Matthiessen, and Maurice Firuski, who owned the Dunster House Bookshop where Richard Blackmur worked. In addition to his works on personality, Murray edited Herman Melville's *Pierre* (New York: Hendricks House, 1949; rpt. 1962).

CHAPTER VI
Allen Tate

ALLEN TATE TO
LINCOLN KIRSTEIN
22 January 1930

Dear Mr. Kirstein:

I should like very much to review Hart Crane's forthcoming book, *The Bridge*, and I should like to review it for the *Hound and Horn*.[1] The special edition of the Black Sun Press will arrive in this country in about a week, and the trade edition (Liveright) will appear in February. I could therefore have the review ready for your March number, if it will not go to press earlier, say, than the fifth of February. I have the proof of the book here, and could proceed immediately with the review.

Please let me congratulate you on taking Katherine Anne Porter's "Flowering Judas." I have read it in ms., and in my opinion it is the finest short story written by an American in years. Miss Porter is one of the few American writers of fiction who have a genuine style.

Allen Tate (1899–1979) was asked to contribute to the *Hound and Horn* by Bernard Bandler, who considered Tate's "the best critical mind in America at the time." Tate became southern editor of the magazine from 1932 to 1934 and provided the impetus for an increasing emphasis on the publication of poetry and fiction by southerners. Tate stressed as well the importance of a purely technical criticism that helped to place the *Hound and Horn* in the forefront of American literary journals of the period. *Hound and Horn* published his reviews of T. S. Eliot's "Ash Wednesday," Edmund Wilson's *Axel's Castle*, Hart Crane's "The Bridge," and Phelps Putnam's *The Five Seasons*; two essays, *In Memoriam: Hart Crane, 1899–1932* and *The Fallacy of Humanism*; two poems, "Aeneas at Washington" and "The Meaning of Life"; and his first published short story, "The Immortal Woman."

[1] Tate's review of *The Bridge* was published in vol. 3, no. 4 (July–Sept. 1930). It is a mixture of praise for the "richness of rhythm and style" which makes for a quality of "immense poetic interest," and of criticism of Crane's lack of focus and of definition of theme that at times results in "a sentimental muddle of Whitman and the pseudo-primitivism of Sherwood Anderson and W. C. Williams. . . . Crane's vision is that of the naturalistic romantic poet, and it vacillates between two poles. A buoyant optimism of the Whitman school and the direct Baudelairean pessimism exist side by side, unfused."

2   ALLEN TATE TO
          BERNARD BANDLER
          7 February 1930

Dear Bandler:

Thank you for your letter of yesterday. I don't see how any sensible writer could possibly hesitate between the *Hound and Horn* and any other journal in this country.[1]

There are several matters I want to communicate to you.

Do you wish to run my review of Hart Crane in the March issue? I can have it ready.

What plans have you for the Humanist symposium? I should like to review it somewhere. Perhaps you will let me review it and the anti-Humanism book together. I am not contributing to the latter. This review might be done for the summer issue.[2]

If Cowley and Burke *were* getting up the antidote I should feel sympathetic towards it. The editor is C. Hartley Grattan, a worthy and I am sure an able man with whose views I have no sympathy at all. Moreover, I am not anti-Humanist at all; I differ with the Humanists on the question of method. Babbitt's *Forum* essay makes the point of departure very clear. He looks to education in the strict sense; I look to it in the larger sense and the more radical sense of the total background. If the homes of college boys are one thing, you can't make Humanists of them with another thing that will not be relevant to their parochial needs after college. I think Babbitt falls into the hands of the enemy by proposing the mechanical and external methods of the educational committee—a proof of my contention that the underlying mental habits of Humanism are *naturalistic*.

I have been commissioned by a popular journal here to write a short sketch of Babbitt's life in relation to his ideas—about 2500 words. It will be very light stuff, but it may help to get the man's books read by a wider public. The method will be anecdotal, and I need anecdotes. Perhaps I ought to see Babbitt. I doubt if it would be wise to warn him in advance of my purpose; I think it would be necessary to show him the article before it is presented—otherwise I couldn't go to see him. My purpose in not warning him would be the prevention of self-consciousness. Could you undertake to introduce me to him if I came up to Cambridge? Unless it could be done without inconvenience, I shouldn't want it done. I should appreciate any help you would give me.[3]

I will send you one of my essays along in May: I hope to get the book out in September or October.[4] I am very grateful for your interest in the matter. The essay will be on Timrod, Lanier, Poe, and Hayne as a background to the modern Southerners, Ransom, Davidson, Warren, etc.[5] It will be called "The Lost Tradition."

The galleys of my reply to Mr. Shafer are due any moment. I must ask you not to forward them to him unless this would help to get you out of the difficulty I got you in.

[1] Tate's essay "The Fallacy of Humanism" was published in the *Hound and Horn*, vol. 3, no. 2 (Jan.–March 1930). Robert Shafer published an answering article, "Humanism and Impudence," in the *Bookman*, Jan. 1930, pp. 489–98. Tate attempted to place his answer in the *Bookman* but, when refused, asked the *Hound and Horn* to publish it. Bandler agreed in a letter of 3 Feb. 1930, only to receive in the same day's mail a note from Tate withdrawing the essay because the *Bookman* had changed its mind. He offered Bandler instead an essay by John Crowe Ransom, "Humanists and Schoolmasters." Bandler refused and sent an angry letter to Tate, who apologized the next day, explaining that his only reason for the change was to reach the same audience that read Shafer's attack on him. He offered the *Hound and Horn* anything he wrote in the future. Then Bandler apologized: he had thought Tate felt "that the *Hound and Horn* was a sort of minor league affair compared to the big-time *Bookman*" (6 Feb. 1930).

[2] The revival of interest in Humanism in the late 1920s was promoted by a series of articles in *Forum* magazine in 1928. Tate's question about the Humanist Symposium refers to *Humanism and America* (1930), edited by Norman Foerster. The anti-Humanist book *The Critique of Humanism* (1930), edited by C. Hartley Grattan, contained essays by Edmund Wilson, Malcolm Cowley, Kenneth Burke, R. P. Blackmur, Yvor Winters, and others. Tate changed his mind and did contribute "The Fallacy of Humanism" to Grattan's book.

[3] Tate wrote me on 17 June 1976 that although he visited Babbitt, no article ensued.

[4] The essay was not written, nor was the book finished (letter to me 17 June 1976).

[5] John Crowe Ransom (1888–1974), writer and critic, was a member of the faculty of Vanderbilt University from 1914 to 1937, where he taught most of the *Fugitive* group. He went on to become Carnegie Professor of Poetry at Kenyon College from 1937 to 1958, and founder and editor of the *Kenyon Review* from 1939 to 1959. In *The New Criticism* (1941), Ransom set forth his deeply influential theory that criticism of a poem should consist of close textual analysis rather than an emphasis on its period or any other consideration. Donald Davidson (1893–1968), poet, critic, and historian, was educated at Vanderbilt University, where he later taught for many years. Robert Penn Warren (*b.* 1905) was a member of the *Fugitive* group of poets and a founder and co-editor of the *Southern Review*. He was later professor of English at Yale, a position from which he retired in 1973.

3   ALLEN TATE TO
     ALAN STROOCK
     [Undated]

Dear Mr. Stroock:

Your point about my review of "Ash Wednesday" is very well taken. I am only sorry that I did not include some of the analysis of the poems that I wrote out in my first version of the review. The more I thought about it, the more imperative seemed the necessity to clear the ground for a direct discussion of Eliot's poetry before proceeding to such a discussion. In other words, I felt that because of the atmosphere of opinion that has been gathering about his work in the last three years, it was not safe to assume that the poetry could be properly analyzed to good effect. However, the main reason why I omitted such an analysis was the lack of space; I felt that the defense of Eliot required all the space I gave it.

Yet it is not so much a defense of Eliot as the plea for a sound critical procedure. Edmund Wilson's review of "Ash Wednesday" seems to me to be very unsound; it ends up with some very disconcerting speculation on Eliot's private life which has no significance at all.[1] When a man of Wilson's great gifts succumbs to the zeitgeist, it is surely powerful enough to justify comment at length.

I will rewrite the review, and get it to you in a very few days. I see your point of view perfectly. I wrote you the other day about payment in advance of publication; since the review will be postponed until January, this would be even more desirable for me, if it is convenient for you.

What shall we do about the review of Ransom's book?[2]

This letter is a reply to Alan Stroock's suggestion that Tate's review, although "splendid as far as it goes," contain a critique of "Ash Wednesday" as poetry rather than a defense of Eliot.

[1] Wilson's review of "Ash Wednesday" appeared in the *New Republic*, 20 August 1930. The closing lines, to which Tate took exception, were "'Ash Wednesday' . . . is distinguished above all, [by] that 'peculiar honesty' in exhibiting the essential sickness or strength of the human soul . . . which . . . even at the moment when his psychological plight seems most depressing and his ways of rescuing himself from it least sympathetic, still gives him a place among those upon whose words we reflect with most interest and whose tones we remember longest."

[2] John Crowe Ransom's *God without Thunder* (1930), in which he set forth his preference for "the thundering God of the Old Testament to the God that has been set up as the deity of the scientific world." In his *Memoirs and Opinions, 1924–1974* (1975), Tate writes that Ransom repudiated "the liturgical Christianity advocated in *God without Thunder*, but that I still agreed with the main argument of the book—that is, I don't see how Christianity can survive as a humanistic doctrine; there must be a theistic God, apodeictic and menacing as well as merciful."

4   ALLEN TATE TO
         BERNARD BANDLER
              [Undated]

Dear Bernard:

I am mighty glad to hear that you are back in this country. I do hope you will come to see me: I will probably be in New York at Christmas, but not for long; it is too expensive.

As to the Eliot review, I have read it over several times, your letter in mind, and I conclude that your criticism is partly just, partly unjust. It is very just in demanding more clarity at some of the crucial moments. But perhaps I might demand in turn a little more concentration from you as reader. For example, you say that I offer in proof of my assertion that Eliot's poetry may be the only religious verse we have, two merely technical reasons—the rhythm and the imagery. This does not do your powers of attention, my dear Bernard, full justice. I describe these technical points in terms of moral and religious aims and can only advise you to read the passage again. Now for the question about the irony of the opening lines. I do mean, as you suggest, and as I stated, that the lines permit us an insight into Eliot superior, for the moment, to his own. We know, in fact, that he is far more considerable as a person than he makes himself out to be: we know that the practical values which he repudiates are quite secondary to the quality of his character and mind, and this conflict gives us the irony. We know what his real powers are, and the passage pretends to ignore these and to lament the loss of less important powers. But again I must ask you to reread the review.

In general, however, I am not inclined to admit the justice of your criticism—where you regret the controversial element. I have struck out all but one reference to the minions of darkness, and I believe the five-page preliminary statement is necessary. In long critical works where we have time to set forth the full grounds of the Truth, so that by long and unconscious persuasion we displace error in the reader's mind, not much explicit notice of error is necessary. But in a comparatively brief discussion, it is difficult to show the reader just how a true opinion is related to his false one unless we take explicit notice of the false. In short, reviewing, or one good method of it, must proceed by comparison, and where the subject under review has been widely misunderstood, it is better to take into account the terms of the misunderstanding. In this case, it would be feeble indeed to praise the virtues of a religious poetry without defending them from some of the bad thinking which undermines them.

I have reread four or five reviews from recent issues of the *Hound and Horn*. I am naturally pleased that you set me a higher standard than you do most of your reviewers. I can well understand how you might feel that I could do better, or that some one else could; but I can't understand your hesitation in printing the review. I can only return it with some minor corrections for your final decision.[1] Wilson's book[2] isn't out: so I will have to wait a while before I begin the Wilson-Ransom review.

[1] Tate's review ("Irony and Humility") of *Ash Wednesday* was published in vol. 4, no. 2 (Jan.–March 1931). He discusses various forms of criticism, such as the Humanist and the Marxist, resents the judging and rejecting of Eliot's poetry in terms of his religious belief, and finds it astonishing that reliance on poetry as a source of gratification and "as a mirror of one's needs" should exist to the neglect of its quality as poetry. His review concentrates on what he considers to be the essential qualities

in *The Waste Land*—irony—and in *Ash Wednesday*—humility—and ends with a
discussion of Eliot's rhythm and imagery.
[2] Wilson's book was *Axel's Castle*, reviewed by Tate in vol. 4, no. 4 (July–Sept.
1931). "Mr. Wilson's sensitive and finely modulated prose style, the emotional sub-
tlety of his insight into the sensibilities of his six writers, betrays a curious sympathy
with them that his argument cannot cancel out. In spite of his belief that they are
lost in an age that is all but history, in spite of his conviction that an age indifferent to
their attitude is at hand, he is yet involved in that stage of the humane tradition
which they stand for: he cannot predict coherently another kind of art than theirs.
Writing about them he is precise, lucid, the master of his subject; as a prophet he is
confused."

5   ALLEN TATE TO
LINCOLN KIRSTEIN
2 November 1931

Dear Kirstein:

I have mislaid or lost the issue of the *Hound and Horn* containing
Blackmur's essay on Cummings;[1] so will you send me that issue and
charge me for it? I am writing a piece on *Viva* and need it to refer to.
. . . Your remarks on Steffens in the current number are extremely
brilliant; I am astonished throughout to see how accurately you've put
your finger on the general malady of liberalism.[2] I kept thinking that
you were really writing about Edmund Wilson—"reaction against pu-
ritan conformist morality goes only far enough to kick over the traces
of convention without providing any substitute except *nervous curi-
osity*." Again: ". . . two sides to every question . . . absolves one from
doing anything more about it than investigating the next question."
This applies perfectly to the liberals of our generation. Wilson is al-
ways *investigating the next question with nervous curiosity*. I wish you'd
examine some of these people in the near future.

P.S. Is the All*a*n Tate whose review of Yeats (not to be) is adver-
tised the same as the All*e*n Tate whose poetry you announce!

[1] "Notes on E. E. Cummings' Language," vol. 4, no. 2 (Jan.–March 1931).
[2] In vol. 5, no. 1 (Oct.–Dec. 1931). In this review of *The Autobiography of Lincoln
Steffens* (1931), Lincoln Kirstein writes, "This book is not only the history, the ex-
posure, the muck-raking of the character of Lincoln Steffens but it is also the story
of the American Liberal soul. It is a story of the triumph of the equivocal, the con-

quest or assimilation of circumstance by curiosity, without conviction or direction. . . . The feeling of confusion which is so present . . . is the general liberal fever and its causes lie somewhere in liberal, or in what is nowadays called, progressive education."

6   BERNARD BANDLER
TO ALLEN TATE
10 November 1931

Dear Allen:

I am delighted that you will review Dewey and Spingarn for us. I am sending on Laski and Russell as well. In case you are not doing Burke for the *New Republic*, I will also send you that.[1]

I think I shall soon take advantage of your invitation to come down and see you. About two months ago, when the last *Hound and Horn* was going to press, Fergusson, Mayor and I sat down with *I'll Take My Stand*,[2] to do our type of *New Republic* editorial, but I laid down my Davidson's chapter and thought it was pretty good, and Mayor weakly confessed he liked Ransom, and Fergusson was impressed with whatever he read, so instead of doing you in an editorial, we all but bought tickets for Nashville. I thought of doing a short article on your movement and to do it thoroughly, would like to see the movement in action.[3] This is a most ungracious way of telling you how much I should like to accept your invitation. A visit to Nashville needs no further excuse than the pleasure of renewing our acquaintanceship.

P.S. I am delighted you like the *Hound and Horn*. When I see you I hope to talk to you about it in more detail.

[1] John Dewey, *Philosophy and Civilization* (1931); J. E. Spingarn, *Creative Criticism and Other Essays* (1931); Harold Laski, *Politics* (1931); Bertrand Russell, *Scientific Outlook* (1931); Kenneth Burke, *Counter-Statement* (1931). These books were not reviewed in *Hound and Horn*, probably because it preferred to allocate its space to books that would not be reviewed by other magazines such as the *New Republic*, the *Nation*, and the like.
[2] *I'll Take My Stand*, a collection of essays by a group of southern writers. Donald Davidson's essay "A Mirror for Artists" deals with the deadening effect of industrialization on the arts and urges the artist to "enter the common arena and become a citizen to fight against the infection of our times"; in "Reconstructed but Unregenerate," John Crowe Ransom calls for a combination of western farmers and the old-

fashioned South, along with those who are tired of progressivism, to unite into a "formidable bloc" to defend the rural life of America against encroaching industrialism; Allen Tate's essay "Remarks on the Southern Religion," although not mentioned in Bandler's letter, clarifies his position as a southerner. He finds that the southern religious impulse is "inarticulate," that it "tried to encompass its destiny within the terms of Protestantism, in origin a non-agrarian and trading religion; hardly a religion at all, but a result of secular ambition. . . . because the South never created a fitting religion, the social structure of the South began grievously to break down two generations after the Civil War." How may the southerner take hold of his tradition? Tate calls upon the southerner to enter into political action, to get back to the roots, to reestablish a "private, self-contained, and essentially spiritual life."
[3] The movement was, of course, Agrarianism, started by a group of southern writers who had written for the *Fugitive*, principally Tate, Warren, Ransom, and Davidson, as well as those others who wrote essays in *I'll Take My Stand*.

7 ALLEN TATE TO BERNARD BANDLER
23 October 1932

Dear Bernard:

. . . Business: I am finishing up a review of Miss Glasgow's new book—which will surprise you, but then I was surprised by the book.[1] It is superb. It meets very well Leighton's demand for a maturer fiction. (Leighton's case was weakened by his refusal to grant Hemingway even a gift for pleasant prose). Now I would like to do up a long piece on Eliot's new book, the *Selected Essays*, and the three new essays just advertised; then I might add to it Hugh R. Williamson's book on Eliot which has been published in England. This, for the spring issue. Please let me know at once.[2]

Suggestions: Get Ransom to review the next important book on economics that comes in. Get John D. Wade to do some biographies, or invite him to write an essay on Lytton Strachey. Wade is by far the best writer of the Tennessee group. Wade is at the James Robertson Hotel, Nashville. And try to get some of the best work of Achilles Holt.[3]

I have a suggestion about Eliot. Can't you prevail upon him to write an essay on contemporary American poetry? He has said very little on this subject, and he might not be very keen on the notion; but it would be a great thing for the *Hound and Horn*.

A suggestion about H. B. Parkes (whose essay on Emerson is the best evaluation that old son of a bitch has ever received).[4] Get Parkes to turn his attention to some of the Southern political writers—Ruffin and Calhoun, Jefferson of course, George Fitzhugh.[5]

The last two issues are the best you've ever put out, I was glad to see Cunningham's work;[6] though I thought his survey of poetry a little magisterial in tone. But it was very keen and intelligent. His verse not quite so good. Fergusson's poems amply prove your analysis of his mind,[7] Gertrude's masticatory ruminations on the father of our country seemed to me dull, pretentious and without excuse.[8] The Joyce piece is splendid.[9] Adams on Babbitt is a little naive, but he would be readable if he were not so long-winded.[10] However, the two issues are very fine. Let me hear from you.

In a letter dated 31 Oct. 1932, Kirstein wrote Tate that he had assigned the Eliot books to Henry Bamford Parkes for review, not knowing that Tate wanted them, and that Bandler was leaving the *Hound and Horn* to prepare himself to be a psychiatrist. He hoped that Bandler's departure would not affect Tate's serving as "regional editor and general help," stated that the magazine would continue indefinitely, and said that Winters and he were "in a little closer cooperation."

[1] *A Sheltered Life* (1932) by Ellen Glasgow.

[2] Eliot's *John Dryden* and *Selected Essays* (1932) were reviewed by the historian Henry Bamford Parkes in vol. 6, no. 2 (Jan.–March 1933).

[3] A young southern writer, whose literary promise was lost to mental illness.

[4] In an essay on Emerson in vol. 5, no. 4 (July–Sept. 1932), Parkes wrote, "Throughout the nineteenth century there was a steady deterioration in the tone of American life and character. A study of Emerson may illuminate some of the causes for that deterioration. Emerson himself was a person of great moral strength and integrity, but the whole tendency of his philosophy was to destroy the tradition in which virtues such as his own could be cultivated. . . . Emerson's mistake seems to have been due to the very perfection of his own character. He was an optimist because he was himself innocent of evil."

[5] Edmund Ruffin (1794–1865), agriculturist, publisher, ardent defender of slavery, and one of the first secessionists in Virginia.

George Fitzhugh (1806–1881), lawyer, sociologist. A defender of slavery, he felt that the economics of a system—like that in the South—which relied on slavery, answered every constructive purpose. He was hopeful of eventually seeing the southern aristocracy, which he regarded as socially superior to the northern, dominant in the Union.

[6] Tate refers to J. V. Cunningham's "Two Poems" and his Poetry Chronicle about the magazine *Poetry*, an estimate of twenty years of the magazine which embroiled him in controversy with Harriet Monroe. Both of these were published in vol. 6, no. 1 (Oct.–Dec. 1932).

[7] Two poems by Francis Fergusson, "Ruth and Boaz" and "Pioneer and His Children," vol. 5, no. 4 (July–Sept. 1932).

[8] "Scenery and George Washington," a story by Gertrude Stein, in vol. 5, no. 4.

[9] "From a Banned Writer to a Banned Singer" by James Joyce, vol. 5, no. 4. Cf. Chap. V, Letter 10, n. 1.
[10] A review by James Luther Adams of Babbitt's *On Being Creative and Other Essays*, vol. 6, no. 1.

8   ALLEN TATE TO
              LINCOLN KIRSTEIN
              30 December 1932

Dear Kirstein:

(I do wish you wouldn't address me as "Mr.") I am very much pleased that you are going to print the story.[1] I will have a new version in your hands some time in January—as early as possible—and if I may say so, it will be vastly improved.

But the most interesting news is your discussion of Pelham. I can't tell you how delighted I am. He was one of my boyhood heroes: when we played soldier in the backyard, all of us clamored to be the Gallant Pelham. I am enormously interested in what you will do with him. As you have found out, the materials are slight so far as the printed record is concerned. It is very difficult to find out much about his personality; at least that is my impression now. Next summer I want you to come down to see us. I will take you to Alabama, where we shall have little trouble in finding some of the family and perhaps some letters and papers of various sorts. I can see after a moment's reflection that Pelham, just because he was a pure soldier, offers a fine opportunity for a study in the Southern mind of his age. The preceding generation was the age of statesmen; Pelham's age was the age of action, in which the Southern "system" had to defend itself. If I can answer any questions or be of any service to you at any time, please let me know. I've been over the military campaigns in Virginia so much that I know them asleep.

I write this hurriedly; I must go out immediately. I am glad to hear that you are having my books reviewed. The Davis book is the better; . . . By the way, my essay in "I'll Take My Stand" should be read by Mr. Buck, since it summarizes some general views of the South. I'll write more at length a little later. Meanwhile, best regards.

On 8 December 1932, Kirstein wrote Tate that his biographies of Jefferson Davis and Stonewall Jackson were being reviewed by Paul Buck in vol. 6, no. 2 (Jan.–

March 1933); that he (Kirstein) was spending most of his time gathering material for a biography of John Pelham, Jeb Stuart's "artillerist," whom he hoped to make out "a kind of typical Sydney, without any sentimentality, but considerable valor and glory"; and that he had been in Virginia looking over the battlegrounds.

John Pelham (1838–1863), called the "boy major," was one of the bravest and most capable young officers in Lee's army. He became to many southerners a romantic hero because of the glamorous description of him in John Esten Cooke's *Surry of Eagle's Nest* (1894). When he was killed in battle at Kelly's Ford, 17 March 1863, there was widespread grief in the South at his death. In a letter to me, 1 Dec. 1975, Lincoln Kirstein wrote, "I was mad for the Civil War, and never got anywhere with the book on Pelham, but I had a long correspondence with Thomason, the man who wrote a brilliant book on Jeb Stuart. . . . I went all over the Virginia battlefields; some of this comes into *Lay this Laurel*, my book about Robert Gould Shaw," who led the first black volunteer regiment in the Civil War.

[1] Tate's first published story, "The Immortal Woman," vol. 6, no. 4 (July–Sept. 1933). Yvor Winters, as an editor of *Hound and Horn*, called it potentially a very fine story and made a number of suggestions to give it clarity. Tate followed his advice and wrote Kirstein that it made for a greatly improved story.

9   ALLEN TATE TO
              LINCOLN KIRSTEIN
              22 January 1933

Dear Kirstein:

I am hoping to hear from you soon about my story and poems, and for heaven's sake don't hesitate to deliver your decision should it be in the negative. But meanwhile there are more interesting things to write to you about:

1. I do think by all means that you ought to do the book on Pelham. In fact, the more I think of it the more it seems to me that your proposed way of treating him is the correct way: he is not large enough in quantity to fill out a regular biography. Knowing your style, I am convinced that you would be able to present all the facts and give them a body of your own insight that would make them live. I am sure that ordinary biographical treatment would yield almost nothing but the portrait of a dashing boy. Go ahead, and please let me see some of it as soon as it is ready.

2. Caroline and I have made a discovery of an unknown masterpiece of 19th century American literature. It is a book called *The Life and Times of Elder Reuben Ross*, by his son James Ross, who was born in North Carolina in 1801 and died in Montgomery County, Tenn., in

1878. Only four copies are known to exist: the book being inaccessible, I gave up the idea of writing an essay on it, and have now determined to get it republished.[1] It will require editing; much of it is about obscure pioneer preachers, the colleagues of the subject; but from a large volume a masterpiece of about 60,000 words can be extracted by simple omission. The magnificent parts of the book are concerned with the trip across the mountains from Carolina to Tennessee in 1807. There are two chapters of this that can be lifted out bodily, called The Journey Commenced and Beyond the Mountains. They would take together about 15 pages in The *Hound and Horn*, and they are the kind of prose that Hemingway thinks he is writing. I offer some samples:

"On the 6th of May, 1807, according to appointment, all bade adieu to their friends and relatives, the scenes of their early life, the graves of their fathers, and many objects besides around which memory loves to linger, and turned their faces towards the setting sun. It was customary then, and I believe is so still, when a family was about to remove from a place where they had long resided, and seek a home in a distant country, for the near neighbors and intimate friends to call and bid them farewell. This is usually a time when there is much tenderness of feeling; many, in taking leave, would not venture to speak; a tender embrace, a silent tear, and a pressure of the hand, in many cases, would be all. But few of the aged men and women now living do not remember such parting scenes. In those early times, the emigrants that left Carolina or Virginia to settle in Kentucky or Tennessee, hardly expected ever again to see those from whom they parted, especially if somewhat advanced in years. The great distance, the intervening mountains and rivers, the difficult roads, and the cruel savages that roamed in and around these states forbade the indulgence of this hope. They parted much as do those who part at the grave."

If you think it is interesting I will copy out the two chapters and send them on.

The new *Hound and Horn* has not arrived, but I hear it is in town, so doubtless ours will be here shortly. With best regards,

---

[1] Nothing came of the plans to republish Ross's book because Tate "lost the rare book!" (letter to me from Tate, 17 June 1976). Caroline Gordon was Tate's first wife.

10   ALLEN TATE TO
LINCOLN KIRSTEIN
3 February 1933

Dear Kirstein:

I write this hurriedly to ask whether you have assigned for review the forthcoming book of Crane's posthumous poems? [1] I am very anxious to say something about them. My "In Memoriam" was very general, and I want to supplement it with some more detailed analysis of his style. These poems, many of which are early, offer a good opportunity for this. Won't you cable me the answer, at my expense—that is, by deducting it from my next cheque the *Hound and Horn* sends me?

The new issue is splendid. Holt's prose piece is one of the finest things you have ever printed, and the poems by Bishop and Baker are very good, Bishop's particularly. Bernard's essay is one of his best; its conclusions, I should think, would teach him the futility of practical psychiatry. The Monroe-Bunting-Winters affair adds amusement, but Winters should have known better than to reply to Bunting, who is obviously a fool. Miss Monroe, as usual, is valiant, but misses the point at issue. Which is that she is not as intelligent as she ought to be. The review section is one of the best you've turned out. You yourself on Hemingway are extremely good; the trouble with Hemingway's worship of physical courage is that it acts in a vacuum, and I think you have touched his weakest spot when you ask whether he will have the courage to acquire knowledge of other men—a knowledge that he lacks. If he acquires that, he will develop a new kind of courage, or become a coward. Leighton is so perfect on Wilson that had I ever had a conversation with him I should be sure to think he had taken the words out of my mouth. (That sentence sounds a little funny, but I let it stand). Parkes is very fine: I'm delighted to see him crush Waldo Frank—who I understand has written 5000 words of the same pretentious piffle on Crane: Crane is a great seer because he doesn't see anything clearly. I like Buck's review of Hollis and myself, and I am grateful to you for getting the books reviewed. [2]

By the way, since Parkes is an Englishman studying American thought, why don't you get him to examine some of the ante-bellum Southern political writers. They would be a sure antidote to the bad taste that Emerson seems to have left with him. Rhett, Calhoun, Harper, Fitzhugh, Ruffin, Dew, Hammond, etc.[3] Their immediate purpose was political theory, but a whole philosophy is set forth.

P.S. These men knew their Marx thoroughly, and it is amusing to see the neo-Communists discovering Marx for the first time in U.S.

[1] Crane's posthumous poems were not reviewed in *Hound and Horn*.

[2] Tate refers to vol. 6, no. 2 (Jan.–March 1933)—"A Glass of Wine," a short story by a young southern writer Achilles Holt; "Perspectives are Precipices" by John Peale Bishop; "Travelogue" by Howard Baker; "Joyce's *Exiles*," an essay by Bernard Bandler; Correspondence—Harriet Monroe defends her magazine *Poetry* against the criticism of J. V. Cunningham in the previous issue of *Hound and Horn*; Basil Bunting lashes out at Yvor Winters's negative view of Louis Zukofsky's *Objectivist* anthology; and a short reply from Winters to Bunting construes Bunting's letter as a challenge to an encounter—"any kind of prose or verse—with or without gloves, Queensbury [*sic*] rules"; Kirstein's review of Hemingway's *Death in the Afternoon*; Lawrence Leighton's review of Edmund Wilson's *The American Jitters*; a review of T. S. Eliot's *Selected Essays* by Henry Bamford Parkes; Paul H. Buck's review of three books, *The American Heresy* by Christopher Hollis and Tate's biographies of Stonewall Jackson and Jefferson Davis.

[3] Robert Barnwell Rhett (1800–1876), statesman. He fought hard for secession, wanting South Carolina to secede alone if need be to lead the way to a southern Confederacy. His last energies were spent in defense of southern civilization against Davis's proposal to arm—and free—the slaves.

William Harper (1790–1847), nullification leader and judge. In 1837 he wrote a memoir defending slavery.

Thomas Roderick Dew (1802–1846), economist, professor of political law at the College of William and Mary, Va., who later became its president. He wrote articles in favor of slavery, feeling it to be in the economic interests of the tidewater states.

James Henry Hammond (1807–1864), governor of South Carolina and United States senator, who wanted the withdrawal of the southern states from the Union and thought slavery "the cornerstone of our Republican edifice."

11   ALLEN TATE TO
LINCOLN KIRSTEIN
5 February 1933

Dear Lincoln:

I shall be delighted to see "Aeneas at Washington" in the *Hound and Horn*. "Picnic at Cassis," alas, has been sold to *The Yale Review*. Heretofore I have always offered my verse to the *Hound and Horn* first (with what success you know), except the Alice poem; but this time something like desperate need of money compelled me to offer the Picnic and another called "Shadow and Shade" where I could be paid immediately and, for poetry, handsomely.

Since you are using Aeneas and the short story, (the second cleaner copy is the one to use), perhaps there will be no room in the next issue for a review by me of Crane's posthumous book; or perhaps the review could be used in the summer issue. Please let me know what you think about this. I seem to foresee difficulties in any attempt I might make to write about it in the *New Republic*, since Frank[1] is a contributing editor there: I mean that his preface is bound to be piffle and I shall want to say so.

With your letter arrived a copy of Davidson's Sectionalism essay, and I am very much puzzled as to what advice to offer on the occasion. For what he has to say, it is nearly twice too long. The writing is largely wooly journalese, and his tone is that of the advocate, not the critical investigator. I remember when Bernard opened the question with him that I gave warning to that effect. Nevertheless, I hope you will, after some labor spent on cutting it, use the essay,[2] I suggest this: cut it to the proportions you think best, *forward it to me*, and I will persuade him to accept the situation. I think the point of view set forth is valuable; our problem is to get it in decent form. Unless I am very much mistaken, the revolution of the land at this moment in America bears out his main contention; the belief held by New York liberals and communists that the only solution to the crisis is some form of machine or proletarian control simply means that they see the country only in terms of abstract domination from some remote center. This will not happen in our lifetime, if ever. So I think it would be well for the *Hound & Horn* to get into the record the other point of view. . . .

Davidson remarks that you found *I'll Take My Stand* without any great significance. This may be true. If I may say so, and I ask you to believe that I say it in no unpleasant spirit, I suspect that you have been influenced by Tom Mabry's view of the book and of our group. This would be quite natural; Tommy was your friend long before you knew anything about us. I feel that Tom's reaction was motivated by his revolt against his father's tobacco business, and this too influences him in his humanitarian sentimentality about negroes and the underdog.

However, there is another way of arguing the insignificance of the book—that it is the sort of thing that can have no political effect. That remains to be seen. Rousseau died in bed, not on the barricades; we can't do both. The trouble with the neo-Communists is that they want to do both.

Esther Murphy[3] is here with wonderful stories of the late campaign, of the toilets in the Empire State Building, and of the Communists in New York. It now seems that Christ was a proletarian victim of the class struggle—he had attacked the capitalists of Palestine. With that instance of intellectual integrity on the part of our saviors of society, I bid you temporary farewell.

[1] Waldo Frank (1889–1967), novelist and social critic.
[2] An essay by Donald Davidson, "Sectionalism in the United States," vol. 6, no. 4 (July–Sept. 1933), in which he discusses the importance of recognizing the existence of a variety of sections in the United States, each with its customs, folklore, literature, attitudes, and so on. Heretofore, the emphasis was placed on the autonomy of the federal government, as if the United States were "a compact and well unified body, neat and coherent as a European state." He finds, rather, that people have become interested again in reaffirming ties in "a revolt against the excessive centralism of the machine age"; in their "different yet related traditions the sections—that is, Westerners, New Englanders, Rebels, Yankees, or what you will—have a common interest to maintain what is organically American against what is synthetically imposed."
[3] Esther Murphy—personal friend of many of the artists and writers of the time.

12   LINCOLN KIRSTEIN
            TO ALLEN TATE
            16 February 1933

Dear Allen:
    . . . I am terribly glad that you are having those poems printed in the *Yale Review*. We are printing "Aeneas at Washington" next time. I want very much your review on Crane's book whenever you want to do it, probably for the summer number.

My Pelham thing is absolutely held up for the present. The material is all lying to hand and next September I'll start in with all my pent up excitement in it. At the present time I have been doing nothing but trying to relive the period of 1909–1914, with the Russian Ballet, and seeing everybody in this country[1] who had anything to do with it. It of course fascinates me completely, but I find as I go into it more and more, that it is a period further from us by a thousand years than the Civil War. It is a period as neatly pigeonholed as the time of the moguls in India.

I have suggested to Parkes about Calhoun and he wants to do it very much. I also want somebody to do an article against the Northern Abolitionists and their complete misunderstanding of the South. Who could do that?

The next issue will contain an extremely good article on Marx and Bakunin, by Max Nomad, an essay on D. H. Lawrence, by Francis Fergusson, a fine review of Winters on T. Sturge Moore, and an excellent review of the eighteenth century by Mrs. Stillman.

I intend to be in Paris towards the end of May. Will you be there then? If I possibly can, I want to get to Russia for four weeks, for documentary purposes.

Please give my best to your wife, and write to me.

[1] France.

13   LINCOLN KIRSTEIN
          TO ALLEN TATE
            24 April 1933

Dear Allen:

Thanks so much for your letter. I am so glad you approve, particularly about those four articles on the Civil War.

My Nijinsky book may take me to Europe almost at once.[1] Your story appears in the next number of the magazine, and I think it is one of the best numbers so far, all the way around.[2] Please send us your young unknowns at once. I am in constant communication with Winters, who behaves as if he were tired out. If I go abroad I'll be back by August anyway, and I would like to come down and see you. I have several very ingenious plans, I think, to put our whole gang in a position of considerable power, particularly if things get worse, and I would like to talk to you about it.

[1] Kirstein was helping with the research for Romola Nijinsky's biography of her husband, which was published in 1934.
[2] This issue was vol. 6, no. 4 (July–Sept. 1933). It is a composite of the interests of the editors: Tate's in Agrarianism and the New Criticism, Winters's in western regionalism (Don Stanford was a protégé of his), and Kirstein's in Marxism. It contains a short story by Tate, "The Immortal Woman"; "Three Poems" by Don Stanford; "Theseus: A Trilogy" by Winters; an essay by Donald Davidson, "Sectionalism in the United States"; essays by John Brooks Wheelwright on Remington and Winslow Homer, and Jean Charlot on Ben Shahn; "Christian Science" by Fred T. March; Chronicles on Film ("Eisenstein and the Theory of Cinema") by Harry Alan Potamkin and on Music by B. H. Haggin. There are also book reviews by Francis Fergusson, Richard Blackmur, Yvor Winters, Kenneth Burke, and a review of three books on Russia by M. R. Werner.

14   LINCOLN KIRSTEIN
        TO ALLEN TATE
        8 May 1933

Dear Allen:

I am sorry not to have written before, but I have been terrifically busy. As you know, Winters is no easy character to handle. I really share your opinion of him, and I appreciate his kindness to me, and his great taste and wit, more than I could possibly say. However, very often I don't know really what he is talking about, and I have to dismiss so much of his excitement as either induced by insomnia or physical exhaustion of some sort, which, since I don't know him, I never can exactly figure out.

On the whole I like Warren's essay[1] very much, although I agree with you and Winters about it, and I think it's a good thing to publish. I rather hesitate, however, to go in for a long controversy about irony as I feel at this time we have many better things to do. I don't think Winters, however, would write on Ransom, probably out of pique or impatience. Will you write to Warren, or do you want me to, about the essay?

My plan for the seizure of power as such would perhaps disappoint you. I am merely trying to jockey myself into a position where eventually I can act as I like in relation to the employment or cooperation of the artists of merit in this country. And while I should never attempt to assume the career of a Diaghilev, nevertheless the parallel is useful. Political power interests me less and less. In fact, the hypnosis of accelerating anarchy which we seem to be in for for a long while, is rather, in these crazy times, a fertile ground for all sorts of interstitial experiment.

P.S. I am enclosing a thing by Katherine Anne Porter which impressed me very much indeed.[2] I hope you like it. I think it's really quite extraordinary. Please send it back when you are done with it.

[1] The Warren essay is on the poetry of John Crowe Ransom.
[2] Katherine Anne Porter's "A Bright Particular Faith, 1700 A.D." in vol. 7, no. 2 (Jan.–March 1934).

15   LINCOLN KIRSTEIN
            TO ALLEN TATE
            23 May 1933

Dear Allen:

I think you will be very pleased with the next number. There are a lot of excellent things in it, and the whole thing shapes up into the definite sensation of a direction. You will also see that our next year's announcements are pretty distinguished as well. I had a note from Johns,[1] telling me that *Pagany* was going out of existence, so that leaves us more isolated than ever.

I want very much to see John Bishop in Paris, to discuss with him the possibility for a ballet, to be called "The Defense of Richmond," or some such romantic title. A ball at the capitol during the last days of the war, with the soldiers dashing off in the middle of a dance, giving the chance for elaborate farewells, and then the tragic return. This seems to me to be in an idiom which the Russian dancers could understand much better than jazz, possibly a starting point for a nationalist movement in lyric subject matter. I could also think of other ballets— one to be called "Doomsday," the essentialized New England graveyard with one of those Cotton Mather angels cracking tombstones; and another one called "Flying Cloud," which would be the return of a clipper ship to Salem harbour, with the fire company in attendance, sailors, negroes, and the people of 1840. We could do so much popularizing general notions in the form of ballets. It is one of the world's finest instruments.

¹ Richard Johns, editor of *Pagany*.

16 ALLEN TATE TO
LINCOLN KIRSTEIN
18 October 1933

Dear Lincoln:

I have been trying to write to you for a week; but I have been in a swivet.

I am getting Warren's essay on Ransom to you in a few days:¹ he has had it all summer working it over. There will also be a poem by Ransom, one of his very best.²

You ask for suggestions. Of course, the series of articles on the background of the Civil War should be completed. I will have my essay on Ruffin for the January issue. Lytle will have his on John Taylor by then.

Here are some other notes:

1. An essay on Marxian esthetics. The only thorough piece I've seen was Burnham's article in *The Symposium*, but it was so clumsily written that it was almost unreadable. I suggest Parkes for this.

2. An essay on Dewey's philosophy of education with emphasis on his esthetics. I suggest Lyle W. Lanier, at Vanderbilt. He knows Dewey upside down.

3. An essay on the relation of literature and propaganda. How about Leighton? We might get Ransom to do it.

These three essays would cover much the same ground from different angles. There might be a fourth:

4. An essay revaluating the poetry of the last ten years. I suggest Howard Baker.

How about the two poems that I sent you? I mean Stevenson's and Baker's? I'd like to hear from them right away. I enclose a new one by

John Bishop. I urge you to keep it several days and reread it: it gets better.

I've been expecting the new issue with interest.

[1] Bandler had been lukewarm about Warren's essay from the start, so that even though it was rewritten, the editorial reservations about the essay, as well as the fact that there were only three issues remaining in the life of the magazine, explain why it was not published in the *Hound and Horn*.

[2] "Prelude to an Evening."

17   LINCOLN KIRSTEIN
TO ALLEN TATE
17 October 1933

Dear Allen:

This letter may be sort of a blow to you, but I have got to tell you sometime. Bernard came in here and we had a terrifying half hour's talk. As a result the policy of the magazine is changed and solidified for the rest of its natural life. I can't tell how long this life will be, anyway till next September. We have decided to eliminate all articles for the magazine not of a distinctly literary nature. By literary I mean really technical. That all critical articles must have something to do with questions directly involving the materials of writing. This means an end to any political or philosophical essays. I have cancelled the series of 19th Century Russian revolutionists, and articles on Catholicism and related subjects, except as they have to do with Catholic poets. If the magazine has any function at all, that is, any real special function, it is of a literary quarterly. Our chronicles and reviews will have to take care of whatever political sidelights or philosophical implications that interest our writers. Magazines like *The American Review* will have to take care of the South. It's really a much better place for them than *Hound and Horn* anyway.

We finally decided to have our Henry James number in the spring, and have asked for contributions from Marianne Moore, Bandler, Mayor, Ezra Pound, T. S. Eliot, Gertrude Stein, Stephen Spender, Edna Kenton; Newton Arvin has written on James and Money. Is there anything you would like to do for it? I assume that you have Warren's essay on Ransom. It's not here in the office and I know I didn't send it to anybody else. The *Criterion* just came in, with Caroline's story in it, and I am most eager to read it.[1]

I think after a while you will probably see that Bernard and I really have a pretty good point in this. I hope you like the last number of the magazine. It should be in your hands very shortly.

[1] Caroline Gordon's "Old Red."

18   ## ALLEN TATE TO LINCOLN KIRSTEIN
29 October 1933

Dear Lincoln:

I am sorry that I have not been able to answer your letters sooner. My father died up in Kentucky ten days ago, and I am just getting back from the funeral; so I am getting around late to the course of life.

I am not shocked at your change in policy. If you will consider it a moment, you will recollect that I have never written a political article for you. Owsley and Lytle have written reviews in that direction, and Davidson one essay.[1] I think you will have available from us as much material as before. Ransom at this moment is finishing up a fine essay on poetry, which he promises to pass on to me for you. Warren will send in his essay this coming week.

I am glad you took Stevenson's poem;[2] and although I like Bishop's better than you do, I don't like it well enough to argue about it. I'm getting up some more poetry for you right away.

The new *Hound & Horn* came in while I was away. I haven't had time to read in it yet, but I will soon. And you will hear from me again in a few days.

[1] Frank L. Owsley wrote "Two Agrarian Philosophers; Jefferson and DuPont de Nemours," a book review, for vol. 6, no. 1 (Oct.–Dec. 1932); Andrew Lytle reviewed two books, *Robert Barnwell Rhett, Father of Secession* by Laura A. White and *Edmund Ruffin, Southerner* by Avery Craven in vol. 5, no. 4 (July–Sept. 1932); and Donald Davidson contributed *Sectionalism in America*, an essay, to vol. 6, no. 4 (July–Sept. 1933).
[2] "Icarus in November" by Alec B. Stevenson, vol. 7, no. 2 (Jan.–March 1934).

19   ALLEN TATE TO
                     LINCOLN KIRSTEIN
                      18 December 1933

Dear Lincoln:

I have just received Ransom's essay[1] and poem, accompanied by
Blackmur's letter. This letter is profoundly incomprehensible to me.
There's no use arguing about it. One statement he makes convinces me
that he did not read Ransom's essay or that, if he read it, he did not
understand one word of it. He quotes a line of Racine to prove that idea
may be seen as image, thinking that this refutes Ransom. It is absurd;
it really supports Ransom's argument, which Blackmur evidently
doesn't understand.

As to the poem,[2] I take it that you have let Blackmur reject it for
you too. He says it is rough and awkward! My God, Lincoln, what
kind of nonsense is this? There are better poems in this world, but this
poem is a very subtle piece of versification, or a refinement so intense
that it is almost decadent.

Now what shall I do? I think I shall have to ask you to remove my
name from your masthead. I don't like to do it, but I think I can be of
as much service to you this way as before. This Ransom essay is, I
think you will admit, the only piece of writing I have ever insisted
upon for the *Hound and Horn*. With Ransom I went rather far; I
wanted it so much for the *Hound and Horn*, and I thought it was such
a fine piece of work, that I told him he could count on its appearing. I
had no authority for this; I did it wholly on my own responsibility. I am
assuming that responsibility by "resigning" from you.

My conclusion is brief. Ransom's essay is so revolutionary that it
frightens your advisors. Blackmur, in particular, can't follow the argu-
ment, so he picks out little uses or words like a schoolmaster. I don't
mean to say that a loose vocabulary can ever be right, Ransom's is not
loose; it is rather that Blackmur can't follow the context, so the details
seem confused.

You have lost the best essay that has come your way in your whole
career. How under heaven you can turn this essay down, and yet print
MacLeish's absurd outburst from which you might have protected

him, since he can't protect himself, is more than I can ever understand. But so be it.

[1] "A Note on Ontology," described by Tate earlier in Nov. 1933, as "the best thing I have ever sent you" and "the best essay Ransom has ever written."
[2] "Prelude to an Evening."

20   LINCOLN KIRSTEIN
TO ALLEN TATE
20 December 1933

Dear Allen:

You misunderstand me or else I misunderstand you. I didn't refuse Ransom's essay or his poem. I didn't have time to. First I sent it to Winters, and then I sent it to Blackmur, as I always do. In the meantime you said you had to have an immediate answer, which I was not able to give you, so I sent it back to you as per request.

I liked the poem very much. I am not able to judge as to the value of the essay. I only know that we would of course publish it, inasmuch as I have published many things which I was far less sure about. Only you said that Ransom needed the money at once, and that Seward Collins would publish it, so I sent it back, because we could not possibly publish it until next fall, and I am not sure by then what is going to happen to *Hound and Horn.*

21   ALLEN TATE TO
LINCOLN KIRSTEIN
15 February 1934

Dear Lincoln:

You know how news travels: I have recently heard something that convinces me of my own error in the recent controversy over Ransom's essay. I didn't give you time to read the essay yourself. So I hope you will accept my apology for the harsh things that I said.

22   ALLEN TATE TO
LINCOLN KIRSTEIN
7 May 1934

Dear Lincoln:

I write these belated congratulations upon your James number. When your letter about it came, some weeks before the issue appeared, we were just out of a bad automobile wreck. We are now barely recovered, though no one was seriously injured. But the car, a new one, was a total loss.

The James number is the best thing of its kind I have ever seen. Wilson, Fergusson, and Blackmur are extremely good. Miss Moore is at her worst in this sort of thing. The whole issue is impressive, and I urge you to get up other symposia not only on other writers but on periods and groups. One a year would be just right.

I have finished three chapters of a history of Southern literature. If you are interested I shall be glad to send you in about a month the chapter on Poe, which is a separate essay.[1] I have tried to revaluate Poe from all sides.

---

[1] Neither book nor essay was finished, Tate wrote me, 17 June 1976.

CHAPTER VII

Homage to Henry James

LINCOLN KIRSTEIN
TO EDNA KENTON
21 August 1931

Dear Miss Kenton:

Mrs. Muriel Draper [1] tells me that you have been working for years on the various problems of the Figure In The Carpet. The *Hound and Horn* is planning an international tribute to Henry James for its Spring 1932 issue. We are going to devote the entire issue of the magazine to articles and original material on James. We have in our possession several extremely interesting letters and the unpublished scenario for *The Ambassadors* which he sent to his publishers to get an advance from them, which we intend printing at this time. [2] It differs from the original in a very great many ways. We wonder if you would be interested at all in helping us with this scheme and perhaps editing the scenario. We have hopes of having personal reminiscences from Mrs. Wharton and Bernard Berenson, with critical articles by Eliot, Pound and others. At the same time we will print a check list of all of James's novels, criticism and biography, as well as the most important criticism of him.

I would prefer you kept this letter in confidence. We have not approached any of our prospective contributors and, of course, we may not be able to get any of them, although our connections will probably make it possible to obtain some. I wish you would let us hear from you about this at your earliest convenience, as we should get started pretty quickly.

> Vol. 7, no. 3 (April–June 1934), the memorial to Henry James, is the most famous issue of *Hound and Horn*. Henry James was not always held in the high esteem in which he is regarded at present; Bernard Bandler remembers that, when he was at Harvard, people thought of James as "a funny little man" and wondered at Bandler's admiration of his writing. The idea for a Henry James issue had existed almost from the inception of the magazine, and Bandler and Kirstein started working on it in 1931. The only previous memorials to James in literary magazines had appeared not long after his death in 1916—in the *Egoist* in England, Jan. 1918, and in the *Little Review* in America, Aug. 1918. Among the essays that were published in the *Hound and Horn*, two have become classics—Richard Blackmur's "Critical Prefaces" (published as the Introduction to *The Art of the Novel: Critical Prefaces* by Henry James in 1934) and Edmund Wilson's "The Ambiguity of James." The issue certainly stimulated an interest in James and resulted in the publication of some very fine essays that would not have been written until long after, if at all. Leon Edel, the noted James scholar, wrote me 19 November 1975, "I was then still in the student stage of my work—and it is my great regret that I was not qualified then to participate in that fine symposium. I would have been among those who would have written some of those essays later—and I did."

> Edna Kenton (1876–1954) was one of the leading James scholars in America at the time. In a letter to me 4 Dec. 1975, Leon Edel wrote, "She was way ahead of her time in her work on Henry James and her appreciation of his genius. In editing the scenario to *The Ambassadors* she made many bibliographical discoveries about James, which are included in the Issue. Edna Kenton was so devoted a Jamesian, that she almost thought she was James, even to dying on the date of his death."

[1] Muriel Draper (1886–1952) writer, wife of Paul Draper, the distinguished lieder-singer, mother of Paul Draper, the dancer, and good friend of Lincoln Kirstein, who described her to me as "the last of the great saloneuses." Letter to me, 22 November 1976.

[2] The scenario was bought by Bernard Bandler at an auction and given to Hyatt Mayor as a wedding present—"the only act of generosity I ever subsequently regretted," Bernard Bandler told me. In 1975, Mayor gave the scenario to the Morgan Library in New York City.

2 # EDNA KENTON TO LINCOLN KIRSTEIN
24 August 1931

My dear Mr. Kirstein:

I have your letter of August 21st, and assure you that I shall hold it as confidential. I shall be most interested in seeing the scenario of *The*

Ambassadors and am sure I should be equally interested in editing—at least annotating—it. Your scheme sounds alluring and whatever aid I can give you in the way of suggestions or material I shall be glad to give. I am sure I can help you in your check list. I have several items dug up at great pains which appear in no bibliography—or anywhere else.

Do you know of the "scenario" for *The Awkward Age*, of which James speaks in his Preface to that novel—of drawing for the editors of *Harper's Weekly* "the neat figure of a circle consisting of a number of small rounds disposed at equal distance about a central object. The central object was my situation, my subject in itself, to which the thing would owe its title, and the small rounds represented so many distinct lamps, as I liked to call them. . . ." This correspondence was of 1899— possibly 1897. That cabalistic page might reproduce very amusingly. Since you are reproducing scenarios.[1]

It is just possible that I may be able to get for you—if you want it— a letter or two from an unpublished correspondence extending over nearly sixty years, to which I have had access.[2] The particular letter I have in mind is an extraordinary one on the war—so confidential, so vehement, so illuminating on the whole moot little question of his final gesture of British citizenship, that it may not be given out. But it might be. The name of his correspondent would be of itself enough. I saw these letters so confidentially that I don't give you the name, and I am sure that their guardian would have to be assured of the "dignity" of the whole proceeding before release of this letter would be even considered.[3] I mean that your final table of contents and the contributors to it would be a very large determining factor. So this is a matter that would have to wait for some time.

Be assured of my interest in your project and let me know how it fares.

[1] This was not reproduced in *Hound and Horn*.
[2] Leon Edel suggests that possibly the correspondence refers to the E. L. Godkin papers, now in the Houghton Library at Harvard. Godkin was editor of the *Nation* from 1865 to 1881.
[3] This letter was not used in *Hound and Horn*.

3   LINCOLN KIRSTEIN TO
                  EDMUND WILSON
                   16 January 1933

Dear Mr. Wilson:

   I have no idea whether or not you would be interested, but I should like very much to know whether or not you will care to write about Henry James from the point of view of his social background, not necessarily in relation to Marxian criticism, but with a definite occupation with his social environment and his ideas about money. We happen to have in our possession the unpublished manuscript, which is the length of a short novel, of the scenario of *The Ambassadors*. We also have letters in connection with this and other James material. I wanted to issue a number of the *Hound and Horn* which would be a kind of homage to Henry James, and as an excuse for its publication, although perhaps it doesn't need an excuse, to make it an enquiry into the state of James's reputation at the present, in the light of what younger novelists and critics think about him. I would like to have as many opposing viewpoints as possible. Some people I thought of asking are Mr. William Troy,[1] whose article on James you may have seen a year ago in *The Bookman*; Miss Constance Rourke,[2] and Mr. Newton Arvin.[3]

   I know you have a great deal of work, and perhaps this subject is not in the least seductive to you. I would greatly appreciate it if you had anybody else you could suggest in place of yourself. Any article you might choose to do would not need to be ready before next July or even later, if this would be any inducement. Our rates are depressingly low, only $2.50 a page. I would be delighted to hear from you.

[1] William Troy (1903–1961), critic and essayist.
[2] Constance Rourke (1885–1941), writer, whose book *American Humor, A Study of National Character* (1931) contained a chapter on Henry James.
[3] Newton Arvin (1900–1965), educator and author.

4   LINCOLN KIRSTEIN TO
EDMUND WILSON
17 January 1934

Dear Mr. Wilson:

I should be very much interested in an article by you on the subject of the truth in *The Turn of the Screw*, or anything to do with James' neuroses. I wonder if you could possibly let me know at once if you really will do it, and whether or not you could have the article in by February tenth, or the fifteenth, at the very latest.

It would really be a privilege to include you among the list of contributors. I daresay you have seen who they are, in the present number of the *Hound and Horn*.

5   EDMUND WILSON
TO LINCOLN KIRSTEIN
[Undated]

Dear Kirstein:

This has turned out longer and more elaborate than I had intended—due partly to my having become embarked on a retelling of *The Turn of the Screw*. I thought, however, that this might be worth while, as the case for this interpretation has never, so far as I know, appeared in print.[1] Let me know if it is all right.

Perhaps the better title would be simply, "The Ambiguity of Henry James."[2]

[1] Wilson got the idea for this essay from a combination of his own psychoanalysis and an earlier article written by Edna Kenton, in which she pointed out that the governess was the only one who saw the ghosts. "The children do not see them. Wilson took off from there." (Letter to me from Leon Edel, 19 Nov. 1975.)
[2] This statement is handwritten at the end of the letter.

6 LINCOLN KIRSTEIN TO
EDMUND WILSON
14 February 1934

Dear Mr. Wilson:

It has been extremely behind-handed of me not to thank you for your essay before this. I read it with great interest and I deeply appreciate both your kindness in writing it and its inherent excellence. It seems to me one of the most searching and genuinely curious articles on James I have ever read and it will lend a great deal of distinction to our number. The only thing that rather worries me is the detailed recapitulation of *The Turn of the Screw*. Perhaps I have been wrong in believing most people know it. It somehow stands as a block at the very start of your essay. Nevertheless, it may be necessary and I shall of course abide by any decision you wish to make in regard to it.

7 LINCOLN KIRSTEIN TO
EDMUND WILSON
9 March 1934

Dear Mr. Wilson:

I am terribly sorry to have to ask you to do this, but it is absolutely necessary in relation to other contributions to the *James* number.

If you look this proof over could you possibly cut from it anything that you do not think integral, without rewriting the manuscript. Five or six pages saved (your article now comes to twenty-seven pages, which is seven more than we had allowed), would mean the inclusion of things for which we now have no room and which must absolutely appear in this issue.[1]

I would greatly appreciate whatever cooperation you could give us.

[1] The article in its final form was twenty-one pages long.

8   LINCOLN KIRSTEIN TO MARIANNE MOORE
10 October 1933

Dear Miss Moore:

In April the *Hound and Horn* is going to bring out a whole number of a Homage to Henry James. We hope to have articles by Hyatt Mayor, Bandler, Peter Quennell, Stephen Spender, and Gertrude Stein. Have you anything you would care to say about Henry James? Newton Arvin has written an extremely interesting article on Henry James and Money. Would you care to write about James in relation to any particular phase? Any ideas which you might have on this subject would be very interesting to us.

9   MARIANNE MOORE TO LINCOLN KIRSTEIN
13 October 1933

Dear Mr. Kirstein:

Could you allow me to say something about Henry James as A Characteristic American? I hesitate to try even to touch Henry James, I am so fervent with regard to him but do let me submit something to you as soon as I can get it ready, that you may make up your mind whether or not you want it.

10   MARIANNE MOORE TO MARGARET JAMES
19 January 1934

Dear Peggy,[1]

Lending things is sometimes a bad business; the reason for lending is the reason for not lending; but I have received a request which I am transferring.

Mr. Kirstein—Lincoln Kirstein of the *Hound and Horn*—asks if I have an unpublished photograph of Henry James—or document or drawing or other thing—that I would allow to be reproduced in the next number of the *Hound and Horn*. At the *Dial* we sometimes had framed drawings photographed through the glass; Mr. Kirstein is a craftsman himself—a photographer, I mean—and I know he could safeguard one's treasures. I don't know what magazine deity could guarantee that Henry James would like the coming Henry James number of the *Hound and Horn*. There are a great many things I don't know, and I do know I have lost things I have lent, so be kind if you can but stern if you must.

I could ask questions of my own about the years between Bryn Mawr and now, but sporadic letters to answer are an abomination so I would try to lessen the task I am offering by saying don't write to me; and if you should be lending a drawing or other possession, please feel free to accompany it with this letter of mine—to save a little the bother of self-statement—and for this reason I am typing rather than writing. I shall suggest to Mr. Kirstein that Miss Alice Boughton[2] may have more pictures than have been reproduced. Perhaps you could tell him of an owner of a picture or thing not yet photographed? though I should think he might be humble in the matter of the not-yet-reproduced and repeat the frontispiece to A Small Boy and Others.[3]

Yours with happy memories,

[1] Henry James's niece, Mrs. Bruce Porter.
[2] Alice Boughton was one of the first great women photographers in the United States.
[3] A charming photograph of Henry James as a small boy, standing hand in hand with his father.

I I   LINCOLN KIRSTEIN TO
           MARIANNE MOORE
           27 January 1934

Dear Miss Moore:

Thank you ever so much for your letter. I am particularly eager to know if I can't get either some photographs by Coburn[1] or by Miss Boughton. There is a marvellous photograph by Miss Boughton of James in a top hat looking in a mirror. There is also another small picture of James in top hat outside in the open air.

At the present moment I have two unpublished photographs which are of considerable interest and a wood cut that Timothy Cole[2] did of an early photograph which came out in the *Century* magazine in November 1882. I particularly want to find photographs of James as a young man.[3] The James family are absolutely no help directly to me. I regret to say that I studiously avoided taking any classes at Harvard with Bliss Perry,[4] because now he has all the manuscripts at his own disposition and I think he feels the magazine's antagonism. For this reason I'd greatly appreciate it if I can get any possible material by way of other sources.

[1] Alvin Langdon Coburn (1882–1966), pioneering American photographer whose photographs were used innovatively by James as frontispieces to the New York edition of his novels and tales.
[2] Timothy Cole (1852–1931), an American wood engraver born in London and brought to the U.S. when he was six.
[3] Four photographs and a portrait of Henry James were reproduced in the magazine. Three photographs taken in 1906 were by Alice Boughton and show James "wearing a top hat several sizes too big, and looking like a Daumier," in Miss Boughton's words; one shows him observing a painting, another gazing into a mirror, and a third looking startled by a request from Miss Boughton to look into the camera. The fourth photograph, by Van der Weyde, shows a quizzical James, and the portrait, a wood engraving by Timothy Cole reproduced from *Century* magazine (November 1882), depicts a youngish, full-bearded, balding James.
[4] Bliss Perry (1860–1954), professor of English literature at Harvard University.

12   DORIS LEVINE TO MARIANNE MOORE
27 *April 1934*

Dear Miss Moore:

Thank you so much for your note. It was nice to get it. I am enclosing a check for twenty-five dollars for your contribution to our Homage to Henry James. Need I repeat how glad we were to have it?

13   HENRY JAMES TO
             LINCOLN KIRSTEIN
             31 January 1934

Dear Mr. Kirstein:

Miss Alice Boughton has a number of good photographs of Henry
James, and you have my permission to reproduce any one of them you
like. I am much interested in your announcement of the special num-
ber of *Hound and Horn.* "James and Money" will be a truly novel
topic. I hope that Mr. Blackmur knows the book *The Prefaces of
Henry James,* by Leon Edel, published by Jouve et Cie, in Paris. This
is a very good piece of work and seems to be little known.

P.S. Miss Boughton's address seems to be 319 East 17th Street,
New York City. However, if you are not able to get in touch with her,
please write to me again.

> This letter is the response of Henry James (nephew of the author) to a letter from
> Lincoln Kirstein informing him of the contents of the Homage to Henry James is-
> sue and asking if he had any photographs suitable for reproduction.

14   HENRY JAMES TO
             LINCOLN KIRSTEIN
             15 February 1934

Dear Mr. Kirstein:

I return herewith the copies of the letters from my Uncle to Gilder
and Heinemann, and cordially give my consent to their publication;
although I am bound to say that I don't much enjoy seeing trivial and
insignificant things turned into magazine copy, and that the note to
Gilder does strike me as being, although harmless, of this trivial order.

> This letter is the reply to a request from Lincoln Kirstein for permission to publish
> two of James's letters which he (Kirstein) had acquired many years earlier at an
> auction in England—one of them from Richard Watson Gilder, editor of *Century*
> (1881–1909) from Geneva, Switzerland, in 1889, regarding an article on Daumier;
> the other to British publisher William Heinemann (1863–1920), thanking him for
> William Archer's translation of Hauptmann's "Hannele"; both of them ultimately
> collated and placed by Edna Kenton.

15   LINCOLN KIRSTEIN
TO GERTRUDE STEIN
7 October 1933

Dear Miss Stein:

In the spring the *Hound and Horn* is issuing a number dedicated entirely to the work of Henry James. We hope to make this more or less an international homage to his genius. In this country he is almost completely forgotten by our younger writers, and we hope this issue of the magazine will be in the nature of a testimony of faith in his innovations and genius.

I wonder if you would have any interest in writing about James? The passages in *The Autobiography of Alice B. Toklas* dealing with him struck us as so evocative that we hoped for the possibility of an extension of these remarks.[1] Any ideas you might have on this subject would be extremely interesting to us.

Gertrude Stein (1874–1946), American writer, who spent a large part of her life in Paris, where she came to know such post-Impressionist artists as Picasso and Matisse. Her home was the center for many writers of the twenties, including Hemingway, Faulkner, and Sherwood Anderson, with whom she discussed her radically experimental theories of writing.

[1] "She contends that Henry James was the first person in literature to find the way to the literary methods of the twentieth century. . . . But oddly enough in all of her formative period she did not read him and was not interested in him. But as she often says one is always naturally antagonistic to one's parents and sympathetic to one's grandparents. The parents are too close, they hamper you, one must be alone. So perhaps that is the reason why only very lately Gertrude Stein reads Henry James." Gertrude Stein, *The Autobiography of Alice B. Toklas* (New York: Harcourt, Brace, 1933), p. 96.

16   GERTRUDE STEIN TO
LINCOLN KIRSTEIN
1 November 1933

My dear Mr. Kirstein,

Your idea of dedicating an entire number of the *Hound and Horn* to the genius of Henry James pleases me very much and I will be glad to send you something for it very soon. It seems the moment to definitely affirm his unique position.

17   LINCOLN KIRSTEIN
                TO GERTRUDE STEIN
                 14 November 1933

Dear Miss Stein:

It was so very kind of you to write me your letter of the first of November. We are delighted that you seem to be as enthusiastic about the idea of our James number as we are. The following is a list of the table of contents as far as we have it:

R. P. Blackmur: "The Critical Prefaces of James"
Lawrence Leighton: "James as an Expatriate"
Marianne Moore: "James as a Typical American"
Newton Arvin: "James and Money"
Edna Kenton: "New Light on *The Turn of the Screw*"
Peter Quennell: "The Younger and the Older James"
Stephen Spender: "Henry James and Problems of Behaviour"

We have asked Mr. Pound and Mr. Eliot. Mr. Eliot has refused twice. Perhaps he will accept the third time. Mr. Pound I have not heard from. Should you see him, I wish you would speak to him about it. As I believe I told you, we are also publishing a large portion of James's unpublished scenario for *The Ambassadors*.

I very much hope that I will have the pleasure of meeting you at the premiere of your opera in Hartford.[1]

> An additional letter and two telegrams urging Gertrude Stein to "please rush James immediately" failed to elicit an essay in time for the Henry James issue.

[1] *Four Saints in Three Acts*, with music by Virgil Thomson.

18   EDNA KENTON TO
                LINCOLN KIRSTEIN
                 4 May 1934

Dear Lincoln:

I'm enclosing that *Times* bit I spoke of Wednesday night which you said you hadn't seen, and also two columns from the *Saturday Sun*. It was inspiration I felt at the time and now am sure of that I so suddenly switched from the article I was intending to do, to another. The number did need something more like it, and that article really disposes of "expatriate" for all times.[1] However, I feel the Sun critic was too severe, and he was certainly much more interested in what he was about to display of erudition of his own—which is not so much—than in *criticising* the Henry James Number. He gave about one-fourth of his space to that small matter—the rest is the usual tosh.

The Edith Wharton book, by the way, has just one thing in it worth preserving. It may be an apocryphal story—she doesn't seem to swear to it; but it is the sentence with which James told Mrs. Prothero—who told Dearest Edith—he faced the first slight stroke. He said that just in the act of falling—he was dressing at the time—he heard a voice surely not his own which said, "So here it is at last; the distinguished thing." I congratulate the fabricator, if fabricated it is.[2]

I hear from a Washington friend that many good things have been said in the Washington papers about the James number and am promised the clippings. It strikes me that Melville is the best of the several you mentioned,[3] and I suggest you get in touch immediately with his granddaughter—Raymond Weaver can tell you all about *her*—before she faces "the distinguished thing." She is not at all young—she may have passed on already. But surely she would have portraits, old pictures. . . .

Yours in the triple faith (G. and J.
and S.),[4]

---

[1] James's expatriation was a major topic of criticism in the twenties. Van Wyck Brooks had triggered it in *The Pilgrimage of Henry James* (1925), when he argued that James's late novels were "difficult" because he had uprooted himself. Many Americans could not forgive James's seeming defection in having adopted British citizenship on the brink of the grave, as it were. "James was a failure in Brooks's eyes because he had long before ceased to take nourishment in the American soil; and to take such nourishment he should have stayed at home." Leon Edel, ed., *Twentieth Century Views. Henry James* (Englewood Cliffs, N.J.: Prentice-Hall, 1963), p. 3.

[2] Edith Wharton, *A Backward Glance* (New York: D. Appleton-Century, 1934). Fanny Prothero was the wife of George Walter Prothero (1848–1922), the editor of the *Quarterly Review*. They were James's neighbors at Rye, Sussex, and in his later years Mrs. Prothero kept a close eye on James's servants and his house.

[3] The Herman Melville issue was only a vague idea, never "really in the works," wrote Lincoln Kirstein to me, 10 Feb. 1976.

[4] Perhaps Gurdjieff, James, and ?

CHAPTER VIII

Stephen Spender

I   STEPHEN SPENDER TO
               LINCOLN KIRSTEIN
               2 June 1933

Dear Mr. Kirstein,

Thank you very much for your letter. I am glad that you liked my poems. I am very glad that Mr. MacLeish should be reviewing them. Will you also apologize to him for my extremely inadequate and inaccurate review of his poem *Conquistador*. I was given only three days to review it in, and some of my review was omitted. I made the mistake of describing the metre as founded on blank verse when of course it is a form of terza rima. I am really extremely sorry, but I did not have time to reflect on the poem. I mentioned that the poem superficially resembled Anabase, though I think the influence of Apollinaire is more marked, and I reviewed him as pre-eminently a poet of death (the death that is complementary to a spurious life, not "The Waste Land" kind of death) but these remarks were omitted.

I shall be very glad to meet you in London. I shall be there on July 21st at latest, and, till then, I think I shall be here.[1] I hope you will be in London till after the 21st.

I look forward to seeing your review and also MacLeish's.

When I was in Florence I was staying with Mr. & Mrs. Roger Sessions whom I have often heard speak about you.

Will you let me know soon whether you will be in London in the last ten days of July. Perhaps it is safer if you write to my London address, and then it will be forwarded.

Stephen Spender (*b.* 1909), British writer, contributor to *Hound and Horn*, became a personal friend of Kirstein's. *Hound and Horn* published his poetry; a short story, "The Burning Cactus"; and an essay in the Henry James issue, "The School of Experience in the Early Novels."

[1] Near Spezia, Italy.

2   **STEPHEN SPENDER TO LINCOLN KIRSTEIN**
8 October 1933

Dear Lincoln,

I am awfully sorry that I have not answered the last two or three of your letters, or acknowledged your story [1] and Billy Budd. Thank you very much for all the books. [2] Tony [3] and I were delighted with them. We have not written because we have been occupied in moving to the above address, our new flat, and so have lived in a whirl, which I found very disconcerting. However, we move in tomorrow and shall settle down soon, I hope.

The story is remarkable, I think. It has a very upsetting effect which makes me feel distinctly unhappy: I felt this also in your novel, and it seems peculiar to you. You are in some ways a Russian writer. I think the description and characterization in your story were excellent: but I mean, you are Russian, because like the Russians, you give the impression that the behaviour of your characters, has the quality of *Life*. The difficulty about the story is that it leaves one simply with an impression: a strong sensation that life is cruel and perplexing, but no feeling of direction. However perhaps I am asking for something that should not be there.

I look forward to your dictator book. [4] Dictators seem to be the factor that one must realize now. The worst of it is there are so many intruding external factors pushing themselves on to one, and all of which are undoubtedly important and affecting the cultural side of each person. The factors are so many one wants to realize which are significant: but they are really mostly only significant of a disruption which has no real purposive significance at all. But one has to see that lack of significance, to enclose it in one's understanding as well. One has to realize that things like the attempted assassination of Dollfuss,[5] and Germany's resignation from the League, are symbols of an overwhelming and intruding *un*reality, of mere change taking the place of growth, of mere sensation. One is dazzled by the succession of flying images, above all because one is oneself compelled to stand still and to resign all idea of progress.

I shall keep you posted with all Auden's work,[6] so please don't bother to get it.

Glad that the *Hound and Horn* will do my story.[7]

Since I wrote the first page of this we've learnt that Tony has appendicitis and has got to be operated on next week. He's going to take your books on gangsters to hospital with him.

Tony seems more lovely the more I get to know him. He is such a natural, unaffected person.

He is quite simply grateful to me where I had learnt to expect people to be resentful and jealous. He also likes being loved which is the rarest of qualities for an Englishman. He is one of those lucky people who knows that he needs love all the time and who can accept it. He is also very kind and gentle.

I liked Archie MacLeish's review very much. When the *Hound and Horn* comes out I'll write and thank him for it.

I'll write again soon, now that we've finished painting the house and have got settled.

                                        Tony and I both send love

[1] Refers to a "long unpublished tale which he [Spender] very correctly advised me not to try to have printed" (Lincoln Kirstein in a letter to me, 1 Dec. 1975).
[2] As Stephen Spender remembers them, they were books of poetry by James Agee, Malcolm Cowley, Wallace Stevens (possibly *Man with the Blue Guitar*), and Horace Gregory (letter to me, Nov. 1975).
[3] After a break with Christopher Isherwood, Spender writes in his autobiography *World within World* (New York: Harcourt Brace, 1948), "There was no one whom I could ask to travel with me or share a flat. . . . I did not want to live alone and I did not consider marrying. . . . By chance I met a young man who was unemployed, called Jimmy Younger [Tony]. I asked him to live in my flat and work for me. . . . Jimmy had run away from home at the age of eighteen, and been in various jobs,

including for three years the Army. He was pleasant-looking, friendly, quickly intelligent in certain ways, and capable of learning. He read a good deal and had a response to poetry which often astonished me" (p. 156).

[4] The "dictator" book was not written.

[5] Engelbert Dollfuss was chancellor of Austria in 1932. He survived an attempted assassination in 1933, but after putting down a socialist revolt in 1934 and establishing a corporate state similar to Germany's, he was himself killed by the Nazis in July 1934.

[6] The English poet Wystan Hugh Auden (1907–1973) was the acknowledged leader in the thirties of a left-wing group of poets—Spender, C. Day Lewis, Louis MacNeice, and Christopher Isherwood—known as the Auden Circle.

[7] "The Burning Cactus," vol. 7, no. 2 (Jan.–March 1934).

3   STEPHEN SPENDER TO LINCOLN KIRSTEIN
18 December 1933

Dear Lincoln,

Thanks very much for your letters and for the prospectus of the ballet school.

First of all, I enclose a poem as a sort of Christmas Card. Secondly, to answer your questions, I would like very much to contribute to the *Hound and Horn* in April, on Henry James.[1] We would both love to come over in the Spring, but I don't see really how it is possible: I am still badly in debt and keep going by doing hack reviews. I want to work very hard this winter and finish the James Essay by March and then we thought of going abroad as usual during the summer and working at some place where we can be quiet. I want very much to do a long poem, perhaps a dramatic poem. First of all I thought of the Reichstag Trial as a subject, but now I am considering Nijinsky's life.[2]

After the James book,[3] Tony and I are going to do a short "social document," a study of his life in the army.[4]

I did not like the Dance of Death, either.[5] I thought the lack of any protagonist showed a curious element of nihilism which one often finds in his work. I suppose his danger is to write too easily.

London is very cold and hideously dirty now. We have got a flat which is really extraordinarily nice, and which we get to like better and better. Tony is really happy, I think, and so am I. It is much nicer now that we know each other so much better, and are not partly afraid of some unknown element in each other.

We haven't seen Laurens[6] much, as I believe he's mostly in the country looking for a farm. William[7] lives just over the road, so we are always seeing each other.

I saw David Garnett over at the N. S.[8] office and I liked him, but I haven't seen him since. If I do, I will ask him for the *Mint*. . . .[9]

I met Yeats a few days ago. A very fine tall man with a mass of white hair, bronzed complexion and sensitive features: particularly that slight sensuous lift of the nostrils which one notices sometimes in artists. He stoops slightly and is curiously potbellied. He held forth a great deal.[10]

Tony is still having trouble with his stomach. I think he should probably have been operated on a long time ago. He is going to be examined this afternoon.

We are both extremely glad to hear that you are so happy and that the ballet school is doing so well. I love the symbol.

                                        With best love,

[1] Spender contributed an essay, "The School of Experience in the Early Novels," vol. 7, no. 3 (April–June 1934).

[2] Spender published no single work on these topics, although the Reichstag Fire was mentioned in his poem "Perhaps," written in 1934:

Chancellor Dollfuss clutching his shot arm
The Reichstag that their own side set on fire
And then Our Party banned.

The Reichstag, the German Parliament building, was burned down on Hitler's orders in 1933 so that the fire might be blamed on the Communist party, which was thereupon banned in Germany.

[3] *The Destructive Element* (1935), in which Spender analyzed "the deep consciousness of destructive forces threatening our civilization, which was to be found in the work of James, Joyce, Eliot, and some more recent writers" (*World within World*, p. 129).

[4] A study of Tony's life in the army was not written.

[5] The title of a play by W. H. Auden, published in 1933.

[6] Laurens Van der Post (*b*. 1906), British novelist born in South Africa.

[7] William Plomer (1903–1973), British writer, born in South Africa.

[8] *New Statesman*.

[9] T. E. Lawrence's account of his life in the R.A.F. The book had come out in a limited edition and was not readily available to the public.

[10] This meeting with Yeats at Lady Ottoline Morrell's house is amusingly described in *World within World* (pp. 148–49).

4   STEPHEN SPENDER TO
     LINCOLN KIRSTEIN
     15 April 1934

My dear Lincoln:

Thank you for your letter. I'm afraid the *New Republic* has the best version of the Van der Lubbe poem,[1] but I enclose two other poems and two further ones from which you may choose the third: or you may publish all four if you wish to do so.

I have been feeling very guilty that I have not written to you. But I did not feel capable of writing a sensible letter from London; we were so overwhelmed with people—most of them very nice people, but the crowds of them made me more and more irritable. I have also had to do more journalism, and I was beginning to feel discouraged about my poetry. My poetry is rather irrelevantly and dangerously linked to my self-respect: and I sometimes wake up in the night and feel as if I have eaten dust when I think of what I have written: and I feel also that perhaps my sensibility is too coarse, or I am too far lacking in the ability to commit myself to any religious or social belief which would provide me with a ready-made point of view: or I have too much of a common amiability which always makes us surrounded by people to be able to do the best work. Please do not console me about this: because, now we are away I feel quite differently about things: and also I know you know that I do not fish for compliments about things for which I really care.

Your book about the occult also rather stumped me.[2] I will read it again when I get home, but when I read it last I could not really make anything of it. It seems to me slightly sordid—like the Charing Cross Road—in some way, but that only shows how much prejudice I must overcome to understand it.

Thank you awfully Lincoln, for sending us so many books. The novels have not yet arrived, but it will be a great pleasure when they do.

Tony is more wonderful than ever. We have really learnt to trust each other now, and he seems very happy.

This place is incredibly lovely. It is almost five miles outside Dubrovnik, right on the Adriatic at the foot of mountains with cypresses on them. It is a tiny village, very quiet and restful.

I am working hard. I am writing a play which is absolutely *the* test of whether I can do anything. It is about German justice,[3] the thing I feel most strongly about. I'm also at the James book.[4]

Could you send me the cheque for the poems again before they appear? I am so sorry to bother you, but this is only our address till July. We stay here till then. Write.

[1] Van der Lubbe was the young Dutch communist who was blamed for the burning of the Reichstag in 1932. The poem described the first in the chain of events that Spender saw as characterizing the moral decadence of Nazi Germany. This, along with his long poem "Vienna" and play *Trial of a Judge*, was the beginning of his bitter indictment of Nazism.

[2] G. I. Gurdjieff's *The Herald of Coming Good*. See Chap. V, Letter 24, n. 1.

[3] *Trial of a Judge*, a tragedy in five acts, published in 1938.

[4] *The Destructive Element* (1935).

5   STEPHEN SPENDER TO
    LINCOLN KIRSTEIN
    16 August 1934

Dear Lincoln,

Thank you very much for your letter, which interested us both extremely, and which I have read through several times.

I think you are quite right about the *Hound and Horn*, though I myself am very disappointed as I had a dream of how nice it would be to publish something every quarter in it. But you obviously can't give out spiritually and financially in every direction. By the way, I did not get the money for my poems. It may have got lost in the post, or be delayed, as my movements are so varied. But if you haven't sent it, could you send it to this address, as since Tony's illness we have been rather short.

I met a young man called James Laughlin who gave me the addresses of various American magazines which I might write for.

I liked your letter very much. I think you are very right and greatly to be admired in so many things, such as not seeing your pupils out of class. Laughlin also told us about the row you made over Upton Sinclair's version of Eisenstein,[1] which made us both very pleased.

Tony has quite recovered from the operation and is about 10 times better than he ever was before.

While we were in Vienna, I have been having a friendship of a more or less intimate kind with an extremely attractive and intelligent American woman whom I met there.[2] Tony has been terribly upset about this, although he was extremely generous about it, and never felt in the least resentful. In fact, he was very fond of her. But all the same, it has made a break, and we have decided now that each year we have a month's holiday from each other, and that we try and remain fundamentally independent, so that our friendships won't ever threaten any final break between us. So he is going to London now, and I am going to Vienna, and after a month, I shall either join him in London, or else we shall both meet in Paris. I am trying to make him have more work, and I am hoping he will form relationships with other people, and that being with me, and being independent will give him a basis for such friendships: so that in the last analysis, even if I married, it wouldn't form a separation, because we want to live together for our whole lives. I used to hope that he would marry, but it doesn't seem very probable now.

I am writing by far my best poem—my only mature poem, about Vienna.[3] It is in four parts, between 650–850 lines. I shall send you a copy in September. If you like the idea, I shall suggest also writing a version for a ballet. It is essentially dramatic and full of movement.

After that I shall do Roger's libretto.[4]

What about your novel? Will you ever finish it? I want very much to read you on dictators.

Laughlin also told me that there were several poems of yours, in private circulation, which you had done recently. I saw the one you sent at Christmas, which interested me v. much. So, if there are any others, could you send them to me at this address.[5]

I have finished the James book.[6] I like the James part v. much, the rest not so much. I have had a job to revise and rewrite a good deal of it.

I'm sorry we can't get to America, but it doesn't seem likely for some time now. Next year we are going to settle in a cottage in the English country, so that means, I think, that we won't get abroad till 1936. I am very anxious to live quietly and within my income, so that I don't have to take any more commissions. It is ridiculous to make debts that prevent me doing the work I want.

Tony sends love and grüssen.

[1] Cf. Chap. IV, Letter 40, n. 6.
[2] Stephen Spender met a woman he calls "Elizabeth" at Mlini, Yugoslavia, whom he continued to see in Vienna. This meeting is described in *World within World*, p. 168.
[3] "Vienna," published in 1935, a long poem expressing Spender's indignation at the suppression of the Viennese Socialists by Dollfuss, Fey, and Starhemberg, and in part also concerned with a love relationship. "In a world where humanity was trampled on publicly, private affection was also undermined" (*World within World*, p. 174).
[4] The idea for the libretto was with Roger Sessions—"The Nightingale" by Boccaccio (letter to me, November 1975).
[5] Kirstein does not remember which poems are referred to here, but they could have been published in his book of poetry *Low Ceiling* (1935).
[6] *The Destructive Element* (1935).

6   STEPHEN SPENDER TO LINCOLN KIRSTEIN
13 October 1934

Dear Lincoln

Thank you very much for the poems. I think they are extremely interesting, and I am very pleased about the dedication. I like mostly the first—about Hitler—then Salesman, then Byrne. But I don't know yet which I will really like most. Your world is very effectively conveyed, but seems very strange to me. There is always a feeling of something metallic, which moves me very much. I like lines such as "My beauty in my bullets builds me best."

I would have written before but I have had an attack of poisoning, lasting in various forms for several weeks. This week, I had some teeth removed and am now much better, but still have rather a headache.

Enclosed is the Vienna poem. I hope this may interest you, though I am not as sanguine as I was that you will see in it a subject for ballet.

We came back to London a month ago. I am revising my prose book.[1] Then I am going to write some stories and the libretto for Roger.

Yes, please do send some books, if there are any of interest. But don't if it's a bore or an expense to you.

Tony is v. well and happy.

Write and say how you like this.

---

[1] *The Destructive Element* (1935).

7   LINCOLN KIRSTEIN
        TO STEPHEN SPENDER
        October 19, 1934

Dear Stephen. . .

I met Roger in the street today and he showed me "Vienna," which I really think is marvellous, so far and away the best thing you have ever done, the most sustained and the largest.

There is an excellent magazine here called *Dynamo*,[1] of which I am sending you copies. The boys who are running it are not Communist Party members as far as I know, although they have very strong Left leanings, and as you see, they print as good verse as we get here. They can't pay you for it, but you reserve the copyright in any further publication in a book. I very seriously doubt if any other magazine in America would take this poem, although you might try. You see it's very long and the subject matter would automatically count out most of the so-called literary magazines.

I have been seeing something of two young boys, both actively engaged in revolutionary activity in America, where conditions are less apparently melodramatic, but no less violent or terrible than in Europe. One of these boys, called Wirt Baker[2] is a southerner and is facing a thirteen months' sentence on a road gang for obstructing traffic, which is the only charge they could get him on. If he serves the sentence he will be unquestionably killed, because he has done his best to foster unionization in the southern center of the steel industry, against the time when that would be the artery of ammunition in case of war.

He is a very sad and impressive boy whom I like more than I can say. Unfortunately there are too few like him. They stick out like sore thumbs and they get hit and there is hardly anybody to take their place. The other is a Polish boy called Walter Petras. He is only nineteen years old, but he led the strike in Rhode Island, which ended in murder and the strikers making their own tear gas and using it on the State Troopers. He is very determined and tough, but very unorganized and he sees the whole world as his small town. It's all too sporadic and feeble now, but there is no telling what might happen in ten years' time.

There is a very lively organization in New York called The New Workers' Theatre. They have already produced a very successful play about negro and white dock workers, called *Stevedore*. I spoke to them about your Reichstag Fire play, and they want very much to have it. I am going to do with them some time during the winter a big spectacle tentatively called *Red Hydra*.[3] It's a kind of a symbolic history of the Communist Party in Germany before, after and during the Revolution. They have put more or less at my disposal about eight hundred people who are organized into various singing societies, dance groups, etc., and it will be a very interesting thing to work on.

I've got a book of verses ready to be published if anybody will print them, and I am sending you under separate cover some things that came out in a book something like *New Signatures*. I am proceeding with my history of dancing, but slowly.

If anything happens about the play, why don't you come over and see it done? I'd always take care of you. I saw Harold Nicolson. He is staying with Lindbergh and very much enjoying himself. He seems to be very agreeable and spoke affectionately of you. . . .

Our ballet opens its public productions in December, and I am very much occupied with all the details. Our School is going very well. We have seventy students and a company of thirty.

How is Tony? Please give him my love. I don't suppose you ever see Laurens van der Post? Again, many congratulations on "Vienna."

[1] *Dynamo*, a journal of revolutionary poetry, published from 1934 to 1936.
[2] Lincoln Kirstein wrote me, "I was much involved with a young CP activist called Wirt Baker; he was a boy who had been in jail in Alabama whom I liked personally. Actually I never had much use for his friends but I adored him" (2 July 1975).

[3] "As for *Red Hydra*, I flirted with a lot of young communists in the early Thirties but I can't recall *Red Hydra*. I wrote a lot for *New Theatre*, a CP publication" (letter to me, 2 July 1975).

8   STEPHEN SPENDER TO LINCOLN KIRSTEIN
7 November 1934

Dear Lincoln,

I am awfully sorry not to have written to you since your cablegram and three letters. I feel extremely ashamed of myself, but the things you write about are really so interesting and so important, that I have not felt able to answer them; until I got through a little of my reviewing work, I did not feel I could attempt even to do so. I am still at the James book, I think it will be quite good now, as I have rewritten a great deal of it.

I am very glad you like the "Vienna" poem. It is really, I suppose, in the nature of an experiment, and I think it is written in a manner I shall not return to. I wanted to write something which was as directly about contemporary affairs in its reference as say "The Vision of Judgment,"[1] or some of the Elizabethan plays. I think the point of writing a poem of this sort is in order to describe the surface of what one is attacking; the next stage is to get below the surface. Now I have actually named the actors, Dollfuss, Fey, etc., I am free to invent symbols, for the forces which I discover in them.

You are quite right about the last part. It is much too personal, I think. The whole poem is meant to be symphonic in its structure. The first movement is allegro, and statement of a problem. The second is a scherzo (of a serious and satiric kind) enclosing a trio which begins 'if only one can silence every voice.' The last movement is meant to be a kind of exhilarated and mad statement, restating the themes of parts I and II.

I want now to read Aristophanes.

I am writing now a much more personal kind of poetry, of which I enclose an example. I am grateful to the "Vienna" poem for the feeling of release which it has given me. But I have left it far behind now.

To write from the centre of excitement is wrong. One must write from the centre of peace. That is a criticism that applies to my work, and to most modern work.

As far as possible one wants work now to be external. Also as far as possible, cheerful. But to use the external as a means of forcing the internal and promoting a facade, or a shell, is fascism.

I have left your own poems too long out of this letter. I think they are extremely interesting, and that probably I am not the person to do them justice, because there is some discrepancy in me which prevents me getting the most out of them. Anyhow, I find that I like individual passages very much, but I find the whole effect rather metallic. I also like the ideas extremely and agree with most of them. But in poems, they do not interest me as much as in your letters, for example. I dare say it is partly the difference between English and American. I find nearly all American poetry has some quality, something to do with the very brittle surface, that I don't quite like. I find it in Cummings and MacLeish, for instance. It is too worked up, brilliantly visual, but the emotion although very individual, seems somehow generalized. I can't explain. This is nonsense perhaps.

Lastly, a request. I never got the last number of the *Hound and Horn*. Could you send me one?

I have cabled to *Dynamo*. They must ask Random House. Faber objects to anyone else doing it, I believe. But I am willing. It isn't a matter of their not having any copyright: the point is that R. H. and Faber have one.

Tony sends love.

¹ A satirical poem by Byron (1822).

9   LINCOLN KIRSTEIN
TO STEPHEN SPENDER
15 May 1935

Dear Stephen:

Thank you ever so much for the copy of your book which I have just read with the most intense interest and greatest admiration.¹ I think it is much the most important book of criticism that has come out since *The Sacred Wood*,[2] the clearest and the most satisfactory. I think you have exceeded yourself. I want to write you a long letter about it in a day or two, but I wanted you to have the enclosed clippings by the next boat.

I am extremely upset about the accident to Colonel Lawrence.[3] Can't you possibly come over here next winter? I think it extremely important that you see this country, particularly at this time. It's in a most remarkable and interesting state of ferment, and an understanding of it is basic for everything that is going to happen in the next twenty-five years. I'm sure that you could make a go of it financially, if you wouldn't mind talking around, lecturing, and that kind of thing.

If Tony is with you please give him my love. I have two books that I want to send him when you are settled somewhere.

Yours always affectionately

[1] *The Destructive Element* (1935).
[2] By T. S. Eliot.
[3] T. E. Lawrence's fatal motorcycle accident.

10   STEPHEN SPENDER TO
       LINCOLN KIRSTEIN
       8 June 1935

Dear Lincoln,

I expect this letter is crossing the second one of yours which you promised to send, but I shall answer that separately, as I don't want to delay in thanking you for the poems. I admire them very much, they are far better than I had thought them to be from the occasional typescripts you have sent me. "Chamber of Horrors" is really an amazing performance. You are most successful, I think, in violent, sadistic, 100% American stuff. "Kidnapped" is extraordinary, and so is the first poem in the book. I read a review in the *Herald Tribune*, which I thought quite sensible, except that I don't recognize my own influence in your work, I'm glad to say. But if it is there, I am glad that it should have contributed to a poetry that is so tough.

I send a story under separate cover, partly for your amusement, partly because I wondered if you would care to place it anywhere. But it doesn't really matter. I sent an awfully bad version of the same work to *Story*, and they refused it. It is so different now that I wouldn't mind if they had it again, if you can explain that it is a new story. But, if you prefer, send it to one of the smaller magazines which you are interested in. It will also appear in the July *London Mercury*.[1] Does that prevent it from being published in America? But don't trouble: all this is quite unimportant really.

Tony and I are still together, and have just spent 4 weeks in Dalmatia where I have been working on a vol. of short stories, poems, and also a translation of Holderlin, which I am doing in collaboration with Edwin Muir.[2] He is a beautiful and important poet; but I expect you will know that.[3]

I am glad you liked my book. But I am still only in my tutelage. I have done some better poems lately, and in these stories I am learning to present character. In a year's time I shall be able to do my plays. But I don't think I'll come to America until I've got them off my chest. . . . I really travel as much as I can now: to go further would prevent me working and at present, I have work which I very much want to do. I want to produce uninterruptedly for a year until that leads me to the plays.

But now I read everything I can about America, and am becoming more and more interested. I really do want to go there. Yet I think that in two years it may be still more interesting.

I am terribly sorry about the death of Lawrence. It really hung over me for a few days just as the loss of the other, D. H. Lawrence once did. It is an awful loss to literature, and now every civilized being who crashes is a discernible loss to our civilization. He does not seem to have felt his life was worth making use of. At least, I cannot understand the motor cycling, the empire building, and all the other sides of him. I expect you do. To me his life seems almost a waste.

Do write soon and tell me your news.

[1] "Strange Death," published in *London Mercury*, August 1935.
[2] The translation of Holderlin, with Edwin Muir, "remained a project only" (letter to me, Nov. 1975).
[3] Edwin Muir (1887–1959), born in the Orkney Islands off the coast of Scotland. His recollections of the primitive agricultural life of the islands, with its ritual and customs, form the material for much of his poetry.

11   STEPHEN SPENDER TO
          LINCOLN KIRSTEIN
          5 August [1935]

My dear Lincoln

When you write, your letters are so interesting that they make me feel ashamed and afraid that I shall not be able to answer them at all adequately. Thank you very much for the last one. I am extremely interested in what you say about Lawrence, particularly as now I am reading the *Seven Pillars*. Thank you also for the kind things you say about my book. It has been turned down by several American publishers, including Random House, but now Houghton Mifflin have bought 350 sheets from Cape. Cape hopes that more will sell, and that then they may set up an edition in America, so if the *New Republic* will take your article, I expect that will be a great help in getting it going. In any case, I should be very interested to see it.

I am doing a volume of four stories now, for publication in England in the Autumn or Spring. One is the *Burning Cactus*, another I sent you from Yugoslavia, and there are two more.[1] I think you will perhaps especially like one of these stories. In any case I shall send them to you.

It will be fine if you can come to England in the Spring. I am not quite sure whether I shall be able to get away next year, because, as you know, I have intended all this work—stories, criticism, and poems—of the last two years to lead up to the writing of three plays about Europe. I think now that when I have finished the stories I shall be able to start these plays. Also I am rather dissatisfied with my present arrangement of living abroad for six months, when I do serious work, and then living in London for six months when I see people and do reviewing. Humphrey has got a cottage in a fairly remote part of Sussex,[2] and next Spring I'm going to build a hut there with a workroom, a library, where I can get away from London when I want. Then when I do go abroad, I shall take a complete holiday and go quite alone to unknown parts of Greece, or perhaps further East even. If one has work to do, one is tied down to the places where one can find above all a nice room, and, secondly, fairly decent food and living: so, for that reason, during the last two years, I have repeated the same journeys.

Tony has gone home now, and is going to look for a job. I hope awfully that he will be able to find one, but it is very doubtful. If he can't, he is thinking of joining the International Red Cross and going to Abyssinia. Homosexuals of his type are obviously the best nurses, and though it would be a frightful job, I'm not going to oppose his going, partly because I can't hold him back any longer, partly also because I think perhaps he is better cut out for a job of that sort than for being a bank clerk. Our friendship has not altered at all, but our relationship has really had to alter because it developed a logic of its own by which it formed a barrier and a protection for him which prevented him having to make his own way, earn his living, and finally even from having to *be* himself: and a barrier which prevented me also from developing, since I was always having to put this relationship before everything else. I expect you realized that that would happen. In the last few weeks he began definitely to feel restless and unhappy, and finally he decided that he must try to get a job. I suppose it is absurd to ask if there is any chance for him in America? if everything else fails, I expect he could *make* a job for himself with free-lance secretarial work, but this again would depend chiefly on me: the one important thing is that he shouldn't depend on me.

Personally, I don't feel now that I want any "marital" relationship with anyone: not with Tony and not with anyone else. I would like a woman but not marriage: as far as homosexuality goes, it is to me an utterly promiscuous, irresponsible, adventurous excitement: the feeling of picking someone up in a small village and going on somewhere else next day. This is very anti-social, but there it is. What's most important is that I've come to a stage in my work where I feel more and more isolated. What I write about, the interest of a moral and political will in society, is to me intense, but that interest isn't there for most other people. In any case, I enclose a fairly long poem to show you what I am doing now.

Thank you once more for your letter. I am sure that Tony joins me in sending love.

[P.S.] If you want the enclosed poem for any of the magazines you are interested in, please use it.

I am sorry the poem is so badly typed. It suffers from Tony not being here and someone else having volunteered to do it.

¹ *Burning Cactus*, a volume of short stories, published in 1936.
² Humphrey, Stephen's brother. Here Spender meant to write (Lavenham), Suffolk, not Sussex.

12   STEPHEN SPENDER TO
       LINCOLN KIRSTEIN
       8 January [1936]

Dear Lincoln,

I feel very guilty at not having written to you for so long. But when I last heard from you was just before I left London, and then I was extremely busy. Last September I got a very long and interesting letter from you, which was forwarded to Austria. This I certainly answered, but I have an idea I may have misaddressed my letter, since I don't think it ever reached you. Anyhow, it doesn't matter.

First of all about Laurens. I am sure he hasn't grown indifferent to or annoyed with you. The fact is that he never writes to anyone, I believe: certainly not to me, though I occasionally get messages from him through William Plomer. He has a farm which occupies absolutely all of his time: he has to get up at about five in the morning, and he works till late. Also he has extremely delicate health, so I suppose he has decided to have no correspondence. But do write to him: I am sure he would be glad to hear from you.

Christopher Isherwood,¹ Tony, a German friend of C's and I, have taken this house here.² It is an extremely beautiful place, and we can live here cheaply and quietly. Later on we may be going to take a larger house, where Heinz, the German, will be able to farm. As it is, we are content with a few animals, hens, a dog, rabbits, etc.

I am working hard, and am at last doing the play which I told you about three years ago. So far, it is going very well, and I feel more confidence in it than in anything I have as yet attempted. Apart from that, I am learning Greek simply in order that I may read Greek tragedy in the original with the help of a translation, and get a certain amount out of it. We are jointly writing a travel diary which we shall probably make into a book of sorts.³

I've just refused a contract to write a book of political opinions.

First of all I thought I could do so: but when I came to think more closely about it, and even start writing it, I found that I can't make positive factual statements; that all my arguments are much better expressed by political-historical and economic writers; and that I am not interested in my ideas as "autobiography". What I do feel in myself is a strong and consistent tendency, a habit of always thinking in the same way; but this is quite different from making up one's mind, and being able to present a completed account of what one believes, and thinks one always will believe. So I had to give that up. In fact, the play is the only way in which I can write such a book.

I am so glad that the Ballet School is doing so well. In *The Listener* this week, I read an account of The Metropolitan Opera, in which it said they had taken over the American Ballet School. Is that you? I suppose so, because it said it was a "young" organization.

I don't know what to think about politics. During the English election Tony and I canvassed—Tony more gallantly than I—but with no success. The amazing thing was that all our most gloomy warnings and prophecies were so spectacularly fulfilled in the Hoare-Laval plan.[4] Now we wait here, half expecting a war between England and Italy at any moment. On the other hand, it now seems quite possible that Mussolini will be thrown out, and that *may* mean a set back for German Fascism as well. We are living in an age of very obscure movements. I get more and more satisfaction now out of reading history. I think I may write two or three plays: the most ambitious idea I have is to write a play about Hoelderlin:[5] because that would be much the most interesting way of writing a play which implied the whole of industrialism. My feeling is that the German romantics almost consciously lived at the edge of the immense gulf—the industrial revolution that divides their world from ours: they saw what was coming: the force of their appeal is an appeal to the imagination and to the standards of Greece to prevent their age from perpetrating what they saw as a crime. Hoelderlin is the person one might write about, because he is a man outside his age, like the hero of *The Sense of the Past*:[6] he is both as modern as Hamlet and more Greek than, say, Shelley.

I shall have finally to write about Hoelderlin, because as long as I write about the contemporary, people will think of my stuff as a kind of journalism: they won't see that I learn Greek in order to write about

Hitler, and that I am trying to make "communists read Friedrich Hoel-
derlin." Well, it's my own fault that they don't see it, because my stuff
isn't good enough yet.

In a couple of months I'll send you a vol. of short stories I did,
which will appear then.

This letter is too long already. When you come to Europe do visit
Lisbon, and come over here for a few days. There is an air line to Lis-
bon. And there is a very cheap and excellent hotel, a few minutes dis-
tant from here.

Also you will meet one of my greatest friends, and one of the most
interesting of young Englishmen—Christopher.

Tony joins me in sending love,

[1] Christopher Isherwood (*b.* 1904), British writer, born in Cheshire, England, be-
came a naturalized American in 1946. He is best known for his prewar Berlin novels
The Last of Mr. Norris (1935) and *Goodbye to Berlin* (1939), published in 1946
under the title *The Berlin Stories*, adapted by John van Druten as the play *I Am a
Camera* (1951), and adapted for the Broadway musical and movie *Cabaret*.
[2] Sintra, Portugal.
[3] "This work, a travel diary with Isherwood, about life in Sintra, Portugal, did not
materialise" (letter to me, Nov. 1975).
[4] A plan, co-authored by Sir Samuel Hoare of England and Pierre Laval of France in
the middle thirties, which proposed, after Italy's attack on Ethiopia, to appease Italy
at Ethiopia's expense.
[5] No play on Hoelderlin was written (letter to me, Nov. 1975).
[6] Published in 1917, this was the second of the two novels by Henry James left
unfinished.

13   STEPHEN SPENDER TO LINCOLN KIRSTEIN
8 November [1936]

Dear Lincoln:

Thank you very much for your letter. I am awfully glad that you
should have written as I am so bad at letter-writing that I am indeed in
danger of losing touch with my friends when they are away. Especially
now when I have so much journalism to do that the very act of writing
prose reproaches me with the poems I would like to have written.

Firstly, it was just rudeness that I didn't reply about your *Burning*

Cactus letter. The fact is I lost all interest in that book shortly after it was published. I only prayed that it wouldn't appear in America. I do think it may interest someone some day if people are at all interested in me; but it is a very inappropriate book for the present time.

Secretly, I quite like some of it but I have forgotten what or why.

Next, I never got your Ballet book.[1] I suppose it was lost, like so much else, in the Portuguese post. Would it be too much to ask you to send another? If you send that and anything else especially interesting I shall send you any books you want from here. Only I am at a disadvantage since most good English books are published in America, whereas comparatively few good American books seem to reach us here.

I shall almost certainly come to America next winter, i.e. the winter of 1937–38. Curtis Brown has written me that one of the better lecture agents wants me to go for a tour of six to ten weeks. I shall be paid my return fare plus an advance on 50% of my takings. I suppose that is usual and all right. Anyway, I am extremely anxious to go to America and to meet the Left Wing writers there, and try and find out all I can about conditions. You will be able to help me.

I have done a book on politics—about the position of Liberals in relation to Communism[2]—which will interest you, I think. It is coming out in January with a thing called the Left Book Club, an amazingly successful propagandistic enterprise which has some 30,000 members, and is still increasing at the rate of 5000 a month. Also I am now really writing hard at the play which I always promised you I would do. I have done about ½ of it in three years, and I think you will like it very much. I can't guarantee when it will be ready, though I think now that I can finish it in a few months. I see my way very clearly, but then find that a speech which I have stretched out in my mind takes three weeks instead of three days to write as I want it. I promise that as soon as it is ready I shall send you a typed copy.

Tony is very well and happy. He has a job now with a magazine called *Left Review*, which I shall order for you, I think, as it is rather interesting. It strikes me that *Partisan Review* is considerably better, but we are hoping to make something of the *Left Review*. Tony has also joined the C.P. who make him work for them from 8 till midnight most evenings. They are self-sacrificing and admirable as an organization. They are the only party that have collected large sums of money and organized effective protests about Spain. They take the trouble to educate their followers: Tony is taught Marxism and also to speak in public. He is extremely sincere and hard-working about it, as also about his *Left Review* job. The L.R. is only a halftime job and the rest of the time—which is not much—he types for me. So we still see a great deal of each other, though we have separate flats.

Yes, I have come back from Portugal. Actually I only stayed there about 3 months during which it rained all the time and I wrote at my play. I don't think really that kind of ménage of 2 writers and 2 friends is very satisfactory. It is necessary for Christopher since his German boy can't get a Pass to England: in fact the Passport difficulties make them exiles from one country after another. But it isn't necessary for me, so I suppose Tony and I were sound really to go away. Christopher is now in Brussels as he found that the German consul in Lisbon was arranging to ship his friend back to Germany, so they had to fly. The Portuguese are a bloody German-Italo-Hispano-Fascist colony. I think the Spanish business is the most terrible European disaster to date. The English bourgeois don't care though: they are on the upsurge of a Boom which makes them think they are unaffected by the rest of Europe. The boom is due to armaments.

I had a feeling (a) that I won't be able to live abroad so much in future because I daily become more entangled in doing what I can to help make a Popular Front in England (b) that I probably wouldn't be able to see Europe in a few years time, because it won't be there to see. So Tony and I went to Spain for 4 weeks, and then took a cargo-boat in April from Marseilles to Piraeus; stayed in Greece for six weeks, then went to Vienna where I wrote my political book. We saw a great deal and I enjoyed it all immensely.

Now about our friends. Laurens has gone to South Africa to farm, I believe. William Plomer wears more and more the mask of irony which shuts out all politics and finally, I suppose, interest in everything. Virginia Woolf feels she can't be indifferent any longer—she has claustrophobia about fascism, a very European feeling—so she is writing an article about art for the *Daily Worker*, and she has written a novel which she described to me as "propagandist" (please don't quote this, shd you be tempted to). It is called *The Years*, and she can't make up her mind to publish.[3] She feels that much as she cares, she can't really write about everyday life. David Garnett I don't see; he must be nice as a man, but as a literary figure sitting on the fence and saying that Aldous Huxley is the only novelist who writes about "civilized" people, he's hateful.

Yes, do send me Agee's book; I should like very much to see it.[4] Farrell I have read.[5] I am just reviewing A Note on Literary Criticism. I met Prokosch in Austria and liked him but didn't get to know him;[6] he was always rushing round from Paris to Vienna to Venice to Istanbul; but I expect he enjoys himself. *The Asiatics* was good; the poems repetitive but able, attractive, interesting. There is an American poet called Eberhart[7] who would be spontaneous and natural I think, if his writing didn't have the air of a kitten that has been licked all over by I. A. Richards and other Cambridge dons.

I write a lot. I go about the country talking about various topics to literary and political clubs. I am spending a week in December in Birmingham, Manchester, and Sheffield giving lectures at each university. It will be very interesting.

I look forward very much to hearing from you soon and seeing you in a year's time.

[1] *Dance: A Short History of Classic Theatric Dancing* by Lincoln Kirstein, published in 1936.
[2] *Forward from Liberalism*, in which Spender argues that Liberals must reconcile Communist social justice with their liberal regard for social freedom and that they must accept the methods which it might be necessary to use in order to defeat fascism.
[3] *The Years*, published in 1937.
[4] Probably James Agee's *Permit Me Voyage*, a book of poems (1935).
[5] James T. Farrell (1904–1979), writer, best known for the Studs Lonigan trilogy.
[6] Frederic Prokosch (*b.* 1908), American poet and novelist.
[7] Richard Eberhart (*b.* 1904), American poet.

14   STEPHEN SPENDER TO
LINCOLN KIRSTEIN
13 March [1938]

Dear Lincoln,

I have been meaning to write to you for well over a year. During the past few months I have put off writing because I intended to send you either the manuscript or proof of my play, which I now send.[1] Really, I feel that the play will tell you everything that there is to know about me during the past four years: that is to say, I had begun it some time before you and I met, and completed it this year. Of course, I haven't been working at it all the time, but at intervals, with long gaps between them. For me, that was really the only way in which to evolve the form of the play.

Tony came back in July after a great deal of trouble. He got ill in Spain, and then it was extremely difficult to get him back, and there were a great many complications. The Spanish were very nice about it, the English not so easy to deal with. But in spite of everything, I think he was much better treated than he would have been by a capitalist army in similar circumstances, particularly as he behaved very stupidly.[2]

We are trying over here to make a very good thing of the Group Theatre, and I am trying to get hold of plays which are not only poetic drama, but also naturalistic—but better than the kind of naturalism which appears on the commercial stage. It is suggested by the other Directors of the Group Theatre that you might be a kind of liaison for us. This would not involve much work. For the present, all it would mean would be that you might forward my play to anyone whom you think would care to produce it, and who was competent to do so. I believe that the Workers' Theatre of New York was once suggested. Also, would you look out for any plays which would be suitable for us to do? Plays either on the lines of the Auden-Isherwood productions, or else interesting realistic plays, provided they didn't need too extravagant resources. For example, *Dead End* would require too large a cast and too extravagant production for our resources. Odets plays, on the other hand, would be extremely suitable, but they have already been done by the Unity Theatre, which I suppose, corresponds more nearly to the Workers' Theatre, whereas our Theatre is bourgeois-intellectual.[3]

I won't write any more now, as I have to go out, and if I leave this I may not be able to add any more to it for several days, owing to the rehearsals and other engagements.

Tony is in Vienna, of all places to be today, staying with our friend Muriel Gardiner.[4] He will be back in a month or so. I am very well, as I hope you are.

[1] *Trial of a Judge* (1938).

[2] Tony had gone to fight with the International Brigade in Spain and had become disillusioned about the war. He decided he hated war, "he did not want to die for the Republic," he was a pacifist, and he wanted to be an "ordinary chap." Spender advised him to compromise and to try to get a noncombatant job in the army, but he discovered later that Tony had deserted, had been captured, and had been sentenced to spend two months in a camp of correction. After serving his sentence, he was sent home for medical reasons.

[3] *Dead End*, a very successful play by Sidney Kingsley, which ran from 1935 to 1937, at the Belasco Theatre in New York. It dealt with the contrast between the wretchedly poor who inhabit the streets that dead end in a wharf over the East River and the very wealthy who live in palatial apartments in the midst of the slums.

"Odets plays" refers to plays by Clifford Odets, such as *Waiting for Lefty*, a play about striking workers, produced at the Longacre Theatre in New York by Group Theatre in 1935, plays which required only a simple setting—a bare stage, in this instance—and a relatively small cast of characters.

[4] Muriel Gardiner (*b.* 1901), American, Freudian-trained psychoanalyst, who was active in the Socialist underground in Vienna from 1934 to 1938.

15   LINCOLN KIRSTEIN TO STEPHEN SPENDER
17 May 1938

Dear Stephen:

I was very glad to get your letter of March 13th. I haven't answered it because it was sent to the country and the mail piled up in the office. Then I was on tour with my company and have only just returned to New York.

I liked your play very much, particularly as poetry, but I felt that it had certain formal faults which might restrict it as a dramatic and pictorial production. I took it at once to the head of the Mercury Theatre here, which is the most interesting left-wing organization. They wanted to do it for a series of Sunday nights, but it came too late in the season and they were occupied with something else. They were going to do *Ascent of F-Six*,[1] but then they decided it was too British and too specific. They are very much interested in doing a poetic drama, but Mr. Houseman,[2] with whom I spoke about the play, felt a little the way I did, that the arrangement of choruses and the implied stylization was rather hard to deal with. Maybe we are quite wrong.

There is no workers' theatre left in New York. The so-called left-wing theatres have all folded up, due to acute inter-party difficulties of Trotskyists and Stalinists, and general personal disorganization. I would have liked so much to have seen the show in London. It is possible that I am coming over to England this summer, and I will of course see you then, and discuss other plans with you. I would love to do anything I possibly could for the Group Theatre in New York. I know everybody, of course, but there is a considerable wave of nationalist feeling sweeping the country at the present moment, due in part to our acute unemployment difficulties. And it is increasingly difficult for organized audiences, such as union or left-wing audiences, to interest themselves in foreign problems, or in problems which they consider foreign. It is a very tragic thing, but I have noticed an increasing harshness of feeling both in relation to Spain and Germany. We have our own fascist counterparts right here in America, and the general line seems to be that we should occupy ourselves with the peril at our own doorstep, rather than looking overseas for it.

I fully realize the injustice of this attitude, but as you probably know by this time, the theatre is acutely opportunistic and individualistic. There have to be parts for certain actors or they won't act. You have to be rather close to a repertory theatre to know just the psychological set-up, and you are rather at a disadvantage being across the Atlantic.

I'll write to you if anything turns up. In the meantime, please remember me to Tony, of whom I have the most affectionate memories. I hope you are O.K.

---

[1] A play by Christopher Isherwood and W. H. Auden, produced in 1937.
[2] John Houseman, the stage director and producer.

Epilogue

I   **LINCOLN KIRSTEIN TO
          HAROLD ROSENBERG**
          5 June 1934

Dear Mr. Rosenberg:

Since I last communicated with you I regret to tell you that as far as I can see ahead, *Hound and Horn* will now definitely cease publication after the next number. Miss Codman,[1] who was going in with me, finds that she hasn't enough money, and as I haven't, I'm afraid we're through. Of course there is still a slim chance that a publisher will take us over, in which case yours will be the leading article in the Fall number. . . . However, I would advise you to try to place your article elsewhere, since Thomas Mann is here and you could probably do it.[2]

I will await your instructions about it.

Harold Rosenberg (1906–1978), author and art critic.

[1] Florence Codman, of Arrows Editions, Inc. She hoped to run *Hound and Horn* for a year on a trial basis with Dudley Fitts as editor but was unable to raise the cash.
[2] "An Artist's Attack on Fascism" (on Thomas Mann).

2   ## DORIS LEVINE TO
E. R. BEVERLEY
11 July 1934

Dear Miss Beverley:

. . . We have been receiving scads of really beautiful letters because of the discontinuation of the magazine. Some subscribers even wrote that *Hound and Horn* would be such an unbearable loss to them, that even though they were as poor as church mice, they'd be happy to subscribe at ten dollars a year, as a sort of subscription endowment, if that would help continue *Hound and Horn* publication. It's really touching. . . .

Doris Levine was secretary of *Hound and Horn*; Miss Beverley, secretary to Louis Kirstein, Lincoln's father.

"The Memorial to Henry James" issue was the next to the last issue; a Herman Melville memorial had been planned and excellent articles had been accepted; *Hound and Horn* was well on the way to being regarded as the best of the literary magazines in America when it ended. But, wrote Lincoln Kirstein in an article in the *Harvard Advocate* in 1934, "The magazine died because it cost too much. . . . My father who unhesitatingly put up with it for seven years, used to complain no one could ever understand what we printed, and I always said he and they never took the trouble to read it. . . . We were just learning when we stopped."

The cessation of *Hound and Horn* brought forth some comment from the leading magazines of the day. D. G. Bridson in *Criterion* wrote, "It is desirable that some successor to *Hound and Horn* be found—a successor, needless to say, which is capable of imposing and maintaining the high standards with which *Hound and Horn* will always be associated."[1] Morton D. Zabel commented in *Poetry*, "Its faults were obvious and persistent. Its tone of preciosity, however evident of careful taste, often led to a kind of immature pedantry. . . . However by its suspension the *Hound and Horn* leaves one place less where writing is considered an art rather than a commodity, and where stupidity is not held to be the proper element in which poetry and prose flourish."[2] In the *New Republic*, Malcolm Cowley aired his theory about the magazine's demise. "The *Hound and Horn* followed no political policy; it tried to be merely a repository of good writing. Toward the end, however, there was a division among its contributors like the one that appeared in wartime among the editors of *The Harvard Monthly*; some of them were becoming Marxists, others were neo-Catholics or Southern Agrarians. This wasn't, of course, the reason why the magazine suspended publication. It died for lack of funds or one might expand this statement by saying that in an age of political unrest there was nobody sufficiently interested in a purely esthetic magazine to make the sacrifice necessary to keep it alive."[3] In a conversation with me in 1978, Cowley said that in retrospect *Hound and Horn* was one of the best of the small magazines, and that its non-Marxist alignment had been one of its strengths.

In 1975, Lincoln Kirstein wrote me that he "killed the *Hound and Horn* because I was sick of Cambridge and the un-world." It seems that a combination of three things spelled the demise of *Hound and Horn*. First, Lincoln Kirstein became increasingly bored with the magazine. As he expressed it in a pseudo-diary note in his book on the New York City Ballet, "My father had humored me in providing partial support for *Hound and Horn*, a magazine with which I was no longer involved, since it had been largely taken over by men with a more genuine interest in abstract ideas than I would ever possess. I never thought of myself as an intellectual, but as an artist or athlete." Second, Kirstein's fellow editors had gone off to pursue their own careers in other areas—Bernard Bandler was to become an eminent psychiatrist and Hyatt Mayor, the curator of the Print Department at the Metropolitan Museum of Art. Third, Lincoln Kirstein had found the all-consuming interest that was to dominate his life from that time on—the founding, with George Balanchine, of American ballet as we know it today. The School of American Ballet, which was to become the seed-bed for the New York City Ballet, opened in January 1934.

In his book *The American Literary Review, A Critical History, 1920–1950*, G. A. M. Janssens lists *Hound and Horn* as one of a handful of literary magazines that exerted profound influence on the formation of literary taste in America in the twentieth century, because of its intelligent critical detachment, its imperviousness to commercial or avant-garde pressures, and its ability to provide a common meeting-ground for writers and men of letters. *Hound and Horn* editors thought of following the Henry James triumph with an homage to Herman Melville (Spring 1935) and an homage to Walt Whitman (Spring 1936). Its list of contributors included many of the foremost contemporary American and European writers. Certainly then the death of *Hound and Horn* was a major loss to American letters, but to the editors, occupied with the real business at hand, the choice of their life's work, the *Hound and Horn* had been an exciting and glorious interlude.

[1] "Foreign Reviews," *Criterion*, July 1935, p. 729.
[2] "Recent Magazines," *Poetry*, Dec. 1934, p. 171.
[3] "Midsummer Medley," *New Republic*, 15 Aug. 1934, p. 25.

Index

Italic numbers refer to letters written by the person listed. Unless indicated otherwise, a person's nationality or birthplace is American.